BABEL

BABEL

Review of 60 years of life in medicine

Vignettes

Julian L. Ambrus, MD, PhD, ScD, FACP, KCsHS

and

Clara M. Ambrus, MD, PhD, FACP, LCsHS

Order this book online at www.trafford.com
or email orders@trafford.com

Most Trafford titles are also available at major online book retailers.

Printed in the United States of America.

ISBN: 978-1-4251-8727-9 (sc)

Trafford rev. 12/16/2010

www.trafford.com

North America & International
toll-free: 1 888 232 4444 (USA & Canada)
phone: 250 383 6864 • fax: 812 355 4082

Babel, Languages, and Introduction

This collection of vignettes written in periods "a la recherché du temps perdus" when as Proust I tried to think about past times. Some may be of interest to some, others to others, and maybe some only to those who are very close to me. I beg forgiveness of those whom I may bore at times.

Searching for a title, I came to "Babel." This is a symbol of the event when mankind's single language got mixed up into many. The word translates to the Hebrew word of "confusion." The town's name "Babylon" presumably originated from the same route. In Sumerian it means "gate of the gods." The writer of Genesis, who probably did not like the Babylonians, might have used intentionally a pun.

This all occurred to me when I thought about the languages and cultures in which I was raised. I was born in Hungary. There are only a handful of Hungarians in the world and their language is unrelated to any other except a distant relationship to Finnish and even more distant relationship to the language of a number of small Asiatic groups including the Zurjens, Votjaks, Chechen, Cheremis, and Inguish. Therefore, all Hungarians thought that it is important to learn languages. My first nanny was a Scots woman and my first foreign language was English with a Scottish accent. It took me years to find out that "idea" is not spelled with an "r" at the end. When my parents thought that my English was acceptable, a French madam followed. Then an Austrian "freulein" and a German governess. Many years later, when my wife and I completed postgraduate training at Jefferson Medical College in Philadelphia, PA, we also took a Ph.D. degree. The requirements included exams in two foreign languages. We chose German and French. The German exam had to be taken with Professor Brieger, Chairman of Public Health, who was a Prussian. He knew us well and knew that we are fluent in German. Nevertheless, he insisted on conversing with us in German for a while. At the end, he turned to me and said "I should really flunk you – you do not speak German, you speak Austrian." We both passed though.

Later I worked in Uganda and learned a little of the east African "lingua franca" Swahili. This derived in part from Arab traders who traveled between different tribes with different languages and taught them some of their own. In contrast to classical Arabic which is a highly developed, complex language, this is very simple. For example, "Karibu" means "near," but also means "come in," "here," and "give me." In the morning when my "boy" knocked on the tent post with morning tea, the answer was "Karibu" – "come in." When a wounded elephant charged, I asked my gun bearer for a second gun "Karibu bundugi" – "give me the gun."

When I worked in Saudi Arabia, I tried my Swahili mixed with a little Arabic with my patients. They laughed. They said, "You sound like an ignorant tribesman, stay with English." Some graduated from Oxford or Cambridge and spoke better English than I did.

About languages, I remember other episodes. I was visiting a professor at McGill University in Montreal. Lectures were, of course, in English. But some colleagues came over from the French-speaking Universite du Montreal and participated in patient demonstrations and rounds. The French colleagues insisted on asking their questions in French; it was, of course, mostly "Quebecois." I answered in Parisian French. (My wife and I arrived recently from a sojourn at the Pasteur Institute in Paris.) Our colleagues immediately turned to English. Some were better at it than I.

My wife was born in Rome, Italy, and of course spoke fluent Italian of the northern Italian variety. In the United States, I had to see occasionally patients who spoke mostly Italian. I asked my wife to come and interpret. Most of these patients were Sicilian. When they heard my wife's northern Italian, they quickly turned back to highly broken English; they preferred it to northern Italian.

Once we were attending a medical meeting in Rome. Later at night, we dropped in to a small "rosticeria" for a snack. There were no empty tables, so we sat at one with several local fellows. I tried to be friendly, introduced myself and attempted to chat in my very broken

Italian. One fellow turned to my wife, "Your idiotic brother is trying to make conversations." So much for languages.

The story of Babylon, however, held other interests as well. Probably I agree with the story of Adam, Eve, and the apple. It was interpreted as suggesting that God does not like when people strive to become all-knowing like God himself. I thought that this is only a partly correct interpretation. God does not want anybody to play God. He appreciates the quality of humility and that we should not take ourselves too seriously. He made everything so complex that the more we learn, the more new vistas open up yet to be learned. This is true whether we look at the development of astronomy or medicine. I believe He wants us to try hard to learn more about things which would help us and our fellow man, meanwhile realizing how far we are of "final goals." The last line of Goethe's "Faust" sums it up probably closely translated: "Whoever striving proves himself, he can be absolved." ("Wer immer strebend sich bemüht, den koennen wir erlösen.")

"Medical Odyssee" and "let's be kind to each other"

My wife and I graduated from the University of Zurich in Switzerland and did graduate work at the University of Paris and the Pasteur Institute and Hospital, Departments of Virology, Tropical Medicine, and Therapeutic Chemistry. We worked with and made the acquaintance of such greats as Dr. Jacob, Dr. Lepin, the Drs, Trefuel, and Dr. Montagnier, who first isolated the HIV1 virus, the causative agent of AIDS, and later fought about priority with Dr. Gallo of the NIH. The Drs. Bovet, discoverers of the first antihistamines, just left the Pasteur Institute fulfilling a pledge made during the war to return to their homeland, Italy, after the war if everything turned out well. Later on, they received the Nobel Prize for their work at Pasteur. We were given their laboratory together with their two technicians, the Mademoiselles Eschinar and Mayer. This was right after the war and there were still shortages. One day we asked Monsier Rivoile, another worker, to go to the Institute's animal farm in Garche and get us 50 guinea pigs for an experiment. After a short time, he came back somewhat embarrassed; he had seen the department head and only 25 were authorized. After half a day he returned, triumphantly presenting us with 50 guinea pigs. "How come?," I asked. "I thought only 25 were authorized." "I miscounted," answered Monsier Rivoile.

One day, we asked for an expensive piece of equipment. Mr. Rivoile provided it very soon. We worked with it a few days when a most agitated, angry colleague, Monsieur Silvadjian, appeared. Apparently Mr. Rivoile went to his lab at lunchtime and, without asking, dismounted the equipment and wheeled it over to us. It took Silvadjian several days to find it. But meanwhile, we completed our study and wrote a nice paper for publication.

We worked among others with a Warburg apparatus which at that time was of top sophistication. One day, the apparatus stopped working. I asked one of our technicians what to do. She said to request repair authorization from the director of the institute. In formulating my petition, I asked her, "How do you say 'is become inoperative'?" – in French. "Simple," she answered, "futu," which is a French slang expression meaning something like "busted" or "on the fritz." I went to the director's office saying, "Monsieur le Professeur, mon Warburg est futu." He pushed his glasses down his nose, looked at me, and said, "Monsieur Ambrus, where do you learn your French?" He was shocked by the "cockney" language I used.

Nevertheless, Professor Trefuel liked our work and presented it at the French Academy – a great honor. Unfortunately, by the time it was scheduled, we were on our way to the USA.

Madame Pigrol was our dishwasher. In midmorning, she went around at the animal surgery labs and asked for any rabbit or fowl which was dead but not injected with toxic chemicals or germs. She prepared magnificent lunches for all of us (except for members of the highest command who dined in nearby restaurants). She kept saying to us, "You are poor fellows now and I make lunches for you. When you will be famous and rich, I will be retired. Then you will help me." It did turn out that way. We kept sending her contributions as long as she lived.

We loved France but we felt communism breathing down our necks and would have preferred putting more mileage between us. We applied for positions in England, but were turned down at that time. They did not recognize medical training on the continent. We finally got an offer to teach Pharmacology at the Philadelphia College of Pharmacy and Science, affiliated with Jefferson Medical College, where we could also pursue graduate training. We were told that the Hungarian quota for immigration to the United States was full for the next decade. There was, however, one possibility – we could go on the "extra quota list" of outstanding scientists (Albert Einstein was admitted on this basis) if we could show a teaching and research invitation by an American university and proof that we were teaching and doing research in European universities for at least the past two years. Our chiefs from the pharmacology departments in Budapest, Dr. Bela Issekutz, and Zurich, Dr. Hans Fischer, as well as our chiefs from the Pasteur Institute wrote glowing reports and we were given immigration visas. We sat in the office of the Parisian Consul, Mr. Grant, and he recited the obligatory questions: "Were you ever a prostitute? a communist? a thief?" and finally, "You are going with a professor's extra quota visa to teach and do research. What happens if in a few months a large company offers you a magnificent industrial job with triple salary?" The required answers were obvious, " No," to all including the latter, "we want to teach and do research, not primarily to make money." We received our visas and left. As soon as we were out of the embassy, Mr. Grant came running after us. We were scared to death, "Maybe he will take back the visas?" He said, "Now we are out of the office and I can talk to you as friends. I am a former employee of Smith, Kline, and French, a large American pharmaceutical company. I am here in a temporary position to learn foreign affairs in order to be able to return as Chief of the European Office of Smith, Kline, and French. It so happens that they are looking for a Chief of Pharmacology and asked me to make recommendations. Why don't you visit them when you arrive in Philadelphia and refer to me." We did arrive in Philadelphia but never visited Smith, Kline, and French. We were happy with what we were doing. And maybe we wanted to be true to our statement in Paris, "We don't primarily want money."

The university sent an old professor, Dr. Haas, to pick us up at the immigrant boat (we traveled in steerage and did the first clinical tests underway on the effect of antihistamines on seasickness - published in the Lancet after arrival). They sent this professor because he was of German origin and could talk to us. The university administration was not quite sure how good our English was. Dr. Haas stood at the pier where we arrived (after passing medical exam at Ellis Island) with a big card "Looking for Dr. Ambrus." We were happy to see him. I introduced myself and Clara – "Great," he said, "where is your father?" He was looking for a much older colleague.

When we arrived in Philadelphia, we were notified that the college president expected us for dinner. Our guide told us that he, Dr. Ivor Griffith, was the son of a Welsh miner who immigrated to the United States. Dr. Griffith worked his way up; he was the first member of his family who went to college, earned a doctorate, and eventually rose to a highly respected position. He was also a poet, published several volumes of poetry, lived in a spacious mansion, and was part of Philadelphia society.

When we arrived in New York Harbor on the ship, we counted our money; we had exactly $10.00 in our pockets. Before we landed, we went to the bar on the ship to celebrate; we had a drink, toasted the Statue of Liberty, and arrived with $6.00 in our pockets. This we used to buy flowers and to take to the wife of the college president, leaving us with $00.00.

We were received by the Griffiths most gracefully. Everyone talked very slowly and distinctively because they did not know how well we spoke and understood English. They avoided "ostentatious" topics and in general treated us with tact as "poor relations." On the other hand, we assumed that we were dealing with "nouveau riche" people who came from a relatively simple background. We avoided talking much about our background, about cultural complexities, and tried to stay with simple matters. It was indeed a somewhat comical situation in which we both tried to be very kind to each other, respecting each other's assumed sensitivities. But we became great friends and came to respect each other.

I was, of course, fluent in English with a somewhat strange accent bearing traces of Scottish and Hungarian. My wife was born in Rome, Italy, spoke fluent Italian, Hungarian with a slight Italian accent, and fairly fluent French, but she took her first English lesson on the boat as we crossed the Atlantic. We arrived in December of 1949 during the Christmas vacation. In a week, instructions started and my wife had to take charge of a class in the pharmacology laboratory, and had to start advising graduate students who were assigned to work with her on thesis research toward a Ph.D. degree. Most of the students were working on the basis of the GI bill. They were veterans of the war, older, and more mature than the usual run. Many of them were captains and majors who returned to school after close to a decade of military service. They were most gallant with my wife, polite and helpful; they had a great time working together (one of them is presently a professor at the University of Buffalo). I had to give many of the lectures of the basic pharmacology course. There were over a hundred undergraduates in the class but a few graduate students also sat in. One of them – Howard Cravetz (who later became a respected anesthesiologist) sat in the first row and took special notes of all the words I mispronounced. After each lecture, he came to my office and said, "Please repeat the following words after me…" So I learned, albeit now quite perfectly, speaking American.

We rented an apartment on Osage Avenue, close to the university, and walked to work each day. Much later, we learned from the newspaper that a few houses away a crack house developed with a cache of arms and highly suspicious inhabitants. They resisted police search and finally were bombed by the FBI air force – an unheard of event in an American city – much debated afterwards for a fairly long time.

Our first two children, Madeline and Peter, were born at the University Hospital and returned to this house. But we needed a larger home and found one in the Chestnut Hill area in Whitemarsh Village and moved there. This was a long drive from the university and I had an 8 o'clock class to give every day. I was often late starting and drove fast to make it on time. The local police stopped me several times, "Hello Doc – another emergency?" they asked. A few times the policeman whom I came to know well said "Okay, if it is an emergency, I will give you a lead." He went ahead with blaring sirens and we arrived a little late to the classroom building. Some of the students were waiting on the steps. I told the friendly policeman that they will take me to the "emergency."

The other end of the Wissahikon Drive had some trails where we used to go riding on weekends. Sometimes we took our children in front of the saddle to introduce them early to horses. We usually rode up to the Village Green where there were school children employed to hold the horses while we went in for a snack. The children fed the ducks on the water. Those were nice times.

Some of our work related to cancer research and we made early friendship with many members of the Institute for Cancer Research in Fox Chase, particularly Dr. Theodore Hauschka of cancer biology, the two Dr. Schultz and Dr. Rudkin of genetics. Later, Dr. Hauschka was invited to become one of the founders of the rejuvenated Roswell Park Memorial Cancer Institute in Buffalo and he asked us to join him there.

Roswell Park was the oldest pure cancer institute in the world. It was founded in 1896 when Dr. Roswell Park, Professor of Surgery at the University of Buffalo, went to the legislature requesting a few thousand dollars to establish an institute where, he claimed, he would find the bug which causes cancer – in a few years. We are all still looking for it.

The Institute started out small, it had about 80 employees which included the cleaning ladies as well. In the early 1950s, the State of New York ended its budget year with an embarrassing surplus. Governor Dewey's father suffered from cancer and the governor decided to put some of the money into rejuvenating Roswell Park. It was needed indeed.

The first medical meeting for which I was asked to present a paper since I came into the USA was in Buffalo. We visited Roswell Park; it was not in the same league as the Institute for Cancer Research in Fox Chase or Sloan Kettering Memorial Institute in New York City. Governor Dewey built a renewed institute with a 500-bed hospital and 3000 new employees where planned. We were invited for an interview upon Dr. Hauschka's recommendations. That evening, the president of the university, Dr. Furnass, gave a dinner for us. I sat beside his wife, Sparkle. She turned to me and asked the standard question, "How do you like Buffalo?" "Splendid," I answered, "here in the Midwest everybody is so friendly." There was a deadly silence around the table – I had said the worst possible thing. Everyone considered Buffalo part of the "cultured northeast," but I came from Philadelphia and shared their prejudices.

Dr. George Moore was the new director of the Institute. During our interview, my first question was, "What is my research budget going to be?" "There is no budget," came the answer, "you want something, you order it, there are no restrictions. You want to employ somebody, you bring him to the employment office, you employ him." This was too good to refuse. Much of our budget in Philadelphia was based on grants which required a great deal of "favors" to get. This offer sounded like paradise. We accepted. The "honeymoon" lasted for a few years, then the pressure increased to support our increasing-size department with outside funds. Eventually, one of the incentives to encourage us to bring in outside funds was that our institute budget was to match outside funding. But only those outside funds counted which had a high overhead assignment. NIH paid up to 60%. Some of the private foundations allowed no overhead or only up to 10%. These were not counted. Overhead represented an unrestricted fund for the director. He used it as he pleased. We had to deal with strictly regulated funds "cut to the bone." The more "economical" the grant proposal was, the better were our chances to get it. Once we did, we had to struggle with getting the work done on relatively meager funds. Nevertheless, we managed to "bring in" many millions of dollars during our years at Roswell Park.

In a state institution, we had to deal with some bureaucracy. One day, my wife ordered a number of books to be borrowed from another library. When no notice came of their arrival for several weeks, she went to the head librarian to inquire. "Sorry," she said, "I have not yet ordered them. You know the state is slow and so am I."

St. Gallen Days - School Years

I was sent to boarding school in St. Gallen, Switzerland. I was there until the Fall of 1939 when World War II broke out. On that day at dinner, the headmaster stood up to present the usual "order of the day," and said, "I am sorry to say Russia and Germany invaded Poland; World War II has started. Students from other countries have to decide whether they go home tomorrow or stay for the duration of the war." We were seated at tables according to rotating schedules. At that time, those at my table included the son of Hess, the Deputy "Führer" of Germany, the second in line after Hitler; the two brothers Schiktanz, sons of the Major of Hamburg; and the young Litvinov, son of the Foreign Ministry Commissioner of Russia, a close associate of Stalin. They were all sent there probably to be safe at a critical time of history. At this moment, they all jumped up, started to shake each others' hands, and screamed "together we are going to conquer the world." I do not know what happened to them later except the young Hess whom I have seen on television visiting his father at Spandau Prison when he was the only inhabitant there, much after the end of the war.

I decided to go home even though friends in Switzerland offered to pay my expenses if I wished to stay. I boarded a train and got as far as Innsbruck, Austria. The trains did not run further since German troop transport had priority. I was told to go back to Switzerland or go to a hotel and hope for a train in the next days. This is what

I did, and eventually returned home to Hungary. I had many nice memories from my school days in Switzerland. After the war ended, my wife and I returned to Switzerland to complete medical school.

After completing medical school, I had to take the state board examination. This consisted of written, oral, and practical clinical parts. In the latter, patients had to be worked up and minor procedures completed. Patients might have spoken either of the four Swiss languages: German, French, Italian, or Romanche. Everybody's nightmare was to get a Romanche patient. Very few spoke this language. It originated presumably from the Roman legions who stayed behind after withdrawal by the Roman Empire. There were only a few inhabitants left who spoke the language. Written, it was similar to Latin; spoken, it was unintelligible to the uninitiated. I was the only one in the class to draw a Romanche patient in obstetrics. She was ready to deliver, screaming from pain, in no mood to give me an interview, and, of course, she spoke only Romanche. Soon, a young lady appeared and said, "When part of the practical examination includes a delivery, you may have the assistance of a midwife. I came to help you." "That's fine," I said, "but I am going to flunk – I speak no Romanche." "All right," she said, "I spent years as a midwife in Romanch country – I speak the language well." She delivered the baby, wrote the report of the history, physical examination, and progress, and I passed the exam. She was probably planted. I have my diploma but still do not speak any Romanche.

While at boarding school in Switzerland, I experienced my first human death. We went mountain climbing on weekends, and learned the niceties of rock and glacier climbing. Our group was taught by our Latin professor, an old mountaineer. One day, he was leading our small group, all on ropes. Going ahead, he fell into a glacier "spalte." We were unsuccessful at pulling him out. We tied his rope to poles and went to the nearest village, calling on the rescue squad for help. They came along expeditiously , but by the time we got back, the glacier "spalte" had closed and we would never find our professor again.

Hungarians Everywhere

Cleveland, Ohio, is said to be the third largest Hungarian city. Of course, many with Hungarian names are several-generation Americans and speak little or no Hungarian. Nevertheless, the Hungarian American Medical Association used to have one of its two annual meetings in Cleveland. One year, I received a decoration from them and had to give a talk. I arrived a little late, the meeting was in session, I sat down in the first empty place I found, and found myself sitting beside a great big black man. I introduced myself and asked "are you interested in Hungarian-American medical affairs?" He replied in a true southern-Hungarian accent, "Well, I am Hungarian myself." It turned out that a Hungarian shoemaker immigrated many years ago, bought a small house, and started to work. Sometime later, his neighbor's house burned down. He went in there to see if he could help. He found the whole family dead except for a small black baby. He took the baby out, eventually adopted him, and raised him speaking with a southern-Hungarian accent. The boy went to medical school and wound up to become a popular "Hungarian" doctor.

Some time ago, I was a visiting professor in Singapore. A weekend was coming up and a colleague offered to lend me his car and chauffeur, who would take me on the ferry to Malaysia and drive me around in a lovely rainforest. In the middle of the forest, the driver turned around, white as a sheet, and said, "We are almost out of gas. The next gas station is 300 miles away." "What do we do now?" I asked. "Well," he replied, "There is a small village close by, maybe we can get that far. There is a doctor there, he has a car, maybe he can give us some gasoline." This is what happened. I knocked on the door and presented our problem. He assured us that he would be happy to help us out. I gave him my thanks and said, "Please allow me to introduce myself, my name is Julian Ambrus." "Oh," he said, "you are Hungarian too." It turned out that he was well known and liked in a wide area because he was one of the very few doctors who would be willing to see patients who could not pay.

More on Singapore

I was running a clinic for the medical students. One day, there was a commotion in front of the door. I went to look. The secretary who sat out there pointed out that a Malaysian maid brought her daughter but had only half of the required fee and was told therefore that her child could not be seen in the clinic. I said, "Is it alright if I pay the other half?" The answer came, "Sure." That was the only time I had to pay so a patient could come and see me.

Medical Love Story

My wife and I met in first year medical school. She caught my eye in class, and I noticed that her company included a friend, John Szebehely (who later became a member of the pharmacology department in Stockholm and after retirement a general practitioner in the north of Sweden). I asked him about this girl, but before formal introductions my chance came in the chemistry laboratory when her pencil broke and she came over to my section to borrow one. That evening we had a date; we went to the movies (Monte Christo) and then to a small restaurant in the hills of Buda ("Szederfa" – meaning mulberry tree), famous for its intimate atmosphere and excellent gypsy band. It was a favorite of my father's; we often went there.

In medical school, it was announced in class that students could volunteer to work in research laboratories after classes and on weekends. Clara and I both, as well as several of our friends including John Szebehely and his "steady" Maria Fabinyi, volunteered for the medical biology laboratory. Clara worked with Dr. E. Balazs, a young assistant professor who later worked at the Retina Foundation of the Massachusetts Eye and Ear Infirmary of Harvard and was responsible for the development of hyaluronic acid implantation into the eyes to reposition detached retinas. Later, he became president of a small company which further developed this technique for the treatment of rheumatoid arthritis. In those days, we all had to go to the slaughterhouse, and as soon as cattle were killed and hung up to bleed out, we had to quickly puncture their joints to obtain hyaluronic acid containing joint fluid – quickly before it clotted. In those days of relative wartime shortages, eggs were at a premium. We found that joint fluid can be used as egg white to make delicious cookies, and some of the material was diverted for this purpose. I worked mostly with other young assistant professors, Dr. Fazekas, who wound up as a medical investigator in Australia, and Dr. Vasleisz. Dr. Huzella was the head of the department. I worked on agents involved in directing organization during embryonic development of tadpoles, in the hope that some may "organize," that is return, cancer cells to normal. Eventually, I needed a large number of rats to continue experiments in mammals. An excellent facility was made available at the "Charite Polyclinic" where I took a course in clinical pathology, which also led to a separate certificate under the leadership of Dr. Lenard. I also tried to develop techniques to promote healing of burn wounds – important because of the use of the flame throwers in the ongoing war. Some of these experiments we managed to continue when we transferred to the pharmacology department under Dr. Issekutz after the war and then in Zurich, Philadelphia, and Buffalo. Instead of using toxic chemicals, finding "organizers" to tame cancer cells was a lifelong pursuit for both of us. It resulted in a long series of publications, but the research still goes on.

As a first year medical student, I also volunteered to work in the anatomy department with Dr. John Szentagothai. We worked mostly on cats using the Horsely-Clark apparatus to localize brain centers responsible for various functions. This was a collaboration with Dr. Jack Eccles, who later won the Nobel Prize for those studies. Much later, be became professor in the Buffalo Medical School and we renewed our friendship. He worked very hard together with his physician wife and never had much time to socialize. When he retired and returned to his villa in Switzerland, he told us we were his only real friends in Buffalo. Some of the brain surgery on cats had to be done at the time when the students' laboratory exercises were in course. Some of my friends did the dissections for me, but I was there when we had to demonstrate the results and take a short oral examination. They were given by Dr. Szentagothai, my research chief, and we always passed with flying colors. Dr. Szentagothai later became a representative in the Hungarian Parliament and was responsible for major environmental legislation. His brother, who retained the original name of Schimmert when the family immigrated to Hungary from Germany, later became head of the cardiac surgery department at Buffalo General Hospital. When he had hematological problems, he usually called me for consultations, or Clara when children were involved. The second in command of cardiac surgery was Dr. Tomas Lajos, also Hungarian. Together we were known as the Hungarian Mafia at the hospital.

War Days – Wartime Warriors

During the war, Budapest was besieged for months by the Russian army and defended by the German and Hungarian armies. Most of the population lived in cellars and food was very short. There was a German machinegun unit in our house manned by young boys about 15 to 17 years of age. They were fighting young Russian boys of the same age. In the streets were piles of dead bodies. One had the feeling that these boys should play soccer together instead of massacring each other. The second-line Russian soldiers were older, maybe in their early 30s, manning machineguns; and when the young front-line retreated, they were threatened with machineguns from the back. When the Russians finally occupied our street, they set up their own machinegun units in the windows and we remained in the cellars. One day I went up to find something in my room and noticed a young Russian soldier leaning against his machinegun and turning the pages of my "St. Augustin's Confessions" volume. The book was in Latin. I was happy to see that maybe there was finally a way to communicate. I approached him with my broken Latin. It turned out he didn't understand a word of Latin; however, he did know a little German. We communicated in broken German. I asked him whether he enjoys St. Augustin's. He said he didn't know a word of Latin but it was so nice to have a book in front of him again.

After several days, a Russian group arrived and said that they need some manual labor to push some guns in position. If we would come and help them, they would give everyone a big sack of food. This sounded very good and together with a few friends who stayed with us during the siege, we went to push guns. We soon arrived at a railroad station and found out that they really didn't want us to push guns; however, a shipment of captured SS officers arrived in cattle wagons and when they counted them there were several missing. They needed some replacements lest they were reprimanded by their commanders, so they pushed us into the cattle wagons together with the SS officers. We were told we were now honorary SS officers and we were on our way to a prisoner of war camp. Soon we were unloaded and a long column of German soldiers and "replacement" Hungarian prisoners were marched toward a prisoner of war camp about 60 miles away. This must have been a route taken by armies and columns of prisoners of war regularly, since there were several rest stops on the way with hurriedly dug sanitary facilities. After one of these rest stops, one of my friends decided to use this as a possible escape and jumped into the deep pit. The Russian soldiers probably knew about this trick, and after everyone was out, they went back and machine-gunned into each pit. My friend died there.

After we arrived into a crowded prisoner of war camp, it turned out that there was a large epidemic of typhus. There was only one physician in the whole camp, a diminutive Russian lady physician. She came around after a day or so and asked whether there were any physicians or medical students who could assist her. I volunteered and worked with her. One day, she said that she really envied us because tomorrow a train would pull into the camp and take everyone to Siberia. She wished she could come with us because that was her home. I got together with several of my friends and we decided it was worthwhile to risk a possible escape. We dug in the snow under the barbed wire and tunneled our way out of camp, fearing all the time that the guards in the watchtowers would discover us and machinegun us, particularly after we couldn't tunnel anymore and we had to stand up and walk. Looking back with a great deal of anxiety, we saw that the Russian lady physician was standing on the nearest watchtower offering drinks from a bottle to the guards, having a great time and laughing loudly. I suspect she knew that we were going to try to escape and she intentionally entertained the guards so that we could get away, thus diverting their attention.

We walked to the south, hoping to arrive at the city of Szeged. There, we understood, the front had passed through some time ago and relatively normal conditions had returned, including the opening of the university. At one point, we scrambled up on the metal buffers (cow catchers) of a Russian hospital train and rode part of the time on it. Suddenly, the train stopped in the middle of the tracks and an angry officer went around accompanied by a couple of soldiers with machineguns and called off all the civilians traveling on the buffers. He lined up all the civilians in front of the train and the officer started to shout and make strange gestures with his arms. All the time, the soldiers with machineguns stood around him. It looked like we were being reprimanded for scampering up on the hospital train and we were now going to be shot. Finally, a soldier appeared who spoke a little German and he said, "The commander of this train is very much worried that you are all going to catch a cold, so he stopped the train and he wants you all to follow him in some gymnastics which he is going to demonstrate to warm you up." We did our exercise, got back on our perches, and finally arrived in Szeged. Indeed, there was relative peace, the university was in session, and the dean of the medical school was an old family friend. Together with several of my friends, we registered in the medical school, received university housing, and continued our education. We managed to send word back home that we were safe and staying in Szeged. Meanwhile, there was a great deal of hunger in Budapest: and Clara, my fiancé, and her girlfriend, Eva Fisher, decided to join us in Szeged. They arrived after a long arduous trip, hitch-hiking on various transports, but finally arrived and we met in the street close to the university. We decided to get married. The mayor of the city was a friend and we consulted him. He said that according to the laws, we could not get married without parental approval since we were less than 21 years of age. Our parents were in Budapest. It was almost impossible to regularly communicate between these cities because of the war. The mayor came up with an excellent idea: "I will send out a detective to find your parents. He will come back after a day or so and report that your parents are not to be found. That gives me the authority to name a guardian." We agreed to appoint the only close friend we had, the dean of the medical school, Dr. Purjesz, Professor of Internal Medicine. He became the guardian for both of us and gave his permission to marry from both sides. When we asked him about this, he said, "Okay kids, but no harm should come of it."

At the time, there as a typhus epidemic going on, probably related to the ongoing war. There were so many patients that emergency hospitals had to be established in high schools (straw down on the corridors) and patients were laying all around the buildings. Medical students were assigned to work periodically in these typhus hospitals. We worked after hours of school work and a couple of nights during the week. We were also assigned occasionally to go to various organizations and offer free immunizations. I remember one time we were sent to a Catholic convent and we had a great deal of difficulty in persuading the nuns to allow us to inject them on their bare arm with typhus vaccine.

Our friends assembled at our house to come to our wedding and we arrived just at the last minute from our duty in one of the typhus hospitals. I suddenly discovered with horror that my pants were full of lice (probably picked up at the typhus hospitals loaded with rickettsia prowazekii) and these were my only pants. One of our friends who came for the wedding quickly volunteered that I could use his pants and meanwhile he would stay in our future apartment in his underpants and wait until we cam back from church. Meanwhile, another classmate took my pants with lice to the hospital to be autoclaved. We arrived at the cathedral for our wedding on time. The wedding was to be performed by Msgr. Majtényi, whom we met at our periodic visits to the steam bath where we usually went after a night at the typhus hospital to swim, have some gymnastics, and sit in the steam while our clothes were being autoclaved. We had great theological discourses while sitting in the steam. He was much impressed by the fact that Clara was born in Vatican City, christened in St. Peter's, and educated in one of the best nun-run Catholic schools in Rome. Msgr. Majtényi reminded us that it is the custom that girls christened in St. Peter's receive a dowry from the pope when they get married. He reminded us that one of these days we should go to Rome and collect. We went to Rome several times, we were invested in the Knighthood of the Equestrian Order of the Holy Sepulchre, but we are still to raise the issue of the dowry. After the wedding, we were all worried because it was getting dark and there was a curfew in town. The Russian soldiers shot everyone indiscriminately who moved in the street after curfew. We got home just in the last minute.

At the end of the semester, we returned to Budapest and continued medical school there. It was unusual at the time that people married at such an early age. All our friends and relatives said, "It will never last." All our professors poked fun at us when we arrived together for examinations. We are now married for 65 years.

Ecumenism

I was invited to do a visiting professorship in Amsterdam and my host said that on the evening of the first day, there is an ecumenical meeting to which he would like to invite me. He did warn me that since I would be introduced as a guest who came from far away, I would probably be asked to say a few words. After returned from clinical rounds, which I had to conduct, I found in the hotel several Bibles and even a Koran. I had about half an hour to prepare for my little speech. I started out by saying, "It is nice to see representatives of so many different religions, although of course there are too many for all to be represented here. There appears to be also a minority of Muslims, nonetheless, I want to start my talk with an Arabic invocation which I had to use before each lecture I gave years ago in Saudi Arabia, 'Bism Illah el raman el rahim' (in the name of God, the merciful, the compassionate). This invocation may be shocking to some, but maybe ecumenical meetings are to shock everyone a little. Those whom I haven't shocked yet, I may shock with my verse I will use as my text to initiate my little talk, 'Semaj Isroel Adonaj elauchenu Adonaj echod' (Hear ye oh Israel the Lord your God is one). Some of the biblical texts had specific meanings at the time when they were written but they have eternal meanings even in much later times. At the time when this was written, it might have been referring to the fact that most people were polytheists believing in many gods and it had to be emphasized that there is only one. Today, our problem is more that many people don't believe in any God at all rather than in many different gods. This text also means that there is only one God whether we call him Allah, Jehovah, or the Lord. It's been the same and that is what ecumenism is all about."

I also questioned why Hindus were not invited. I was told this meeting is usually only for monotheistic religions. I pointed out that according to the information I was getting, many Hindus believe that they are also monotheists. Vishnu the creator, Brahma the maintainer, and Shiva the destroyer are a trinity. When Vishnu comes to Earth to check on his people, he is Chrisna or Rama, but all of these are only one. All of the other so-called Hindu deities should be considered as the saints in our pantheon.

History of Medicine – Ancient Medical Schools

We participated in a medical meeting in Ephesus, Turkey, and visited the site of the ancient Hippocratic medical school. We had to put our hands on the column with the multiple serpent sculpture on its base and renew the Hippocratic Oath which we had to take at graduation from medical school. We have also visited Salerno, which prides itself as the first "modern" medical school, as well as Bologna, which was probably second in line. At times, we refer to the medical school of Bologna on hand of a text of comic opera by Puccini. In the opera, Gianni Schicci, a rich miller, dies and leaves all his fortune to the church. His daughter is engaged to be married and counts on this fortune as her dowry. They dress one of the confidants in the clothes of the dead miller (whom they threw through the window into the Po River) and ask for the notary to come and take his final will and testament. He then leaves everything to his daughter, thus making it possible for her to get married. Before the notary arrives, the family doctor comes and asks how the severely ill patient is doing. The man who masquerades in his place says that he is much better and he thinks that he is almost cured. The doctor thereupon sings a little aria: “But I will say in all humility that all the credit belongs to the medical school of Bologna.” Whenever we make rounds together and find that a patient has greatly improved even though this is probably not due to our efforts, we look at each other and say, “La Scuola Bolognese.”

I will never forget the patient with a far-advanced metastatic malignant melanoma who was going to the hospital in a terminal state. I was told that we just had to keep him comfortable and help him over to the other world without suffering. I prescribed intravenous feeding, modest pain killers, and tranquilizers. As the time passed, he improved; and after several weeks, left the hospital cured, even though we had never really treated him. There is an NIH registry of spontaneous cures of advanced neoplastic disease and the majority is malignant melanoma. One case we have witnessed gave impetus to starting a project on the immune therapy of cancer. We are still working on this project.

War Years

In the last year of the war, the Germans occupied Hungary, captured the governor of the country, Admiral Horthy, and put the ill-reputed Szalasi in charge of the government. One of my friends and classmates, Purgly Potyi, the nephew of the governor, was allowed to visit the governor periodically in jail and take to him food. Terror descended on the country and many people were imprisoned, executed, or sent to German concentration camps and killed. One of my father’s friends, Julian Szekfu, Professor of History at the university, was in imminent danger because of his well-known west-leaning political orientation and the fact that his wife was a Viennese Jew. Several friends got together and agreed that they had to be hidden and provided with false identity papers. One of the younger men in the group agreed to hide him in his house and provide him with the identity paper of his deceased father whose photograph was actually not too dissimilar. It was a bigger problem to find identity papers for his wife, since she spoke with a strong German accent. Finally, one of the friends came up with the papers of his mother, who came from the German-inhabited area of Transylvania. This was adequate justification for her German accent. In those days, the concierge of each house was supposed to report to the police anything suspicious. He was required to lock each house at 10:00 in the evening and if anyone, including the owner of the house, would ring the bell after 10:00, he had to be questioned about his activities of the evening and his papers had to be inspected. One day, the concierge appeared and said, "I do not want to go to the police, but I see something very suspicious. The German baroness from Transylvania periodically seems to go into the room of your father at night. I do not want to make an issue out of it, but you better watch out for the old man."

Uganda

During a visiting professorship at the Makarere Medical School in Kampala, Uganda, I had to take medical students with a traveling clinic to small villages in the bush. On arrival, I had to palaver with the village elders to get permission to set up the clinic. At the end of a usually lengthy discussion, a gourd went around with banana wine to seal the agreement. At the gourd went around, I made the diagnosis of those drinking – frambrosia, probably syphilis, herpes labialis, etc. When the gourd came to me, I had to drink. As soon as the ceremony was over, I went to my tent, which meanwhile was set up by my group, and shot myself full of penicillin.

At the time, I also had an ulcer and consumed a lot of milk. At times, I sent a runner to the next village to bring milk. He usually left in the evening and returned the next morning. One early morning, I was shaving in the tent and observed the runner coming in with two large gourds full of milk on a yoke. He hit his foot on a large root, fell, and spilled some of the milk. He looked around carefully, went to the next bush, pushed down his pants and refilled the gourd. It came in nice and warm and foamy. I had to explain to my group that I want to leave some milk in a dish for the jungle spirits to assure further safe travel.

Every morning, I was served breakfast in front of my tent on gleaming clean university-owned china. One morning, I went to the small river behind my tent after breakfast and watched my boys cleaning the dishes. There were round patties of buffalo gunk floating in the river but that did not bother anyone. My good cooks kept spitting on the dishes as they were polishing them, but that evening I had dinner served on shining clean dishes with the university seal on them.

I had a difficult time with students when working in a leper colony. They were afraid to touch patients, examine them, or take blood samples. It was difficult to convince them the leprosy is not as highly infectious as popularly believed. It requires, for the most part, long-lasting intensive contact. Simple hand-washing with antiseptics is effective. Moreover, using modern methods, leprosy is a curable disease.

On some days, we had many hundred patients waiting for us. Some walked a long distance to get there. They started with a large sugar cane for a walking stick and snacking on the way, and arrived with a small stump of sugar cane in their hands. We had no x-rays or EKG, and only limited laboratory facilities and little time for each patient; but we had no fears from malpractice suits and could practice medicine freely without the need for "protective tests."

Many years later, when Idi Amin kicked out all Ugandans of East Indian origin, I helped many of my former students and residents to come to the United States with jobs or training positions which we found for them. For many, we helped to find jobs in Kenya and Tanzania. During a much later visit to Saudi Arabia, one of my hosts drove me from one hospital to another. Bypassing a nice villa, he said, "This is where Idi Amin lives with his large family in exile – do you want to visit him?" I said, "No thanks."

Memories

It is interesting that when recalling hard times, wars, epidemics, floods, and faculty intrigues, one remembers mostly the humorous episodes, the funny side of it all and not the original tragic aspects, the fears, the existential horrors. For example, when returning home after the war, I bypassed mountains of frozen cadavers on the streets, which made little lasting impression. But I saw a dead horse being cut up by a man who was feeding two famished dogs and throwing crumbs to a group of crows – this picture haunts me still.

The Martians (Presentation to the Thursday Club, 1994)

The title of the paper is "Martians" in reference to H.G.Wells's book and Orson Wells's radio performance on "War of the Worlds," which made it notoriously popular. By satellite pictures of Mars, a stone appeared; on closer examination, it looked a little bit like a man's head from a demolished statue. Then they looked carefully – it turned out to be just some old stones.

At the time when the Manhattan Project was on, part of the top scientists were Hungarian, including Leo Szilard, Eugene Wigner, who got the Nobel Prize in physics, John von Neuman, who developed the first computer, and Edward Teller, the father of the hydrogen bomb. Enrico Fermi, the other member of this group, said, "Well, if there is extra-terrestrial intelligence and if there are Martians, how come they are not here yet?" Szilard replied, "But of course, there are here already! But the problem is that they have learned how to speak English, but could not get rid of their thick accent. They said, 'We are Hungarians' and these Hungarians are all Martians." Well, this is how it all started.

This paper originated when, at one time at dinner, we were talking about what should be my next paper. Al Mugel suggested that I talk about the history of Hungary since we know so little about it and that it may be of some interest.

I am going to start at the very beginning. As you know, at about 100,000 B.C., homo sapiens started to move out of Africa. At about 40,000 B.C., a group, the Ugors, found itself in the Near East. Part of this group traveled to Europe; some of them became the Basque and some of them became the Pickts, of the founding stocks of the Scotts. Basque Great Pyrenees Shepherd dog is almost identical to the Hungarian Kuvasz, which is a Hungarian Shepherd dog. This may be one suggestion that these groups probably lived once together and may be relations. My daughter, Madeline, has a Great Pyrenees. Some of the Ugors moved North and became Finns and Ests. The rest of the group moved on to Siberia and found itself near the Ural Mountains. At this point, the group was called the Ural-Altai Tribe. Hungarians were part of this group and eventually this group moved to the West, partly pushed by various other nomadic tribes – the Besengos and the Kuns (Cumans). Part of the Ural-Altai group went to the East and there are some small remainders who are still in Siberia. These are the Vogul, Osztyak, Inguish, Zurjen, and Votjak. One group crossed the Bering Sea and wound up in America. They went down to California and became the Pima Indians. They do not look like Mongoloid Indians. They look more like Hungarians. They had unearthed a while ago the skeleton of the Kenewick man. Anthropologically, he looked more like a Caucasian, possibly Hungarian, rather than an Indian. The molecular geneticists have found a Y-chromosome haplotype mutation which you only find in Hungarians, Finns, Druz, Pima Indians, and some Algonquin Indians. The Mongoloid Indians came later and decimated the Pima Indians, but they are still surviving. Maybe we have to go to request compensation from our Indians and request the right to establish casinos.

The Hungarians contributed possibly at three levels to modernizing warfare. First, they developed the reflex bow and then developed a technique where they made bows not out of wood but out of bone – the ribs of large animals – which is more powerful. Secondly, they also invented the stirrup. An original is hanging on my wall. The story of this is that the dean of the medical school in Munich, Germany, comes and works with us occasionally during the summer on joint projects. One summer, he came along and said, "Well, you know we have a farm near Augsburg; and while plowing, the plows threw up a couple of stirrups. I took the stirrups to the archeology department at the university. They identified them as stirrups of the Hungarians who were massacred at the Battle of Lechfeld near Augsberg, and this pair probably originated there. Your ancestors left them there, and I brought them back to you." The Romans (no matter how developed they were, from a certain point of view) were riding without stirrups – and so did the Greeks and all the Germanic warriors. The Hungarians found out that they could stand up in the stirrups and aim their arrows from a gallop much more accurately. They became highly sought-after mercenaries. The third level was the atomic bomb, as discussed earlier.

At one point, the Sumerians engaged Hungarians to guard the entrance to the Caucasus and prevent nomadic tribes from raiding Sumer. They developed contact with the Sumerians and picked up the Sumerian cuneiform writing with some modifications. I remember the Hungarian cuneiform from my childhood. I had some contact with it due to the fact that we had a shepherd who drove sheep up to the mountain pastures in early spring, stayed out with them all summer long, and the brought them back in early winter. He was allowed to milk the sheep, make sheep cheese, and sell it at the fair. However, they did have to keep records of how many lambs were born and which sheep had which lamb. These records were engraved by cuneiform writing onto willow branches. During the war, I gave a copy of this alphabet to all my relatives so that we could write to each other in code.

The Hungarians became incorporated into various large nomadic tribes. At one point, they were one component of the Hun Empire, and together they raided China. The Great Chinese Wall was built for protection against these raids. At another point, they became a part of the Kazar Empire. The Kazars were courted by the West, the Holy Roman Empire, the Eastern Empire of Byzantium, and the Osman Turks – they all wanted to convert them. The Kazar rulers tried to stay independent from all of these various power blocks. They imported Jewish missionaries and the Kazar Empire converted to the Jewish faith. The Pesenges attacked the Kazar Empire and started pushing them toward the west. The Hungarians started to migrate to the west. There were seven Hungarian Tribes which were joined by three Kazar Tribes, a Bulgarian Tribe (which was Moslem), and a Skitian Tribe of Iranian origin. Multiculturalism started early with the Hungarians. The old Hungarian legend was that they were guided toward Hungary by a hunting eagle. This tradition has continued. We are still breeding these eagles on our farm. We developed breeding techniques for raptorial birds in captivity and did various medical studies on them resulting in several publications. I have a picture of my son, Peter, mounted on his horse with a steppe eagle on his glove. Beside him is my daughter, Madeline, who also participated in these studies. Among others, we showed that raptors have a hematologic variation, they are deficient in clotting Factor XII and thus similar to patients suffering from Hageman's disease, Hemophilia D. Yet they do not have bleeding problems. We are studying the reason for this. These studies may eventually help Hemophilia D patients.

Hungary turned out to be an excellent place to settle due to the fact that it is surrounded by high mountains, all above 6000 feet high; this was excellent protection against the other nomadic tribes which pushed toward the west. The Hungarians settled and for many hundreds of years they were the ones who were protecting the West against incursions of nomadic tribes. Some of these nomadic tribes were actually allowed to cross the mountains and settle down in the border areas. They were employed as border guards. For a very long time, their main function was to protect the West against barbaric incursions.

The Hungarians, themselves, continued the tradition of organizing raids to the west and coming back with slaves and treasures. Very often these incursions were not just to acquire goods, but to actually hire themselves out as mercenaries to the various German Dukes in the altercations among themselves. They continued to raid as far as Spain until they were beaten at Lechfeld near Munich.

At one point, Hungarians were raiding St. Gallen in Switzerland and the local abbot wrote a very detailed manuscript in which he described a Hungarian raid. I happened to be in boarding school in

St. Gallen in my high school years and spent some time in the local public library studying the codex about the Hungarian raids in order to write a term paper.

The first King of Hungary was St. Stephen, who was crowned in the year 1000 A.D. with crowns donated by the Holy Roman Emperor, the pope, and the East Roman Emperor. All three wanted to incorporate Hungary into their power block. St. Stephen had one son, and in those days apparently it was fairly easy to become a saint. His son became a saint and was named St. Emeric. He was fighting against the Bulgarian invaders and became very popular in all of Europe. He became so popular that all over Europe, children were named after him. In Italy, his name "Emeric" was Italianized and was called "Amerigo." Many hundreds of years later, one of his namesakes, Amerigo Vespuci, was one of the first to circumnavigate America, and the name "America" came from him.

St. Stephen had several daughters, and one of them was Agata – Margaret. There was an interesting contact between the Hungarian and British royal houses. At one point, Prince Edward the Peregrine was exiled from England by Canute, the Danish conqueror. Edward went to France, but the French were afraid of diplomatic conflict related to the British Crown, and he was eased out. Edward was sent from one kingdom and dukedom to another toward the East until he wound up at the Court of St. Stephen. There, Edward married St. Stephen's daughter, Agata - Margaret. Their bodyguards were the Argyles. The Argyles were the ones who introduced the bagpipes into Transylvania. Not very long ago, there came a Hungarian music group to Buffalo, and among other things, they demonstrated the Hungarian-Transylvanian bagpipes. This is a modification of the Scottish bagpipes which the Argyles brought along. Edward and Agata returned to England, but after a short time, the Danes again chased them out. Edward, Agata, and their daughter, Margaret, took a ship to return to the court of St. Stephen. A storm drove them up the coast to Scotland. They were rescued by Malcolm III Canmore (which means "great chief"), who was the King of Scotland. He fell in love with their daughter, Margaret, and married her. Margaret had a large dowry from St. Stephen; the most valuable piece of that dowry was the "Black Rood." This was a black box into which had been placed a small piece of wood. This wood was presumably from the cross of Christ. Whenever Malcolm III went into battle, his wife, Margaret (like a good Hungarian wife) rode with him carrying the Black Rood. Whenever she held up the box of the Black Rood, the Scotts were winning; whenever her arm became tired and she lowered it, the Scotts were losing. Margaret founded a great many monasteries and nunneries; she became St. Margaret of Scotland. She is not to be confused with St. Margaret of Hungary, the sister of a later Hungarian King, Bela IV.

Margaret and Malcolm III had a number of children. Three of their sons succeeded each other as King of Scotland. The first was called "The Vassal" because he recognized the superiority of the English King. The next son was called "The Fierce" because he renounced the vassalhood and was interested in an independent Scotland. The third was David I, who was interested in an independent Scotland. A daughter, who was called Edith, the Empress Matilda, married Henry I, who was the son of William the Conqueror. This is the connection between the Hungarian and the British houses. St. Margaret was also known to have magical power over animals. She could talk to animals and she could tame dragons. In a contemporary codex, there is a picture of her talking to and taming a dragon. Nuns from the nunneries which she had founded spread all over Europe. From one of these groups came the original founding nuns of one of the first hospitals in Europe, the Hotel Dieu in Paris. We happened to work for a short time there, and I think some of the nuns from the original founders were still there.

In those days, it was easy to become a saint. Another Hungarian Princess who became a saint was the sister of Bela IV. She was St. Elizabeth of Hungary. She married Otto, Duke of Bavaria. She was very anxious of going out to the slums to visit the poor people and take them food. Her husband however, thought she should not go out and mix with the riffraff. One day, she was walking with her entourage, carrying large bags of food and distributing it to the poor, when her husband, Otto, appeared with some soldiers on horseback. He said, "Lady, I told you not to do this. What is that package you are carrying?" Elizabeth replied, "I am just carrying roses." She opened up the package and all the food had turned to roses.

The Hungarians at that time were very much aware of the fact that they were the protection of the West against invading tribes from the East and the invading Turks from the South. The only way to become protected was to enlarge the country. St. Ladislaus was a major fighter against the invasion of the pagans. He wanted to enlarge his empire as protection against the invaders. He conquered what is today Poland and Czechoslovakia. He extended the country all the way to the Adriatic Sea, incorporating some parts of Italy and today's Slovenia and Croatia. Hungary was at that time one of the largest and richest countries in Europe. Soon thereafter, two major calamities occurred. The Mongols came in a major invasion, beat the Hungarian Army, and occupied most of Hungary, killing off approximately a third of the population before they were repulsed. Soon after they left, a great plague reached Hungary and killed off at least another third of the population. Two-thirds of the population perished in that century. During the Great Plague, some of my colleagues (physicians) dressed in strange get-ups, made everyone think that they had magical powers, and could do something about the plague – even though they did not have the foggiest idea what was the cause and how to fight it. Nevertheless, the plague gradually subsided. As it was moving from one city to another, the citizens went around in self-flagellating processional groups praying for the plague to be lifted. When the plague stopped in an area, they built commemorative columns. I have a picture of my wife, Clara, in front of one of these surviving commemorative columns.

Of the many kings I have not time to discuss, I do want to mention Coloman the Lawgiver. One of his laws in 1111 A.D. stated (in the obligatory Latin official language): "De strigiis quae non sunt nulla litigatio fiat" ("Of witches who do not exist there should be no legal action"). This was at the time when "witches" were burned in most parts of Europe.

The major role of Hungarians continued to be the protection of Europe against the Turks who wanted to conquer all of Europe. King Mathias thought that the way to do it was to become Holy Roman Emperor and concentrate all European countries to fight the Turks. He conquered Prague and Vienna. However, the died in Vienna soon after conquering it. He did not only excel in warfare, but he accumulated one of the largest libraries in Europe. He had a whole monastery doing nothing else but copying manuscripts and establishing the Illuminated Corvina Codexes which is on exhibit today. He continued the war of his father, who played a very impressive role in fighting the Turks. The Hungarian army had a major victory over the Turks at Nandorfehervar and the Pope ordered that in commemoration of this victory, all churches should ring their bells at noon. That is the only help that the Hungarians got from the West, even though they kept asking for help from the Pope and the rest of the European rulers. When the Turks advanced into Yugoslavia, the only help the King of Serbia had gotten was the Hungarian army and the Walachian (Rumanian) army at Kosovo. They were about to beat the Turks when the Rumanians changed position and went over to the Turkish side. The Turks beat the combined Serbian and Hungarian armies. Serbia was occupied by the Turks. The Hungarians continued to keep the Turks out of Europe for another 150 years, but finally the Turkish army beat the Hungarian armies and occupied the central part of Hungary. At that time, Hungary became divided into three parts. The Central part became a Turkish province. The Transylvanian Duke agreed with the Turkish Port to pay them an annular tax and, in return, the Turks agreed not to invade Transylvania. The Western part became part of the Austro-Hungarian Empire. They elected the Austrian Emperor simultaneously King of Hungary. They used Austrian money to build a number of forts on the border between the Eastern and the Central part of Hungary. They were manned by Hungarian military. For 150 years, the border forts continued fighting the Turks and kept them from invading the West. The Turks imposed on the occupied Central part of Hungary very heavy taxes. Part of the taxes was that each village was to submit a certain number of five-year-old boys. These boys were taken to Turkey, raised in a Turkish military orphanage, eventually in a military school, and became the Yanisaries – front troops of the Turkish Empire. They were the ones who occupied eventually all of Arabia, all of Iran, and continued to attack Western Europe. Many of the Hungarian villages were completely devastated by the Turks. They carried away the population into slavery. These areas became uninhabited pampas and stayed that way until the present time. The "Puszia," the great Hungarian pampas, became a communal grazing area where everyone from the neighboring farming areas could graze their animals. Today, part of this is a nature park. Visitors can see Hungarian cowboys who demonstrate their horsemanship. The grass in the middle of summer burns down. Most cattle cannot live there very well, except for the Hungarian grey longhorn cattle, which are probably a direct descendant of the Pleascein aurox, which is now extinct. These cattle are resistant to diseases and get along on just some yellowed grass. There are still large herds of these Hungarian longhorns in that area.

Eventually, the Austrian Emperor got together a large army of Austrian and Hungarian warriors, and they managed to beat the Turks out of Hungary. Of course, the Hungarians were hoping that they would say, "Thank you" to the Austrians and the Austrians would leave. They never left . They established the Austro-Hungarian Monarchy. For some time, this became a fairly prosperous country. The Hungarians became famous for breeding horses: the Lipizzaners were developed there, supplying coach and riding horses for all of Europe. The Hungarians started to develop better relationships with the Austrians. Many were building houses in Vienna and, during the opera season, attended the performances in Vienna. My family and I, as a youngster, stayed at our house in Vienna and attended the opera in season. After the season was over, they were back on the family farm in Hungary. Coaching cavalcades were organized for Hungarian visitors in the riding school of Vienna. Hungarian agriculture developed and modernized. Hungarian wines became famous. One of the specialties was the Aszú wine. Hungarian grapes were allowed to shrivel down to almost raisins. A very concentrated and flavorful wine was made of it.

The Hungarians wanted freedom from the Austrian Empire's heavy-handed rule and they started several revolutions. The first one was in the early 18th Century and the second was in the early 19th Century. Hungarian revolutionaries managed to beat the Austrians out of the country, liberating the country. At that point, the Austrian Emperor teamed up with the Russian Czar and they attacked from both sides, between them the Hungarian revolutionaries were beaten. The Austro-Hungarian Empire was re-established. After the revolution of 1848, many Hungarians escaped execution and prison interment. One of these Hungarians, who came to the United States of America, was Agoston Haraszti. He brought with him a large number of wine cuttings and started the first winery in California, which is today the Bona Vista Winery. At the entrance, there is today a bust of Haraszti. When he arrived, the wines were all properly labeled except for one label which was partly washed away – they could not quite read it. It looks like "zinfandel." Some years ago, there was a wine tasting in Italy and they found that zinfandel is almost identical to an Italian wine from the vineyard north of Rome called Primitivo. But everyone knows that Primitivo came from a Hungarian wine called "Szilvandi," and this is probably where the zinfandel came from and this is how the only American wine really originated.

After a couple of revolutions, the Austro-Hungarian Empire became prosperous again. There was a large building spree. The Hungarian Parliament was built At that time, a large number of Hungarian farms built new buildings. In "Eszterhaza," Hayden was the "house composer."

Prosperity lasted until the Austro-Hungarian Empire occupied what is today Bosnia-Herzegovina. The Austrian Crown Prince visited this newly conquered part and was murdered by a Serbian patriot. This initiated World War I. The Austro-Hungarian Empire attacked Serbia – Serbia brought in Russia, an ally – Russia brought in the Western Allies – World War I was in full force. Eventually, the Austro-Hungarian and German allies were beaten and in the Trianon Peace Treaty, two-thirds of Hungary was taken away. The Northern part, together with a part taken from Austria, became

Czechoslovakia, a country which had not previously existed. The Eastern part of Hungary and Transylvania became part of Rumania; the Southern part became part of Yugoslavia. Hungary was down to one-third of its original size and one-third of its population. Today, there are only 10 million Hungarians in Hungary, about 3 million Hungarians in the surrounding countries, and 10 million Hungarians scattered around the rest of the world. The Trianon Peace Treaty also imposed very heavy financial fines. A tremendous depression resulted. The consequences of this depression in Germany caused the rise of the Nazi Party and the coming into power of Adolf Hitler. In Hungary, a Communist Party came to power In the southern part of Hungary, a group of military leaders assembled an army and arranged a high-level meeting in the cathedral of the southern town of Szeged (the reason this cathedral is dear to my heart is that this is where I was married). They managed to re-conquer Hungary, but there was tremendous bloodshed – this was called the "White Terror." Eventually the White Terror wound down and prosperity started again in Hungary. Hungarian science and scholarship flourished. Several Hungarians won the Nobel Prize at that time. Robert Barany, M.D., was a student of one of my relatives. He discovered the mechanism of the function of the inner ear. During World War I, he was drafted as a military physician. He eventually wound up in a prisoner of war camp in Russia. At one point, the news came into the camp that he had just won the Nobel Prize for his work on the inner ear. The camp physician told Dr Barany that they should try to get him out of the camp to allow him to accept the Nobel Prize in Stockholm. The only way to get him out was to declare him deathly ill, requiring a discharge. Dr. Barany said that he was not ill. The Russian physician replied that he decides who is and is not ill. Dr. Barany was discharged and accepted the Nobel Prize in due time. After he returned to Vienna, which was his Alma Mater, he applied for appointment to the medical faculty. The Viennese turned him down. He went back to Sweden and became Professor of Head and Neck Surgery in Lund. Here happened the famous story when one of my relatives was conduced around the campus and they came to a small bust. Upon inquiring, "Who is that?" he was told, "That is Professor Barany who won the Nobel Prize for developing the mechanism of the inner ear." After a while, they came to a large statue over 30 feet tall. Again, the question, "Who is that?" and the reply, "Well, this is Professor Lindquinst, the Chancellor of the University. He discovered Professor Barany."

A large number of Hungarians at that time moved to the West and here are a few who became well-known in Hollywood. There is Adolf Zukor, who founded Paramount; Vilmos Fox, who founded Century Fox; and Michael Curtis, who directed many famous movies including *Casablanca* and *Robin Hood*. There are also a large number of Hungarian actors who came to Hollywood. It is very interesting that Leslie Howard, considered to be the most British actor, was originally called Laszlo Steiner from Hungary. Another one who was considered to be a very typical Anglo Saxon actor is Tony Curtis, who came from Hungary, as did Fred Astaire (his original name was Austerlitz). There were three famous musicians, Bartok, Kodai, and Dohnanyi – who among others worked together in collecting the Hungarian folk songs from the villages before the songs died out. One of the interesting things is that Dohnanyi became director of the German Musical Academy in Berlin. He was there for a long time, but eventually he divorced his wife and returned to Hungary. His son became a Major in the German Army and Dohnanyi was the one who organized the attempt on Hitler's life, of which many German officers were a part. Dohnanyi, together with Rommel and the rest of the conspirators, were executed when the plot failed.

Hungarians were also prominent in sports at the Olympic Games. The Hungarian rankings were mostly in the top ten among all the countries, even though Hungary was small – only around 10 million people. It was said that Nobel Prizes and Olympic medals per population were highest in Hungary.

We should say a few words at this point about the educational system from which we can probably learn. The main point of the educational system was that teachers were highly honored. High school teachers were called professors. Their place in society was high and similar to that of physicians or lawyers. As an example, on a list of my high school teachers, most were Ph.D.s. At that time, it was customary that if someone wanted a career in academics, he had to start out as a high school teacher and gradually move up to the university. Several of my high school teachers were simultaneously lecturers or assistant professors at the university. Some of us working with them could go to their laboratories and get a taste of their research work at the university. Two of my schoolmates at the Evangelic Gymnasium were Nobel Prize winners (Wigner and Harsanyi). A third schoolmate missed out due to early death (von Neuman), who developed computers.

MY HIGH SCHOOL TEACHERS AT THE EVANGELIC GYMNASIUM IN BUDAPEST

Catholic Religion	Rev. Erno Fuhrman
Literature	E. Remport, PhD, poet pen name Vathly Elek
	D. Kerecsenyi, PhD, Asst Prof Univ Budapest
Latin	S. Klaniczay and J. Ihasz
English and German	F. Endrodi (former fellow Cambridge Univ)
Greek (optional)	V. Dengelegi
History	I. Janossy, PhD
Biology	S Sarkany, PhD, Asst Prof Biology, Univ Budapest; later Chairman of Biology
Math	E. Levius
Gym, Sports, Military Training	I. Miko
Physics	M. Vermes, PhD, Asst Prof of Physics Univ Budapest
Hygiene, Health Affairs	T. Mihailovich, MD
Art	I. Oppel
Music	I. Pesko (father of chief conductor – Vienna Opera)
Speedwriting and Office Skills	E. Ramport, PhD
Philosophy	Z. Losoncy, PhD
Geology and Geography	I. Koch, PhD
French (optional)	D. Kerecsenyi, PhD
Headmasters	I. Mikola, PhD physics (Member Natl Acad Science) I. Renner, PhD physics (Member Natl Otvos Academy) I. Koch, PhD geology
Of 20 faculty:	10 PhDs 3 simultaneously Asst Prof at Univ of Budapest 1 member of Natl Acad of Science 1 member of Natl Otvos Academy

Hungarian science flourished until World War II. In World War II, the Hungarians tried to remain neutral. They, however, used the opportunity to mobilize their army and re-conquer parts of Hungary which were taken away in the Trianon Peace Treaty after World War I. They re-conquered part of Northern and Southern Hungary and part of Transylvania. They came under increasing pressure from the Germans who tolerated this, but in turn expected Hungarians to join in the war on their side. The Hungarians finally agreed to send troops to the Eastern Front and fight the Russians, but insisted that they were not fighting on the Western Front. There was, of course, a large Hungarian group which was against these arrangements. The regime which went along with some of the German demands used the opportunity to turn of the anti-German resistance by Hungarians. As an example, one of my uncles was a Colonel and the youngest member of the General Staff. He was put in charge of a tank company and sent to the Russian Front. He was ordered to attack; at that moment, the Germans on the two flanks withdrew. The Russians managed to annihilate his group and kill all 5000 men. In order to get rid of the one they considered to be anti-German, an important part of the General Staff, they allowed 5000 men to be massacred.

Eventually, the Russians pushed toward the West, occupied Hungary, and there was house-to-house fighting. A good part of Budapest was demolished together with all the bridges. Eventually, the Russians occupied Hungary and established a communist regime. Again, resistance did arise, and in 1956 Hungarian resistance managed to beat the Russians out of the country, occupying parts of the Russian forts and equipment. Very soon thereafter, the Russians returned in force and re-occupied the country. They killed many of the revolutionaries. For a brief moment, the Western border was unguarded and open. A large number of Hungarians left the country and came to the West. They spread out in Western Europe and the United States of America. The Russians continued a reign of terror; but finally, in the period from 1990-1992, the Russian Empire collapsed, left Hungary, and a democratic regime was re-established. When the communist oppression was lifted, among others, Árpád

Gonz, the writer, was released from ten years of imprisonment. He was made the first post-communist President of the country. It was said that in the USA when one completes Presidency, they often try to put him in jail. In Eastern Europe, as in Hungary (and as in the case of Havel in Czechoslovakia), they take people out of jail and make them President. Hungary is now a member of NATO and the European Union.

In a nutshell, this is the most important part of the history of Hungary. One of the conclusions of all this is what Hungarians believe - that all great men are Hungarians!!! If someone is great, and not a Hungarian, he is automatically made an honorary Hungarian to maintain the rule.

Some Problems of the University

Four of us usually drove together to the Thursday Club meetings. Wilmot Jacobsen, Professor of Pediatrics (Peter, our son, stayed at his mansard apartment during his residency around the corner from the Children's Hospital); Winifred Butsch, Professor of Surgery; Seymour (Shorty) Knox, Chairman of the SUNY/B Board; and myself. We had many discussions on the way about the status of our university. We had a great deal of difficulty attracting a first-rate faculty. One of the reasons might have been that whenever candidates came for interviews, they found out from the senior faculty members that when they had come, many promises were made on start-up research funds, salaries for assistants, new junior faculty, and others which were not kept when they arrived. It was also remarkable that in many universities the faculty helped each other in many ways including, e.g., nominations to the National Academy of Science. Here, many faculty members looked at each other as competitors. For example, the Chairman of Physiology at SUNY/B (Dr. Herman Rahn) and the Head of Crystallography at Roswell Park told me that they do not nominate any locals to the Academy and they do not even propose papers of colleagues to be published in the Proceedings of the Academy (I finally got a paper published there, sponsored by a friend from another university). We also have a great deal of difficulty, as do many other universities, with the system that promotions depend on firstly, grants received, and secondly, papers published. Consequently, many faculty members spend most of their time writing and rewriting (when rejected) federal grants. Today's acceptance rates are low. On one committee on which I sit is about 8%. Consequently, much of the teaching is done by graduate students and postdoctoral fellows. The senior faculty is too busy to do much teaching that is not appropriately appreciated or rewarded. Those few who teach enthusiastically and are appreciated by the students are often regarded suspiciously by some of the faculty. For example, at one time, junior medical students had to choose among several optional courses. My group and I offered a course in tropical medicine. This course became very popular and many of the junior class chose this course. Consequently, many other optional courses were left with few students. Soon, a rule was passed that none of the optional courses could have more than a certain number of students, and many who wanted to take our course were told to choose others.

War – Persecutions

During World War II, Hungary was occupied by the Germans in 1944 and by the Russians in 1945 (they stayed until 1990). There were many people persecuted, taken to concentration camps, and killed. My wife (Clara M. Ambrus-Bayer) and her family and my family were part of a network of resistance and efforts to save those persecuted. My wife's father was an architect who built and became manager of a textile factory. It ran out of material during the war, was closed, and all workers were dismissed. The large factory and warehouses stood empty and appeared to be good hiding places for the persecuted. Anyone who asked asylum was admitted – Jews and non-Jews alike. They were hidden in the factory or the family house on the grounds. When the Germans came to inspect, they were told through a loudspeaker that before the gates were opened, the vicious dogs had to be put away. This gave all the people time to go to their assigned hiding places. No one was ever found. My wife also went to ghettos and concentration camps and offered the guards one golden guilder (from the family reserves, since inflation made the regular money not worth much) for each detainee released (this was worth about $5; that, for a human life). These people were then taken to the textile factory or other places in the network. The latter included the large house of one of my uncles who was part of the Italian Embassy with a large Italian flag and a note on the door indicating that this was a diplomatic area. Several houses of the Catholic sisters of social service were part of the network. Unfortunately, one house headed by Sister Sara Salkaházy was raided by the Germans, and all of those hidden, as well as Sister Sara, were executed. She was later beatified by the Pope and is on way for sainthood.

When the Russians chased out the Germans, all those hidden came out and celebrated. But soon the Russians started taking them to concentration camps. Many people had to be hidden again. After the Hungarian revolution against the Russians in 1956, the closed borders were opened for a short time and many people escaped to Austria. Some were later admitted to the USA and put into Camp Kilmer. The condition to be released was to find a job. Many ex-military officers with little English knowledge and not marketable skills had difficult times. At the time, my wife and I worked at Roswell Park Cancer Institute and had a large experimental chimpanzee colony. We employed a number of these ex-officers from Camp Kilmer. The colony never was as nice and clean. It was said that in the morning when the ex-officers came in, all the chimps stood up in their cages and saluted.

While much of this was going on during the war, I was with a resistance group in the woods while the Germans retreated and the Russians came in fighting. We tried to fight both groups. One day, sitting in the tops of trees, we spied a column of Germans through our telescopes with a general on a tall horse leading. I was told that since I was their best sharpshooter, I should shoot the general. I missed. Many years after, my wife and I were asked to consult for a German pharmaceutical company. We worked with them for several days. Before we left, we were asked to come to the president's office for coffee and a goodbye chat. When we entered the elaborate office,

I turned pale and almost fainted. My wife did not know what was wrong with me. Shortly, I recovered, we had a nice chat, and left. After we were out of his office, I told my wife, "The president behind the large mahogany desk was the general whom I missed."

During the war, there was a relative food shortage in Hungary. This was a highly productive agricultural country; however, many products were exported to Germany. Our farm had to submit much of its produce to the authorities; however, some was hidden from them and distributed to the families working on the farm and our own family households. My wife's father was caught at one point carrying a large amount of food (which was needed to feed all of the hidden, persecuted people). He was tortured by the authorities to reveal why he was carrying much more food than a family needs or what its allocated tickets allowed, where it came from, and whether he was hiding unauthorized people with no official food tickets. He did not reveal anything and was finally released. Soon thereafter, he died; the torture and the beatings probably significantly contributed to his death.

Criminality

I had little to do with criminals; however, there were a few episodes which stay in my mind.

When the university in Makarere, a university in Kampala, assembled my traveling clinic, they proposed that among others I take along an African gun bearer who was told to be an excellent game skinner and cook and an intelligent fellow who could be taught to do many things. However, he had a criminal background; he was jailed for some minor infarctions. I decided to take him along. He turned out to be a first-rate assistant. He learned how to take blood, even from people with difficult veins, although he never knew that the heart pumps the blood to circulate. He was also a fine cook of the game which I shot every morning to feed my students, assistants, and even the patients who came to our traveling clinic. The fellow was a Muslim who told me at one point that he could not eat any of the game I shoot unless it is prepared in a special way. He asked me to wound some antelopes rather than to kill them, and to let him take care of it in the way prescribed by his religion. I shot an antelope in the shoulder; he then took his handjar between his teeth and ran hell for leather to catch the antelope, to cut its throat, put a rope on its hind legs, and string it up on the nearest tree branch. This resulted in the animal bleeding out and being acceptable to be prepared according to his religion.

At one time, I was a visiting professor in Mexico City and used the opportunity to visit an old friend, General Umberto Mariles, who was the Captain of the Mexican Equestrian Olympic Team and in the shows that we competed in a long time ago in Europe. I had several of my children with me, some of them very young. General Mariles took us to his horse farm and gave the children advanced instruction in Olympic-type jumping. He then took us on a long trail ride on his farm and again was very careful in instructing the children how to cross deep ravines on their well-behaved ponies. When we returned, his peons unsaddled and washed the horses and again General Mariles explained to the children how to supervise all these activities and make sure that everything is done properly. Several months later, I received a desperate telephone call from his son. Apparently General Mariles was caught in one of the standard Mexican traffic jams in Mexico City and after waiting for a long time he became very agitated, got out of his car, and shot and killed the driver who was blocking him. He was put in jail and was awaiting severe sentencing. His son wanted to know whether I could ask the American President to intervene on his behalf. Of course, I could not do that. Not much later, I was informed that he committed suicide in jail.

We had a contract from the Brazilian government to study disease-related problems among the Indians in the Amazon rainforest. What the government was really interested in was what kind of medical problems may they look forward to when they increased the influx of settlers into the rainforest who were supposed to be sent from the suburban favelas to start farms in the cleared rainforest. One of our Brazilian friends came with us and helped up assemble a group of guides. These included Indians representing various tribes so that all languages we may encounter were covered and we would have adequate interpretation. One of the fellows they recommended to include in our group was a chap whom we were told spoke little English but excellent German and several Indian languages so he could serve as an interpreter. He looked rather European than Indian, and he did a good job except that he tried to get close to one of my daughters, Kathy, and would go off on separate little walks with her in the jungle. We were, of course, not permitting that and everything went on fine after that. Much after we returned home, we found out that this fellow was really a German who went to the Amazon region after the war and made a living as a safari guide. However, he murdered one of the parties he was guiding and took all of their possessions. He was caught and sentenced to be executed. So much for highly recommended guides and interpreters!

We were engaged in much clinical research; but before we initiated treatments on our patients, we often tried these new drugs on ourselves, or we were looking for normal volunteers. We had a small group who went out to Attica State Prison, headed by Richard Shields, and asked for volunteer subjects and also for volunteers to assist us with procedures such as sterilizing instruments, etc. These volunteers received good points in their records which accelerated their receiving early discharge. One of the good points for discharge was having a job. Since some of these people were trained in minor assistant-type procedures, we managed to get jobs for some of them at the Roswell Park Cancer Institute. Everything went well until the Attica State Prison riot, when my group was caught and held as hostage. Fortunately, they were brought out by the National Guard without difficulty. We later received a note from Albany telling us to stop all volunteer experiments in the state prison.

Clinical Research

My group did clinical research and a great deal of basic research on the fibrinolysin system and finally got ready to do some clinical experimentation. The first agent we were going to try was streptokinase. One question was whether streptokinase was strongly antigenic and whether people may have pre-existing antibodies that may produce difficulties. Before we started our study, I decided to try these on myself. I injected myself with this material in the hospital and nothing happened. At that time, I was Chairman of the Main Seminar Program and I was supposed to go to the airport to pick up a foreign visitor who was invited to give a seminar and do some clinical teaching at our hospital. At that time, you could walk right to the steps leading from the airplanes at the airport. I stood there, and when our visitor arrived, he found me on the ground unconscious. Streptokinase did it. He brought me to the hospital and I spent a week on intravenous steroid infusion before it was all over and I would go back to work. This showed that streptokinase is indeed highly antigenic, and it may induce anaphylactoid phenomena and this has to be taken under consideration. In several publications, we recommended that before streptokinase was given to patients they should be given an antihistamine and, if not contraindicated, some intravenous corticosteroids. With these methods we never had significant side effects in our patients. Unfortunately, this was not widely used, as several major reactions were reported from other institutions in the literature.

What we have learned, and what we have not learned, from the Wars

After World War I, the victorious allies imposed heavy fines on the beaten nations. They also imposed heavy loss of territory. For example, Hungary lost two-thirds of its territory, including its ports on the Adriatic Sea. All of this resulted in a loss of three million Hungarians who found themselves as minorities in neighboring nations. Because of these factors a great deal of depression, unemployment and inflation became manifest in the central European countries. Desperation of the population made it possible for Mussolini and Hitler to come into power. We have certainly learned from all of that, and after World War II, instead of imposing heavy punishments, the Marshall Plan helped the former enemies to reach normal conditions and become part of the democratic community. Toward the end of World War I, the central powers helped many communists return to Russia from exile in Switzerland and start the Bolshevic Revolution which took the Russians out from the war against the central powers. What a great mistake this was. It turned out later when Central Europe was occupied by the communist powers for almost 50 years. The Bolshevics imprisoned the Czar and his family but allowed him to communicate with his distant cousins, the Royal Family in England, and ask for asylum. The Bolshevics would have let him go if these arrangements could have been made. Asylum was not granted and the Czar and his family were executed. Hitler started to build up the army, and revolted against the post World War I peace treaty and re-occupied Elsas-Lotharingia, and the Ruhr area. At that time we could have easily stopped him and gotten rid of him, but we did not want another war. We could have prevented World War II and saved the lives of over 50 million people. Hitler then occupied Sudetenland, part of Chekoslavakia with a high German population. Still, nobody objected and he followed up with occupying all of Chekoslavakia, followed by annexation of Austria. Hitler wanted to get rid of the Jewish population of Germany and distribute their goods to his cronies. He would have let them emigrate if they could find countries that would let them in. He was also thinking of sending the entire Jewish population to the island of Madagaskar, but of course this was not practical. Few countries allowed only the immigration of relatively small numbers of these groups. There is the story of a ship full of immigrants who had a visa to Cuba, but when the ship arrived, the Cuban authorities changed their mind and didn't let them land. The ship's captain then decided to run ashore in the United States, become shipwrecked, and then the shipload of immigrants would have to be taken care by the American authorities. When this plan became known, the American government sent out Coast Guard ships letting the Captain know that if he came any closer, he would be torpedoed and sunk. The ship returned to Europe. France allowed some of the women and children to take refuge there. Later, after the German occupation of France, most of these people were killed in concentration camps. The British allowed some of the young men to enter the country. Most of these volunteered for the British army, participated in the D-Day landing, and few of them survived. The rest of the group had to return to their countries of origin and most died in German extermination camps. One of the inmates of the German concentration camps managed to escape and with a great deal of help from various resistance groups, found his way to the United States and had an audience with F.D.R., the President, and Eleanor his wife. He described the extermination camps and asked for help. He was told no direct help is possible; all attempts are to winning the war. Germany has offered several times through various groups to let people from their concentration camps go for small amounts of money or certain goods such as trucks but none of these plans were approved. Close to 10 million people were executed, probably 6 million Jews and numbers of gypsies, resistance groups, anti-Nazi church leaders, severely handicapped and mental patients, as well as homosexuals. Several times there was discussion of bombing the gas chambers of the concentration camps and the railroads leading to the concentration camps. These proposals were always turned down by the allied command since they felt that there were more important targets and no air force involvement can be spared for this purpose. Resistance groups during World War II, as well as during post-war anti soviet revolutions, including the 1956 Hungarian revolution against the Russian occupiers, received little help from western countries. It was thought that this resulted in avoiding World War III, and revolutions contributed to the eventual collapse of the soviet empire.

Cuneiform Writing

Earlier in these vignettes, I discussed how the migrating Hungarians picked up Sumerian cuneiform writing, and how these remained for many centuries among some people in Transylvania. One of our shepherds used this writing engraved on willow branches to record the status of the flock of sheep entrusted to him. I enclosed a copy of this alphabet as I remembered it. I distributed it during the war to many of our friends and relatives, and used it to write each other coded communications.

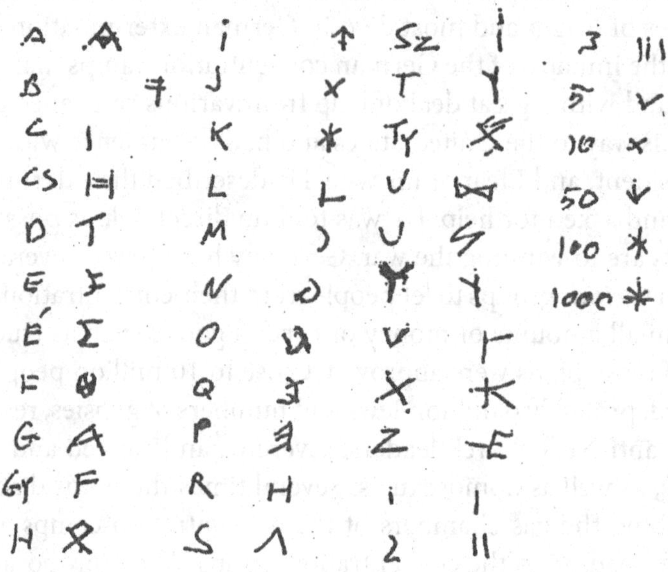

Events 60 Years Ago

For some reason some of our functions during World War II, over 60 years ago, now surfaced and a great deal of fuss was made about it. We had to go to accept medals and listen to many speeches of recognition to New York City, Washington, D.C., Albany, and of course Buffalo, New York. After one of these events, one of the Jewish groups which celebrated us for helping to save the lives of many groups of persecuted people including Jews, invited us for a dinner. I was told to make a brief speech. I was really not prepared for all of that and I asked what they wanted me to talk about. I was told anything, but to try to make a few Jewish jokes in the process. I didn't know many Jewish jokes but I presented a few which I describe here. I tried to find out what kind of Jewish group we were dealing with and it turned out it was not an orthodox, not a reform group, but a conservative one so they reassured me that my first joke would be properly placed. The story was actually told to me by the Nobel Prize winning physicist, Richard Feinman. When he was a graduate student he was assigned the job to build a cloud chamber. He went to an orthodox rabbi and asked him to make a little prayer, usual for new beginnings, called a Brucha. The orthodox rabbi said that cloud chambers must be some new-fangled contraptions and that he really couldn't make a prayer for that, but the student should try a conservative rabbi. He went to a conservative rabbi who said that he would like to help him but the law is not clear about this and he doesn't think he can do something about it. He then went to a reformed rabbi who said, "Well, cloud chambers are fine, but what are Brucha's"?

My second joke was about a Jewish gentleman who went to his rabbi and said that he needs a great deal of help. He sent his son to Jerusalem to learn something about his ancestors. After awhile, the son returned and it turned out that he converted to Christianity. He asked the rabbi what could be done about this. The rabbi said "let's get down on our knees and pray for guidance". As they were praying the ceiling opened up and God himself appeared. God said, "I well understand your problem. You see, I sent my son to Jerusalem and he came back a Christian, the founder of Christianity".

My third joke which was weaved into my brief talk was about another Jewish gentleman who went to his rabbi and said, "I need help. I pray every day to God to help me win the lottery and nothing ever happens. What can be done?" The rabbi suggested that they get down on their knees and pray. As they prayed, the ceiling opened up and God appeared, and said, "My advice is: buy a ticket". All of these jokes were accepted in good spirit. At least nobody at the dinner showed any displeasure.

History of Hungary

In the first volume of Babel, I included an outline of a lecture about the history of Hungary I was asked to give at the Thursday Club. My grandchildren (Christine, Sarah and Karen) who read Volume I, did some research, and gave me some supplements I should include, including an additional list of Hungarians who became famous in the United States. It appears that a little oppression by Mongols, Turks,

Germans, and Russians may be good for you; it makes you work twice as hard to achieve something. They have also included a list of Hungarian Kings and a geneology chart, which are both attached.

Hungarians Famous in the USA

Hungarian Nobel Prize Winners:
Robert Barany, MD – Medicine (inner ear)
George Bekesy, PhD – Medicine (inner ear)
Milton Friedenan, PhD – Economics (monetarist school)
Dennis Gabor, PhD – Physics (holography)
Daniel Gajdusek, MD – Medicine (prions)
John Harsanyi, PhD – Economics (game theory)
George Hevesi, PhD – Chemistry (radioisotopes in medicine)
Inire Kertesz, PhD – Literature
Philip Lenard, PhD – Physics (cathode rays)
George Olah, PhD – Chemistry (carbocation chemistry)
Harold Pinter – Literature
John Polanyi – Chemistry (new reactions)
Albert Szent-Györgyi, MD – Medicine (vitamin C)
Elie Wiesel – Peace
Eugene Wigner, PhD – Physics (symmetry theory in atomic physics)
Richard Zsingmondi, PhD – Chemistry (electron microscope)

Hungarians in Hollywood:

Don Adams (comedian)
Vilma Banky (silent film actress)
Drew Barrymore (actress and part of the famous Barrymore acting family)
Eva Gabor (television actress – Green Acres)
Mariska Hargitay (Emmy-award winning actress – Law and Order)
Jamie Lee Curtis (actress – A Fish Called Wanda)
Steven Spielberg (director and producer – Jaws, E.T., Schindler's List)

Lee Strasberg (director and acting teacher who popularized Method acting)
Rachel Weisz (Academy Award winning actress – The Constant Gardner)
Robert Halmi (TV play – The Iliad)
Tom Curtiz (film maker - Casablanca)
Adolf Zukor (Paramount)
Vilmos Fox (Century Fox)
Alexander Korda (director – The Thief of Bagdad, Red Pimpernel, Henry VIII)
Michael Curtis (director – Casablanca, Robin Hood)
Joe Esterhas (writer – Ninocska)
George Cukor (director – My Fair Lady)
Bela Lugosi (actor)
Zsazsa Gabor (actress)
Leslie Howard (Lazlo Steiner) (actor – Gone with the Wind)
Tony Curtis (Antal Kertesz) (actor – Lobster Man from Mars)
Paul Newman (actor)
Fred Astair (Frederic Austerlitz) (actor)

Musicians:
Paul Simon (singer/songwriter, part of Simon & Garfunkel)
Georg Solti (conductor for the Chicago Symphony, holds the record for receiving the most Grammy awards – 38)
Bela Bartok (composer)
Zoltan Kodaly (composer)
Fritz Reiner (conductor)
George Szel (conductor)
Eugene Ormandy (conductor)
Antal Dorati (conductor)

Politicians:
George Pataki (former Governor of New York)
Jesse Ventura (professional wrestler and former Governor of Minnesota)
Alan Hevesi (former Comptroller of New York State)
Tom Lantos (Congressman)

Nicolas Sarkozy (President of France)

Publishers and Writers:
Joseph Pulitizer (established the Pulitzer Prize)
Arthur Koestler (wrote Darkness at Noon)
Ferenc Molnar

Athletes:
Mickey Hargitay (body builder)
Monica Seles (tennis player)
Don Shula (football coach)
Elvis Stojko (figure skater)

Artists:
Georgia O'Keefe (painter)
Simon Hantai (painter)
Susan Hantai (painter)

Other Famous Hungarians:
Harry Houdini (magician, escape artist)
Calvin Klein (clothing designer)
Estee Lauder (founder of Estee Lauder cosmetics company)

Industrialists/Financeers:
George Soros (financial speculator, stock investor, and philanthropist)
Steven F. Udvar-Hazy (financial CEO, funded a new center for the Smithsonian Institution's U.S. National Air and Space Museum)
Andras Grove (Intel)

Photographers:
Robert Capa
Andre Kertész

HUNGARY'S RANKINGS IN OLYMPIC GAMES 1896-1996

YEAR OF GAMES	HUNGARY'S RANKING
1896	6
1900	10
1904	5
1906	12
1908	6
1912	9
1924	13
1928	9
1932	6
1936	3
1948	4
1952	3
1956	4
1960	7
1964	6
1968	4
1972	8
1976	10
1980	6
1988	6
1992	8
1996	N/A

Accent

I was elected President of the Catholic Physicians Guild - USA - WNY and had to make an inaugural speech. I started by saying that the Catholic Physicians Guild was always doing things first, and this is a first again - the first time that the President is European-born and has a bit of an accent. The story about that, however, is one when President Carter was elected and a reporter went to Plains to interview local residents about how they felt about a local boy becoming President of the United States. One answer was: "This is great. Finally we have a President without an accent". More about the inaugural address will follow.

Health Status in the United States

At my inaugural address for the Catholic Physicians' Guild - USA - WNY Presidency, I discussed recent statistics on the status of health in our country. These data are summarized in the enclosed tables. It appears that we are the country with the highest expenditure for health in the world, as well as the highest level of sanitary factors, nevertheless, from the point of view of infant mortality (which is used by epidemiologists as an indicator of health standards) and from the point of view maternal mortality after childbirth, we are only in the middle of the nations surveyed. Countries like Cuba are far ahead of us. Survival, life expectancy for both men and women also puts us about in the middle of the nations surveyed. Countries like Sweden and Japan far outdistance us. Survival rates are greatly influenced by our bad showing in infant mortality. The major cause of infant mortality is premature birth, largely related to inadequate care and nutrition during pregnancy. Prematurity causes a high incidence of respiratory distress syndrome - hyaline membrane disease. We were anxious to investigate the causes and together with my wife we surveyed cases in the Women and Children's Hospital of Buffalo which is part of our University and our Kaleida Health System. We found that members of the fibrinolysin system develop fully only in the last days of pregnancy and infants which are born prematurely have inadequate levels of plasminogen, devoiding them of a system which can dissolve pulmonary fibrin deposition during birth trauma. Accordingly, we went ahead and produced pure human plasminogen from outdated blood bank blood and used these in 500 premature babies. In the vast majority, we managed to prevent respiratory distress syndrome. In those who developed the syndrome in spite of treatment, we used a ready-made fibrolytic enzyme also produced in our laboratory both by aerosol and by intravenous injection. This resulted in survival in the vast majority of even the infants who developed respiratory distress. We hoped very much that one of the pharmaceutical companies will proceed after these data were published to produce both plasminogen and plasmin for general distribution. Unfortunately, they were afraid of using human blood products because of the possibility of contamination in the early days of the AIDS epidemic and no commercial preparations were made available. It also appeared that inhalation of surfactant may be helpful in these conditions. In our experience, the best results were obtained when plasminogen was combined with surfactant therapy or plasmin when needed. All of these data were published, and we are still hoping for one of the large pharmaceutical companies to return to manufacture these products.

There are a few other comments I would like to make to these statistics. As far as Doctors per Capita are concerned, we are 44th in the world. At one time, there was a tendency to reduce admissions to medical and nursing schools because it was thought that this would save healthcare costs. The consequences of closing several nursing schools and admitting less Americans to nursing education, became by now a significant crisis. We are importing nurses from many countries including under-developed countries that need them very badly. The lack of approving extending medical school admission rates is now projected to become a significant problem in the next decade. In the meantime, we depend heavily on attracting qualified doctors from under-developed countries, again depriving them from probably some of their best graduates.

We are 50th in the number of hospital beds, among the countries for whom adequate statistics are available. We continue to close hospital beds on the idea that this would also save healthcare costs. We neglect to consider, however, that in case of emergencies, earthquakes, floods, bioterror attacks, war, and other major problems, we need available spare beds and if we cut the number to the minimal required under normal conditions, we may eventually be in great difficulty.

We are number one in calories consumed, and obesity is a major problem for us. Interestingly enough, during my first assignments to African hospitals, malnutrition and associated diseases were major problems. On subsequent visits, however, we found at least in some of the large cities such as Nairobi and Abidjan of the Ivory Coast, childhood obesity appeared to be a problem. We studied this issue and found that if women are malnourished during pregnancy, their infants develop mechanisms which make utilization of nutrients more efficient. After birth, in the presence of adequate but not necessarily excessive nutrition, this may lead to obesity. In patients coming in from the outlaying areas, we still found malnutrition so that strangely enough in these same hospitals we found diseases related to malnutrition and obesity at the same time. The following tables summarize these and related data.

Table I
Rank of the USA Among Nations in Healthcare and Related Areas - 2005

	Rank
Money spent on healthcare per citizen	1 ($5,700)
Gross domestic produce % for healthcare	1 (15%)
National debt	1 **(8.6 trillion)**
Federal foreign debt	1 **(2.1 trillion)**
Trade deficit	1
Access to clean water and sanitation	1
Doctors per capita	44
Hospital beds	50
Infant survival rate	34
Maternal survival rate	29
Life expectancy for women	30
Women who already reached age 65	20
Life expectancy for men	28
Calories consumed	1
Murder rates	15
Rape rates	51
Gold Reserves	1
Unemployment	38
Consumption of oil	1
Nuclear energy production	1
Solar and wind energy production	3
Incarcerations	1
Executions	4
Women in managerial or high government positions	5
Voting age citizens who vote	139

Table II
Health Care Expenditures (percent of GDP) – 1991

United States	**13.4%**
Canada	10.0
Finland	9.1
Sweden	8.6
Germany	8.4
Netherlands	8.4
Norway	7.6
Japan	6.8
United Kingdom	6.6
Denmark	6.5

Table III
Life expectancy at birth, years
(1991)

RANK	COUNTRY	TOP TO BOTTOM
1	Japan	82
2	San Marino	81
3	Switzerland	81
4	Sweden	81
5	Andorra	81
6	Australia	81
7	Monaco	81
8	Bali	81
9	Canada	80
10	Singapore	80
11	Iceland	80
12	France	80
13	Israel	80
14	Spain	80

15	Netherlands	79
16	Belgium	79
17	United Kingdom	79
18	Germany	79
19	New Zealand	79
20	Austria	79
21	Finland	79
22	Norway	79
23	Luxembourg	79
24	Malta	79
25	Greece	79
26	Ireland	78
27	Cypress	78
28	Cuba	77
29	Portugal	77
30	Kuwait	77
31	United States	77
32	Slovenia	77
33	Costa Rica	77
34	Chile	77
35	Denmark	77
36	North Korea	76

Table IV
Infant Mortality Rate (per 1,000 live births) – 1991

United States	**10.4**
United Kingdom	9.4
Germany	8.5
Denmark	8.1
Canada	7.9
Norway	7.9
Netherlands	7.8
Switzerland	6.8
Finland	5.9
Sweden	5.9
Japan	5.0

Table V
Death rate of 1 to 4 year olds
(per 200,000 per year) – 1991

United States	**101.5**
Japan	92.5
Norway	90.2
Denmark	85.1
France	84.9
United Kingdom	82.2
Canada	82.1
Netherlands	80.3
Germany	77.6
Switzerland	72.5
Sweden	64.7
Finland	53.3

Table VI
Death Rate of 15 to 24 year olds
(per 200,000 per year) – 1991

United States	**203**
Switzerland	175
Canada	161
France	156
Finland	154
Norway	128
Germany	122
Denmark	120
United Kingdom	114
Sweden	109
Japan	96
Netherlands	90

Note: The murder rate for the above age group is 48.8 per 200,000 in the USA

Table VII
Percent of people with normal body mass – 1991

	Men	Women
Germany	53%	37%
Finland	51	37
United Kingdom	46	38
Canada	52	29
Switzerland	49	30
France	44	30
Denmark	44	25
United States	**47**	**22**
Sweden	44	25

Table VIII
Doctors' Incomes – 1991

United States	**$132,300**
Germany	91,244
Denmark	50,585
Finland	42,943
Norway	35,356
Sweden	25,768

Table IX

USA Status	Approx. No.in Millions
Uninsured, part of the time	75
Uninsured, all times	40
Lives on/under the poverty line (<$20,000)	40
Lives on less than twice the poverty line	90
Illegal immigrants	12

War Medicine

During the war, we often have to deal with patients who were badly injured, in shock, and on the battlefield it was almost impossible to find their veins to give them infusions. I finally developed a technique where we put in a bone marrow needle in to either the spina ilica superior or the sternum and gave the infusion directly into the bone marrow with the help of hyaluronidase for more rapid absorption. This also had the advantage that when the patients were transported, the infusion needle was less likely to fall out particularly on shaky vehicles, or it was less likely that the patients would tear out the infusion in his confusion. We found this method very useful. Later, a collaborator of mine, A. Islam, MD, PhD, spent some time in developing new disposable bone marrow needles for diagnostic procedures. We discussed that he should also develop a bone marrow needle for infusions. This study is still in progress.

Medical Stories

Teaching the First Course of Internal Medicine to Medical Students: In the first course of internal medicine, I usually started out by saying that some of the important characteristics of good physicians are that they are not disgusted by anything, they are not afraid of the medical problems of their patients, and they are very good observers. To illustrate this point, I had a urine sample. I mentioned that in the medieval days, when a patient complained of frequent and copious urination, the doctor would dip his finger in the patient's urine and taste it. If it was sweet, the diagnosis was diabetes mellitus. If it was not, the diagnosis was diabetes insipidus. I said to my students, "Now I'll dip my finger in the urine and lick it, and make the diagnosis. Now you do it yourself." With that, I passed the container around and they repeated the process. They all said the diagnoses should probably be diabetes insipidus. I said, "You have demonstrated that you have two characteristics that I mentioned but not the third. You were not disgusted and not afraid to dip your finger in the urine and lick it. And you made the proper diagnosis. On the other hand, you were not good observers. What you should have observed is that when I demonstrated, I dipped my index finger in the urine, but I licked my middle finger."

I also mentioned as part of my introductory talk to the students that whenever a patient enters a room, we should immediately try to make a diagnosis. As the taking of history and physical examination proceeds, we may continuously alter our diagnostic hypothesis or add new points. However, there is a little history I wanted to mention.

A patient entered the teaching room and the professor said, "Stop! Don't come a step closer. Don't say a word. I want to use your entrance for a teaching exercise." The professor asked the class what their initial diagnostic hypothesis is by just looking at the patient. There was none. The professor then said that they should have noticed how this patient looked around questioningly, somewhat disoriented as he entered the room. This is the typical attitude of a deaf-mute patient. There upon, the patient said, "Professor, the deaf-mute is my brother. He is in the waiting room. Can I bring him in?"

Splenomegaly: At an early session in this course, I brought in a patient with a pronounced splenomegaly and taught the students how to tell an enlarged spleen which is significantly under the costal margin. Then I demonstrated a second patient and I asked them to percuss the spleen. The students did, and when I asked for the results, they all said that the spleen is normal. I then pointed out that all that their examination revealed is that there is no splenic tissue below the costal martin. However, when this is the case, they have to percuss the triangle at the tip of the spleen. If this sounds drummy, as it does in this patient, it means that there is no spleen at all. Instead of saying that the spleen is normal, they should have said that no splenic tissue is appreciable below the costal margin. They should then proceed to determine if there is any spleen. This patient underwent splenectomy a long time ago and there are no visible scars which could call attention to surgery in this area.

Singapore: During a visiting professorship in Singapore, I was to run an outpatient clinic with medical students. One day, I came in somewhat late and the students told me that there was nothing particular so far. They had seen one Malasian maid who has worked for a Singapore family and the students said she has leprosy. They have already called the paddy wagon which is on its way and which will take her to the leper colony. I said that before we let her go, I want to examine her. Her face indeed had the lesions similar to those of a patient with Hansens' disease (leprosy). I took two glass slides and pressed out some tissue fluid from these lesions, stained it, and looked at it under the microscope with the students. It was teaming with leishmania. I said, "This apparently is not leprosy, but post kala azar syndrome." The patient apparently recovered from kala azar, but some of the leishmania congregated in the skin where it is less subject to attack by antibodies. This caused the local lesions. We could take this patient to the hospital, treat her with appropriate chemotherapy, and within a couple of weeks she would be perfectly healthy again. The students appeared unhappy. They said, "But sir, we have already called the paddy wagon. If we have to tell them our diagnosis was wrong and we called them out for naught, we will lose face. The university will lose face. And you, who is in charge of this clinic will lose face. Let us just let her go to the leper colony." I said, "In no way can we do that. If we let her go to the leper colony, sooner or later she will pick up leprosy and her life will be miserable. Instead, we can admit her to the hospital and cure her. I am in charge and this is what we are going to do." I heard some of them murmur behind my back, "barbarian American."

Uganda Story: This was a time when I did a visiting professorship in Uganda. The British colonial rule was just about over and the British troops started to withdraw. My traveling clinic, which was supposed to teach students how to practice "jungle medicine" without the benefit of laboratories, X-rays, and consulting specialists, arrived into a small village. However, there appeared to be no one in the village. Flies were buzzing around. In the central square there was a large Banyan tree. There were a number of cadavers of babies with their skulls fractured against the tree trunk and their brains spewed out. It turned out that the village was raided by their arch enemy, a neighboring tribe, which killed most of the men and children and drove the women into slavery. As we were leaving the village, members of raiding party came and said that they are happy to see us. They had a number of wounded after the raid and thought we should take care of them. I said that we can make a deal. "We will take care of the wounded if they release the women whom they have carried away." It was a deal. They were released. We left soon thereafter and I never found out what happened later. Were the women recaptured? Were they left alone? How did they make a living? How did the new central government of Uganda react to all of this?

Szeged: While World War II was still going on, my wife and I were medical students in Szeged, in the southern part of Hungary. There was a large typhus epidemic but fortunately, we had some vaccines and medical students were assigned in the evenings to vaccinate certain parts of the population. One evening I was assigned to vaccinate nuns in a nunnery on the outskirts of Szeged. I had a great deal of difficulty in convincing them that I should be allowed to see them partly undressed so that I can do a quick physical examination and administer the vaccine. I mentioned that Jesus Christ was often described as a good physician. "He could cure people by just laying his hand on them or sometimes from a distance, not even seeing them. I'm only trying to follow his example, but of course we cannot do what he did. We have to work intensively with our patients. We have to use physical examination, drugs, operations, and pray that all of that should work. Accordingly, we have to do our jobs the only way we can." My little speech seemed to have worked and I managed to vaccinate all of the nuns in the monastery.

Dying Patient: I will never forget the cancer patient who was probably in his last days when I saw him. He said to me that I should promise that when things really turned bad, I would not institute any major procedures, any attempt to prolong his life and with it his suffering, but I will just let him go quietly. I had assured him that everything will be done to minimize his suffering. He was treated with intravenous infusions of drugs and electrolytes and blood. He watched the droppings of his infusions and whenever the infusions bottles went low he hit the panic button and requested the nurses to put on the next bottle. From his attitude, it was very clear that what he says is one thing but what he really feels is that he wants to hang on to life as much as possible. This taught me that we always have to consider that there may be a discrepancy between the patients expressed wishes and his real feelings. It is a frequent problem that the family requests that intensive life support should be stopped and the patient appears to agree. Yet, there are indications that the patient's real feelings are to hang on to life.

Medical practice: One of the patients I saw in the clinic was a retired professor of dermatology who had fallen on hard times. He had difficulty getting around and came in a cab and ordered a cab to take him back home. At the end of the visit, he asked for $40 to pay for the cab fares. It was one of those cases when I had to pay for seeing a patient.

Clinical research: We collaborated with a group of medical chemists at the university. We had joint meetings of our two groups and together designed chemical structures to be synthesized for possible therapeutic use. The head of the chemical unit was Thomas J. Bardas, PhD. Usually we assembled on time, but Tom and I were often a little bit late. It was then said that there are three types of times: a.m., p.m., and A.B. (which stood for Ambrus-Bardas time), which is always fifteen minutes late. Actually, the compounds synthesized had code numbers which started with AB. They went from one to 185. Newly synthesized compounds are tested in our laboratory, first in a series of in vitro experiments then in normal animals, and then in various disease models. We used several inbred strains of mice, rats, guinea pigs, and rabbits, as well as monkeys in different experiments. Before we started clinical studies, if there were any doubts or questions, I often administered the drug to myself. Only once did a serious side effect develop. I did a great deal of work with streptokinase, an activator of the fibrinolysin system and I might have developed some immunity. To make sure the streptokinase does not produce severe allergic reaction, I injected myself with an experimental sample of streptokinase. There were no reactions and all the blood tests were normal. At the time I was chairman of the staff seminar program and the same day I had to go to the airport to pick up a guest speaker who was to arrive several hours before his scheduled presentation. At that time, it was possible to walk out all the way to the steps where the passengers disembarked. When my colleague arrived, he found a body on the ground. I have actually fainted as part of a late anaphylactoid reaction. He picked me up, brought me to the hospital and I lived for several days on cortical steroid infusions. I recovered without sequelae. This showed, however, that streptokinase is indeed highly antigenic, and we recommended that any treatment with streptokinase should be preceded by a test for antibodies and the injections should be given under the protection of an antihistamine and a cortical steroid.

War Time Stories

Gerhard Schmidhuber, a major General of the German army, was one of the commanders of Budapest when it was besieged by the Russian army in World War II. He had previously been in Hungary several times and was known by some of our friends who actually took him out hunting. He was an old fashioned soldier from an old line of military ancestry. In the German military tradition, he was loyal to his government, even though he really didn't like the Nazis. When Budapest was surrounded by the Russian military, he found his position hopeless and asked Hitler several times to be allowed to leave the surrounding Russian ring and save his soldiers from certain destruction. Each time, this was refused. He was told that his position had to be held until the last soldier because Budapest is the gateway to Vienna, which should be attacked after Budapest fell. Many of the Jewish inhabitants of Budapest were hidden by friends in a network of resistance workers, but about 90,000 of them remained concentrated in a ghetto. The Arrow Cross, the Hungarian Nazi party which collaborated with the Germans, continued to round up resistance workers and presumed anti-Nazis. This activity was an excuse for doing less dangerous assignments rather than actually fighting the Russians on the front lines. At one point, the Arrow Cross decided to invade the ghetto and kill the 90,000 surviving Jews. The German commander, Gerhard Schmidhuber was informed of that. He pulled off German soldiers from the front lines, surrounded the ghetto and ordered them to prevent the Arrow Cross from invading the ghetto. Very shortly thereafter, the Russians invaded and the Germans deserted the city. Schmidhuber and a small group of his army tried to break out and escape to the West. During the fighting, Schmidhuber was killed but the 90,000 Jews in the ghetto were saved. It appears that there were some good Germans.

Truth and Hope

I have learned over the years that it is important to tell the truth to all patients but also it is most important to maintain a glimmer of hope. Unfortunately, the two are sometimes contradictory. It is sometimes difficult to tell a patient if the chances are that he has only very limited time left to live, and at the same time maintain some hope for improvement. I worked out a simple strategy to solve these contradictions. I tell patients the truth, the prognosis expected according to the present status of medicine, but I also point out that there is some very promising research going on and there is a reasonable chance that something will develop while they are still alive. Sometimes these refer to some research ongoing within my own group. I have large numbers of investigators working with me and we usually had a number of clinical research projects ongoing. Sometimes it referred to research going on elsewhere in our University community, with investigators in charge with whom we are in continuous contact. At times it referred to research going on elsewhere in the country of which I was aware and to which I could refer the patient. This also allowed me to recruit volunteers into ongoing research projects.

Triage and Diphtheria

My grandmother, who was trained as a nurse during World War I, made patient visits and triaged for the 80 families who lived and worked on our farm in Europe. I remember at one time there was a small epidemic of diphtheria and a number of children had to be sent to the nearby hospital. I accompanied my grandmother on her rounds and helped her as much as I could as a youngster. When she asked children to open their mouth so she can inspect their throat and pharynx she noticed that I was sometimes hesitant to take a look at the lesions that she pointed out. She told me in between visits that the most important thing is never to show patients that we are afraid of them, that we are afraid of contracting any of their diseases, and that we have a feeling of disgust to some of their lesions. Sometimes she said we have no medicine to cure a disease and all we can do is psychological support. Therefore, we cannot show disgust or fear from their problems. She said there is a small possibility that we might pick up the disease. The best thing we can do is to say a little prayer and have trust and no fear. I admired this and remembered it for the rest of my life. At that time there was no vaccine available against diphtheria, but there was antitoxin. This was produced in horses and it was important to know whether patients who are to receive the antiserum are allergic to horse serum. My grandmother had a small vial of normal horse serum of which she dropped one drop into one eye of the patient. By the time the patient arrived to the hospital the presence or absence of inflammation should have shown whether the patient is allergic to horse serum and whether he can get the antiserum. I remembered this well and used it particularly when I was working in Africa.

Patient

One of the early patients I saw in medical school in Zurich, Switzerland, was a patient who had a large palpable liver and his liver function tests showed multiple deficiencies. I suspected alcoholic cirrhosis and asked the patient about his alcohol consumption. He told me that he never drinks alcohol and eats mostly in the special Swiss alcohol-free restaurants. They don't serve alcohol, neither do they use it in any of their foods. I continued to ask him if he has a glass of wine now and then, if he takes a night cap in order to sleep better, or if he has an occasional cognac after a good meal. He said, "No, no, no". Finally, I ask him if he takes a little rum into his coffee. The answer was yes. I asked him how much. With a smile he said, "Well, about a ring finger height of rum into a half cup of coffee". "How many cups do you have a day?" "Well, about five or six. Some times seven". Nevertheless, he continued to insist that he does not drink alcohol.

Dr. Wigner

Another main scientist of the Manhattan Project who occasionally consulted me was an old high school colleague of mine, Eugene Wigner. He won the Nobel Prize in physics and was an important contributor to the development of the atomic bomb. I also saw him at various scientific meetings to which he and Jack Eccles, another Nobel Prize winner, made arrangements to put me on the list of invited speakers. Unfortunately, eventually Wigner became quite a bit senile and the only project that really interested him was the welfare of dogs. Nevertheless, we had some interesting times and heated conversations on many scientific hypotheses.

Gypsy Stories

On our farm in Europe, we usually hired additional help for the Fall harvest. One year we couldn't find anyone else but a group of gypsy workers. I was 13 at the time and my father put me in charge of this group. The biggest fight I had ever heard between my father and my mother was when my mother said that, "This is a dangerous group. They are known to have already knived a foreman who drove them too hard. They may kill the boy". My father answered, "That will serve him right. He will learn something". I wound up getting along well with the gypsy workers. I learned some gypsy songs in the gypsy language although I didn't really know what they meant. The gypsies were musicians in Hungary who played to the Hungarians Hungarian songs, Hungarian folk music. For themselves, they played their own gypsy music and gypsy songs. Many years later friends invited us to a Hungarian restaurant in Niagara Falls, Ontario. There was a gypsy orchestra imported from Hungary, which at that time was still under communist rule and they were supposed to stay here for just a few weeks. When the primas, the head violinist, came to our table and asked what he should play for us, I told him to start with some real gypsy songs. I started to sing some of those I learned in childhood. They played with enthusiasm and then started crying. I still do not know what the words mean. I then said to them that I want them to play some songs from the Revolution in the 1800's against the combined German and Russian armies. The refrain of one of these songs was, "We shed our blood for our country between two pagans". The "Primas" said that he is not really sure if he dares to play that song for us but that he would discuss with his fellows. They all huddled, had a brief chat, and then he came back with a big smile and said that they had decided whatever the risks were they were going to play that for us.

One of the most famous Hungarian gypsy "primas" was Rigo Jancsi (translated: John Robin). He was invited to play in Vienna where a famous Austrian chef constructed a new pastry and called it Rigo Jancsi in his honor. It is still a staple in Viennese gourmet restaurants. He then was invited to come to Paris and play in one of their top restaurants. The Marquis de Chenier and his wife came every day to enjoy his music. Eventually he developed an affair with Madame de Chenier and eloped with her to the United States. One of the relatives, André Chenier, became a famous revolutionary poet, but later as the French Revolution became more extreme, they turned against him and finally he was guillotined. Other members of the family decided to come to the United States. When they landed at Ellis Island, the authorities couldn't quite decipher their name and for simplicity registered them as Cheney. One of their descendents became Vice President of the United States. Another one - Tom - married my daughter Kathy, and they now live in Portland, Oregon.

Family History

When the Hungarian tribes came from Asia and occupied what is today Hungary, their supreme, religious, sacral chief was called Kende, and their overall leader was called Gyula, and the war chief was called Harka. They first invaded what is today Transylvania and left a local chief to be in charge of that area and his rank was called Gyula. The overall chief, however, eventually took the title of King. As time went by, there were altercations between the King and the Gyula in Transylvania and the latter was chased away. In the early Asian days, the Kende was the supreme chief. This leader was killed every three years and a new one was elected, usually from the same family. This office was eventually disbanded. We have, however, a family of distant relatives who kept the name of Kende as a family name. One of my distant cousins, Andreas Kende, was a young boy with whom I almost grew up with. Similarly, Gyula became a name in the family used as a first name for many generations. My grandfather was Gyula, and so was I. The diminutive or nickname was Gyuszi, but this was difficult to pronounce properly for people from other countries, and even more difficult to write, so they used the closest sounding name in their own area. It just so happened that some of my relatives escaped from Hungary when the communists took over and scattered all over the world. Those who went to Italy were called Julio; those who went to Germany were called Julius; those who went to France were called Jules (they did not know that this is also a slang in French for potty); and those who went to England or the United States, were called Julian. Thus, this name came from a hereditary high office, and became a first name maintained by many subsequent generations. My middle name, which in the Hungarian tradition was always awarded during the Catholic confirmation ceremony, was Laszlo, after St. Laszlo, an early King of Hungary. It was anglicized by my Scottish nurse to Lawrence. Originally the Hungarians had no family names, only first names. When the pagan Hungarians were forcibly converted to Christianity under their first king, St. Stephen, in 1000 A.D., they were forced to take on a family name usually fashioned after a prominent saint. St. Ambrose was highly respected and thus the family took the name of Ambrus. In England, the name Ambrose became popular, and in Italy, Ambrosio. Families by the latter names, however, are not related to our family. At the time when the Turks tried to invade Europe the Hungarian Kings built a "cordone sanitaire" by occupying what is today Slovania and Croatia, and built a number of forts and fortified cities or villages with strong military forces stationed there to hold back the Turkish invasion. One of these villages was named after its founder, Ambrus. Recently this little sleepy village was written up in the New York Times, because some gypsies settled in the outskirts and the population chased them away with shotguns and pitchforks. The gypsies went to the Slovanian courts and requested that they should be allowed to return under police protection. All of that was reported at length in many papers.

Not far from these villages, my family also bought a woods which was the best boar hunting country in Europe. This was important for the family because the family tradition required that every boy on his 11th birthday should kill boar. Later on it turned out that these same woods had a marble mine in them, the only one in Central Europe, so what was thought to be primarily for hunting became a very profitable enterprise. After World War I, what is today Slovania and Croatia, was taken from Hungary and given to Yugoslavia. The Yugoslavs said that we could keep our lands and our woods if we move there and continue to work it. My family refused and preferred to stay in Hungary proper. Accordingly, these lands were nationalized. There was a long altercation about compensation and finally after many years a small sum was awarded to the family. This was just before one of my birthdays and my parents took this sum and bought for my birthday a movie projector and a box full of Mickey Mouse and related children's movies. That is all that was left of the woods and the marble mine.

Many years later, when Yugoslavia was still one country, I was invited by the Ministry of Health, to give lectures and make rounds in several medical schools in the country. I was taken around by a minder and spent some time working with students and residents. At one point the weekend came around and my minder asked what I wanted to do since there was no teaching on those days. I said that I would like to visit the old woods near the village of Mohol and the small settlement of Ada. He said that he would pick me up at the hotel on the next morning and take me there. At the appointed time he appeared and he said, "I'm terribly sorry. I couldn't find the place on the map. I even went to the Ministry of the Interior and they said they don't have the foggiest idea either of where the place is. Sorry, we have to do something else". Apparently he was told not to take me there because I may make some trouble. Instead he took me to the skiing place of the area where the Winter Olympics were held some time before. There were a few interesting episodes, however, during these trips. On another weekend, he took me fishing on a large lake which was partly owned by Yugoslavia and partly by Albania. There was a strong wind blowing us toward the Albanian area and our guides became seriously worried that if we wound up in Albanian waters, they would capture us and hold us for a long time before diplomatic intervention could release us. We didn't catch anything but they insisted that we quickly go to shore. Instead they said they would take us to a small lake where there was no such danger. We had a nice lunch and afterward wound up in a small quiet lake and in a very short time we caught a bountiful mass of fish. When we came to shore I found out that this was actually one of several lakes of a fish hatchery where fish were passed on depending on age from one little lake to another and we found we wound up on the lake for the adult fish. It certainly didn't appear to be very sporting.

Another episode during this trip was a visit in Lipica where the Lipicaner horse breed originated. They still had an army-sponsored breeding facility with high school training facilities. I was most pleased when they allowed me to ride one of their stallions and gave me a morning of instruction about the above ground figure dressage performance.

Another interesting episode during this trip through Yugoslavia was the visit to a dialysis center that we were told was the largest dialysis center in the world. They dialyzed about 300 patients a day. This was in an area where the incidence of kidney disease was extremely high. There were a number of small villages where almost half of the population was on dialysis. They did not know the reason for this — a strange phenomenon of geographic pathology. A few miles outside of the borders of this area there were many villages with no significant amount of renal disease. We discussed various possibilities including the presence of various radioactive isotopes in the soil and consequently in local plants. We made some plans for joint research projects including an agreement that they will send us local soil, mineral and plant specimens, tissues from biopsies and autopsies of local patients, and clinical records. Soon thereafter, Yugoslavia broke up into several countries, including Croatia, Slovania, and Macedonia, and nothing came from our joint project. Recently I found out that a visiting team identified a weed in these fields that produces a nephrotoxic poison. This weed infiltrates the wheat fields as well and their poison contaminates flour. The mystery seems to be solved. A nice report was written about this in the Proceedings of the National Academy of Sciences USA, by AP Grollman, et al. The plant, Aristolochia clematitis seems to produce a toxin, aristolochic acid, which is also present in some "slimming pills", as reported by JL Vanherweghem, et al, in Lancet, 1993; 341(8842):387-391.

During this visit I was told that in the same area there are some large grizzly bears but there is also a hunting prohibition even though there were a few accidents where people were mauled by these bears. I was told that if a request is submitted to the proper authorities about a bear which has caused a great deal of damage, it might even have killed some people, then special permission is given. My host told me that they will try to get such a permission for a nice big grizzly and make arrangements that when I come the next time, as part of our planned joint project, they will make arrangements to let me shoot a grizzly. Of course, nothing came from these plans as well. I wound up shooting all kinds of big game, mostly in Africa (to feed my traveling clinic staff and patients), but never a grizzly in Eastern Europe.

Philippines

During a visiting professorship in the Philippines, there was an international medical meeting in which I participated and read some papers. There was a closing banquet at which I was seated beside Imelda Marcos (of the 300-shoes fame), wife of President Marcos. I mentioned to her that just before leaving, there was an announcement in our church that we should collaborate with Amnesty International, and write letters in support of political prisoners in the Philippines. I asked her intercession for this purpose. After I returned home I wrote her a letter concerning this conversation. Soon thereafter, I received a note indicating that the two individuals in prison had been released.

My hotel was beside a large park, at the end of which was the convention hall where the meeting was held. One day I was walking back to the hotel from the meeting and had just entered the park when a cab stopped with screeching brakes, and the driver jumped out and pushed me in the cab. He took off in a hurry and then turned to me and asked whether I noticed the ring of people who were assembling behind the bushes. They were getting ready to kidnap me and hold me for ransom. He had rescued me in the nick of time. He drove around the block a few times and then dropped me at my hotel, expecting a very good tip. I never found out whether this was real or whether it was just a rouse on the part of the cab driver.

My most memorable experience in the Philippines was a visit to the Rice Institute. This was the place where the wonder rices were developed which later on contributed a great deal of alleviating hunger in Asia, particularly in China and India, and contributed to making these two countries to become exporters of rice and wheat. Most impressive was an early study to bioengineer rice DNA so that it should produce human protein as well as various antigens for the rapid production of vaccines. This study still continues in many laboratories throughout the world and may be eventually a major contribution to bioengineering and immunology.

Songs in the War

In high school during the war, everybody had to undergo military training. We wore uniforms and practiced sharp shooting on shooting ranges. Periodically, distinguished German and Italian visitors came to Budapest, and a large public reception was organized on the "Square of the Heroes". Our military troop was ordered to march to these receptions and stand at attention while we were inspected by the dignataries. We marched in uniform and with rifles on our shoulders through the streets. We were not much in sympathy with the visitors, and as we marched we sang songs of the resistance and British military songs: “It’s a long, long way to Tiperary”, “Pack up your troubles in your old kit bag, and smile, smile, smile”, and others. Most people felt that we are singing some kind of German military songs and nobody reprimanded us, or at least kept silent and smiled inwardly. They understood what was going on. Interestingly, some of our numbers included sons of the leaders of the superficially pro-German government, including the nephew of the Regent, Admiral Harty, the son of the Governor of Rutenia called Tomcsányi, and two sons of the upper house representatives for the evangelical church, the two Barons Botlik.

At Russian prisoner of war camps, prisoners were forced to unload heavy bags of ammunition, various kinds of explosives and arms from railroad wagons and transfer them to lorries. If they didn’t work fast enough they were denied a meal. I was working with the camp physician and was not obliged to participate in these labors. Nevertheless, when there was a great deal of labor and the question was whether it was going to be completed in time so that everybody could have some gruel for supper, I decided to go and help with the labor. As we worked in the blazing sun half naked, we sang songs of resistance or Hungarian folk songs. Periodically we sang what we remembered from Paul Robson movies, the song of the Mississippi slaves in English or in Hungarian translation. We felt that we were just like them.

Earlier while with the resistance, I got home occasionally and at times brought some of my troops with me. We had some violinists and trumpet players who brought their instruments. One day we assembled under the window of my future wife and gave her a serenade in the middle of the night. Many years later we were invited by some of our friends to go with them for dinner to Ft. Erie in Canada, where there was an excellent Hungarian restaurant that just imported a gypsy band from Hungary which was still under communist rule. The leader of the orchestra came to our table and asked what he should play for us. We sang the same song that I had serenaded to my wife that remarkable evening during the war.

Duplications

I use a few minutes here and there between various tasks to dictate into the Dictaphone some additions to the Babel series about which my children continuously press me to continue as much as possible. I sometimes am not sure of what I have already dictated. I am afraid that occasionally duplications develop. I ask all my potential readers to forgive me. Maybe one day the whole series will be properly edited and duplications will be eliminated.

Once Upon a Time – by Clara Maria Ambrus (Fall 1999)
To my husband, about the child he never knew, and to my children.

I was born in Rome and baptized in the Basilica of St. Peter, the center of the Christian world. For that I always felt special, selected for an uncharted destiny. This feeling was later reinforced by comments made by several people independently, who for entertainment or fun looked at my palm or my handwriting; "whatever happens, don't ever give up, something is waiting for you to do, toward the end of your years". This was told me on occasions, separated by time and space, among others, by Lili's "crazy" brother-in-law (when we first met in Switzerland), and by a "gypsy" hired for party entertainment at the Buffalo Club. In an out-of-life experience after a car accident I heard the words, "but you must go back!!". These episodes gave me a steady feeling of anticipation, security, and inner peace. However, today, when so often my mind is cloudy, my health is poor, I wonder what is expected from me? My father was an architect attached to the Hungarian embassy at the Vatican. My mother was an artist-sculptor who made many gifts to the Vatican and to the Hungarian parliament (that of a large eagle is still on exhibit in the parliament). One member of the family, General Hadik, is perpetuated in an equestrian statue in Buda. He was a leader during the revolutionary war against the Austrians.

My brother was born when I was five years old. Until that time, as an only child, I had all the attention of my parents. I was a precocious child, presumably never spoke "baby-talk" but by the age of two could converse and read in two languages, Italian and Hungarian. My maternal Grandmother (Anna) sent me Hungarian books for every occasion and I became an avid reader early.

In my family there was a long line of architects on both my maternal and paternal side. The oldest member we know of was in Sari Grandmother's family. In 1674 he built the Basilica in Kalocsa, in a bishopry established by St. Steven in 1003. His name, "Hadik", is engraved in one of the cornerstones. A few years ago my cousin Eva in Hungary was trying to organize a family reunion in Kalocsa in remembrance of him.

In Rome we lived close to the Vatican. We usually attended mass at any of the many altars in the basilica of St. Peter. Coming out I would run around the big piazza and swing on the chains between the columns. I went to a catholic elementary school. As in any school at that time ancient Roman history and geography was emphasized. Mussolini insisted that Greek and Roman history should be studied early and in great detail, preparing the population for his glorious plans in reestablishing ancient Rome's boundaries. Although I was in a private school, twice a week we had to stay for afternoon marching and singing "patriotic" songs and listening to various talks of fascist indoctrination. One of the songs, I still remember the text, is about the victory of the Italian army in World War I over the Austrians. I did not realize at that time that it was the Austro-Hungarian army that was beaten.

I was a sickly child, and at the age of 10 my pediatrician recommended a change in climate, a fashionable treatment for all illnesses at that time. In January 1936, my father took me to Budapest to be with Grandmother Anna to gain more strength. The train from Rome arrived in the evening. My father hired a taxi to show me the evening splendor of Budapest. The Danube, its bridges and public buildings illuminated; I thought I was in fairyland. Grandmother Anna lived in the outskirts of Budapest (Rakosszentmihaly) in a house built by my Grandfather. It had a large, glass-covered porch in front that served as a living room on sunny days (not unlike our present porch on the farm). In front of the house was a long garden, with a large variety of roses. Grandfather Ivan had two hobbies: cultivating and hybridizing roses, and collecting opera records (these were new at the time). Grandfather died of a heart attack when his daughter Vilma was 15 and Sari was 14.

At the age of 15, Grandmother Sari decided to become a jeweler and sculptor, and entered the Collegeal Institute for

Industrial Arts in Budapest, a four-year study. In the last year, two of her classmates asked her in marriage. She could not make a choice and decided to spend the summer in Rome to mull it over. In Rome she met my father and the two suitors were forgotten.

Finally in June of 1936 my parents also came back to Budapest with my brother Ivan who was five years old. I, of course, came with them and started school.

In the Gymnasium (middle and high school) I was first in my class in all subjects except German (my tongue was attuned to Latin languages; I could never speak German or English without an accent, but could speak Parisian French). I was particularly strong in math and physics and participated in senior year in the citywide scholastic competition in math. Homework took little time; the rest of the afternoon was spent tutoring (I earned my pocket expenses) or reading books that transported me to different worlds (e.g., Tolstoy, Thomas Mann, Proust).

At the age of 15 I formed lasting friendships with two of my classmates, Eva Fischer (today Mrs. Yeoge Klein living in Stockholm and working at the Karolinska Institute), and Zsuzsa Biro, who lives in Paris (her husband,Simon Hantai, became a world-renown painter). We would read and discuss the same books, visit museum exhibits and attend philharmonic concerts together.

My school was called Zrinyi Ilona Gymnasium, named after a Hungarian woman who in the 1500's fought the Turks when they attacked the city of Eger, in upper Hungary, until the Turks gave up and left. When about 50 years later the Turks returned, they occupied Hungary for 150 years, until a European army coalition beat them and chased them back.

At age 16 my physician diagnosed pulmonary tuberculosis and sent me for a semester to the School Sanatorium in the Buda Hills. When I was accepted my first reaction was despair. It did not last long. Everyone was friendly. For every subject there was a teacher,

2-6 students in a class, boys and girls together. Teaching started at 8:30 AM, then one hour of rest at 10:00 AM, resting outdoors on a hassock. We were supposed to sleep, but older ones were allowed to read.

The second rest time was between 2:00 and 4:00 PM. It happened that I was reading Zauberberg (The Magic Mountain from Thomas Mann), and compared my life as he described it in a Swiss Sanatorium. I was supposed to stay the full year, but World War II broke out and everyone was sent home.

Meeting my future husband

At the age of 15, Eva and I read two books that gave direction to our life: "Madame Curie", written by her daughter, and "The Microbe Hunters", written by De Kruif. I decided to devote my life to develop new treatments and new medicines, and after high school enrolled in medical school. Eva, being Jewish, was not accepted to the University and could only enroll after the war was over.

In the first semester the obligatory subjects were anatomy, histology, biology, physics and chemistry, each with corresponding laboratory exercises with written reports and documentation required. One day while working in the chemistry lab my pencil broke, and I turned to my friend Szebehelyi (now a Professor in Sweden) and asked whether he had an extra pencil I could use. He instead indicated that his neighbor would be delighted to give me one, he was frequently asking about me, and he was waiting for an occasion to be introduced. His name was Julian Ambrus. When I looked at him I felt a strange admonition that I could not explain. After chemistry was over, he asked permission to accompany me home (at that time that meant to the doorsteps). During our walk he described the kind of person he was going to marry; it was my description. That I found surprising and unsettling – who did he think he was, I didn't even know him!!. During the Christmas holidays he invited me to the movies, to a small restaurant in Buda and for hiking in the hills.

Szebehely and I were doing volunteer research in the Department of Biology headed by Professor Huzella, while Julian was doing research in the Department of Anatomy which was in the same building. Later he also worked in biology in a different laboratory from where I worked.

In February of 1944, Julian wrote me a poem about two sols resonating to each other. One afternoon, in the Biology Building, Julian asked me to marry him and we kissed for the first time. We were 19 years old. In March, the Germans occupied Hungary and life became a chaos. There were frequent air raids to announce American bombings, at which time one had to go to a bomb shelter. It happened a few times that the nearest bomb shelter was in the house where he lived without me first being aware of that). This was a three-story house on one of the major avenues of the city, each floor occupied by members of Julian's family. There I met his father, who after the air raid invited me to join the family for dinner. I am very glad to have had this opportunity. He clearly enjoyed seeing me, and I was very happy with his warm reception.

My parents were managing a large textile factory. During the war they ran out of material, closed the factory and let the workers go. The factory and the large warehouses stood empty. The family decided to use these facilities as well as their house to hide persecuted people, including Jews. My job was also to bribe guards to bring out people from the ghettos and hide them or take them to other collaborating hiding places, including the mansion of an uncle of my future husband who worked for the Italian embassy. Both of our families worked for the resistance and several were killed.

When the Germans left and the war was over, Budapest was in shambles and without food. Cities in the South were occupied earlier and started to recover. Julian sent word that he and several of his friends escaped from Russian prisoner-of-war camps and are in Szeged, where life was normalizing, the University was functioning, and there was food. Szeged could be reached in one hour by train and two days by foot. With my friend Eva we went to the train station, but seeing it crowded with Russian soldiers decided to hitchhike. Two days later we arrived, went to the University, and met Julian at the entrance of the main building. Two weeks later we were married.

Our first "home" was a room on the main avenue of Szeged, "Boldogasszony Sugarutja", freely translated: Avenue of the Virgin Mary. Every evening the columns of the occupying Russian army marched to their barracks on this avenue singing all along. We listened to them behind closed shutters. At the beginning of April we returned to Budapest and lived with Julian's family until we left for Switzerland two years later. I still remember the early days of the Russian invasion.

On Christmas Eve Budapest was surrounded by the Russian army. Electricity was turned off in the city as well as the suburbs. There was no light, heat, or telephone. A few days after Christmas a group of 30-40 Russian soldiers took over the large house, and we moved into the small servants' quarters. The first day a middle-aged soldier came in the kitchen that opened to the courtyard, and asked me and Sari grandmother to sit down with him; he tried to start a dialogue (that became more of a sign language). After a while he took out from his pocket a faded photograph of a women and a girl sitting around a table, and made us understand that we remind him of his daughter and his wife, and that he misses them very much. While we sat there a Russian soldier came in and said that the "commandant" wanted to see me. I refused to go out. Our new Russian friend, however, went out and we heard a loud argument outside between him and the commandant. I was never asked for again. Clearly the soldier had protected me for the rest of their stay.

The Russian group stayed for almost two weeks. Slowly our contacts became more friendly but from our side very cautious. At noon time a soldier would come in the kitchen, bring a big pot of cabbage soup and leave it on the table (we had nothing else to eat). In the evening a group of 10-12 soldiers would come in, sit on the floor in a circle, and sing Russian songs. These were actually beautiful and sounded nostalgic. There were only a few candles lit and we tried to crouch in the corner out of the light. We were aware that all around us there was mass raping of women and beatings of men, yet in our place these soldiers behaved decently.

After returning from Szeged, the first two years were spent in Budapest. When we returned from Szeged to Budapest, we lived with Julian's family in the house that was bombed, leaving an entire side of the building exposed to the elements (Julian's original room was on that side). The suitable living quarters were significantly reduced and the two of us took over the previous "salon" (in Hungarian this is the name for the room where you entertain guests). We immediately enrolled in the Medical School and in addition worked in the Department of Biology and Histology. Later we transferred to the Department of Pharmacology where we became paid instructors, the lowest rank in the faculty hierarchy of the University. Nevertheless, seldom granted to those who were still medical students. We continued our studies on the basis of fellowship at the University of Zurich Medical School, graduated there, completed an internship and then continued graduate school at the University of Paris (Sorbonne) and the Pasteur Institute in Paris. We received a fellowship to Jefferson Medical College in Philadelphia (at the time there was no salary, but we were also given a teaching assignment at the associated Philadelphia College of Pharmacy and Science which was paid).

At the end of the war President Truman established the GI Bill that gave free education to young men and women who missed education for participating in the war. They were looking for people who could teach. The office that was involved with that was located in New York, under the direction of Bernice Larson. Beside teachers they were looking for eminent scientists, scholars and artists. This office brought Szilard, Einstein, and other scientists to America. This organization made the arrangements for us in the U.S.A. Since they were afraid that we did not speak English, they sent an old German professor to pick us up. He came to the boat with a big sign with our name on it and when he found us asked about our father. He did not expect such young people. He had a small radio with him and he listened all the way to Margaret Truman singing. He took us first to the college to meet the present who was equally surprised at our youth, and did not expect Julian to have a wife. He was reassured that I have the same schooling as him and I will be able to help him teach the laboratory part of Pharmacology until my English developed. Temporarily they placed us in a fancy hotel until we found a place to rent. It was a few days before Christmas. We bought a small tree, a few decorations, and candles. When people came to clean our room they were horrified that we had a fire hazard, and called some hotel administrators. We had to assure them that we will light the tree only on Christmas night, and we asked for a bucket of water to be able to extinguish the fire if we would need it. Of course nothing happened. They were not used to lit candles on a Christmas tree.

The president of the college was Irish, Ivor Griffith, who invited us for Christmas dinner. He entertained us with a movie of the D-Day landing. Other women were also invited. They thought that I didn't understand a word, and very kindly spoke about how difficult it must be for me. One of the women offered to help me find a home. We rented an apartment in the German area close to the college and to public transportation. At that time it was a quiet pleasant area. Recently (in 2004), it was quoted in the newspapers as an area full of crack houses.

At the first Halloween we were not familiar with that custom and we were not prepared for it. As the children kept coming saying "trick or treat," we had no idea what they wanted until our landlord explained this American custom. Then we went to buy some sweets.

Most of our students were older than we were. Julian was teaching Pharmacology and asked one of the students to make notes of his English mistakes, which in the beginning were quite a few. For example, once Julian was explaining how the blood pressure in the "giraffe" is the same in his whole body, in spite of the animal having such a high neck. He kept saying "giraffy", and the students wondered what kind of exotic animal he was talking about. We decided that I would set up the laboratory exercises that required more demonstration than talk. All the students were pleasant and patient with me.

We were anxious to start a family and I got pregnant with our first child, Madeline, who was born in the Children's Hospital, very small and premature, in early December. They did not believe that she would survive and they asked us to take her home for Christmas. She had no sucking reflex and we were feeding her with mild concentrates of milk with cereal (as we learned it from Professor Fanconi in Switzerland) about every three hours, day and night, with a spoon. At that time Julian went every evening to the College of Physicians and he always came home late. I minded that until he confessed that he did not take the bus but walked to save money. He modified Madeline's formula and bought ingredients on the way to the College of Physicians.

The following two years we had two boys, Peter and Julian. I found a refugee Lithuanian woman who had a small child herself; she brought him to the house and watched all four children together. She was very smart and pleasant. When we moved to Buffalo I told her that she is too smart to be a baby sitter and she should return to school for more education. I met her again later at a scientific meeting where she discovered that I was presenting a paper, and came to the meeting to thank me for encouraging her to study more. She listened and became a nurse.

Mrs. Larson continued to be helpful. She asked us to write abstracts in English of articles printed in various scientific journals written in different European languages (mostly German, Italian or French) for the "Excerpta Medica". We were paid by the number of words in the abstract; we wrote very long abstracts.

We moved to Buffalo in the Summer of 1955 and stayed for the time in the house of the Wilson family who always moved to Boston (New York) in the Summer. They were famous for having on their property the cabin of Red Jacket, a famous Indian Chief. The children were invited to sleep in the cabin on the floor on a blanket; we let them go whenever they behaved especially well as a reward. The Wilson's belonged to a group that in the Summer exchanged their children with children from war torn countries. Whenever a new group came, we invited them to come over to the farm and visit our children, see the sheep, or ride our horses. Afterwards, I always offered them some fruit. Our farm is on the highest point of Erie County. On one occasion it was a group of girls from Holland. One of them looked with tears in her eyes to the view from there, and told us that it reminded her of her home.

We found Boston, New York, a very nice place. It was a very congenial community that accepted our family with open arms. Every Friday there was a picnic at Clarksburg Country Club; we were invited to participate. Children from the various families often slept at each other's house (as adults still maintained their friendship). I was asked to join a painting group that assembled three times a week. Harold Olmstead, in his Dutch coat and clogs, was teaching painting. When the class was over before we left, we had to line up and show what we made. He looked at our paintings and always found something to praise. I barely knew how to paint (I had never painted before). He was from an old distinguished family that had established many parks in Buffalo and in St. Louis, which was considered its sister city. The children came with us. We collectively engaged some of the older children to baby-sit, and gave them a small reward.

At that time George Moore, director of the Roswell Park Cancer Institute, decided to expand the operation of Roswell Park to Springville, New York, where he wanted to keep the animal colony needed for investigations. He offered Julian a position of the Director for that satellite institution. Julian gladly accepted, in addition to his clinical research at Roswell Park. I also worked at both places.

We decided to buy a farm that was close to Springville. The farm had a barn where we kept horses, cattle, and sheep. Unfortunately, one summer during a thunderstorm, lightening hit the barn. We were called by our caretaker who gave us the bad news that the barn had burned down. We rebuilt the barn, but this time it was built of stone. All of our children learned how to ride. We also built a nice tennis court, and dug a pond large enough to swim and to fish. Summer was not only for pleasure. As the children became older each one of them was given a task in the Springville laboratory. They also assisted in the farming operations.

As the children grew older they were exposed to more sports, but their father saw to it that they learned fencing, skating, skiing, and tennis, but the most time was spent on riding. Old friends who were part of the Hungarian equestrian Olympic team and later became trainers of the Canadian teams, Major Rethy and Captain Nadasy, came over and gave every body lessons in dressage, three day eventing and show jumping. It came in handy when the family joined the Genessee Valley Hunt and then Julian became Commissioner of the Lake Erie Pony Club. This was something like boy- and girl-scouts on horseback. They also learned polo and for many years their team won the pony club polo championship as well as the three-day event championship. Major Rethy was also one of the instructors to the junior Olympic team in Hungary – candidates to future Olympic teams. Julian Sr. was part of this team. When Major Rethy finished giving private lesions to the children at the farm, he gave a high level dressage lesson to Julian Sr. All the children were lined up at the fence and watched. When Major Rethy roared, "For 50 years I was telling you, don't do these foolish things," all the children roared with laughter. These were nice days.

Vacations

Our children really were responsible for writing Babel, by pestering us for an autobiography for many years. They also asked us to write something about our vacations. The interesting thing is that, since starting out in Philadelphia, and continuing in Buffalo, we almost never took real vacations. We did a great deal of traveling, mostly lecturing in various medical schools, or doing more prolonged visiting professorships. And of course, "while there," we always took off a few days and enjoyed the sites or whatever was available locally.

Often we took our children with us, and faculty wives were often obliging to entertain them while we were working at the hospitals. A meeting ended in the Netherlands with a banquet at which prizes were awarded to the best papers. We were surprised when we were also awarded a prize, and it was said by the Chairman of the Women's Committee that they spent several days traveling around with our children in the country. If we put up with them all the time - we deserved a prize.

One of the medical meetings we attended was in Casa de Campo in the Dominican Republic. There was at this resort a large polo stable and well-kept polo grounds. Several of us were interested in playing and we formed Europe vs. America teams. I was Captain of the latter and we had a wonderful time. Unfortunately, I had a bad fall and my wife Clara thereafter made me promise that this would be my last polo game. Interestingly enough, my son Peter, who played with the Myopia team in Boston, had a serious fall about the same time and his wife also made him promise to quit polo. I thought that if one's son stops playing polo, one is indeed very old.

I was also thinking about my favorite vacations in childhood. We often went to the Tatra Mountains, which used to be in Hungary but after World War I was given to Chechoslovakia. At the time I was a skinny kid who never ate much. My parents made a deal: for each major dish which I completely ate, I received a silver coin. I could use this money to go to the main square of the village after breakfast, where around the fountain the mountain guides would congregate offering various climbing trips to the mountains. I used my money to hire guides and to go on a climbing trip each day. At the end we went to a small shop where, for each mountain conquered and certified by the guide, a small emblem was made available and nailed to my climbing stick. Several of us were always competing as to what kind of symbols of our climbing conquests we could be proud of. My main competitor was Mimi Lederer, who much later married a law professor in Oklahoma and helped us in many ways, but this is another story.

Another favorite vacation spot was Misurina, on top of a mountain over Cortina dampezzo. Our favorite day trip was to ski down from Misurina to Cortina, and come up with the small railway car. Two or three runs per day was all for which there was time. In front of the hotel of Misurina, there was a large frozen lake, partly cleared for skating and partly snow-covered. In this area there was ski-joring, where the skiers were towed by a well trained horse. I participated in many competitions for my age group. My main competitor was the son of the Guatemalan Ambassador. We were usually first or second in most competitions including giant slalom, downhill, ski jumping, and, of course, ski-joring.

Another favorite vacation place was Abazia in Italy, close to Fiume (which also used to be part of Hungary in the old days). Every morning we were awoken by fishermen working their nets in front of our balcony singing beautiful Italian folk songs. We later found out that the hotel actually was paying them to sing loudly whenever they fished in front of the hotel. We used to go to a small island opposite to the hotel where there was an excellent seafood restaurant called Picolo Paradiso. You could pick your live lobsters and fish from a large tank. There were also many peacocks and chickens wandering around. One hen kept coming to our table and picking on the shoes of my father. He said, "If you don't stop, I will order you." Somehow I never forgot that. I was offered prizes for eating all of my meal. I used the money to hire fishermen to go rowing and fishing with them.

One of the most beautiful places in Italy I visited was in Sicily. During the early days of the war the Italians were anxious to earn hard currencies. Italians were also interested in increasing propaganda for the Mussolini regime. For these reasons, they had established rather inexpensive travel plans to visit Italy. Once, my family went with one of these travel plans on a trip to Taormina in Italy. Before going there with a group travel plan, the whole group had to go to Rome to a special audience with Mussolini, who berated us to work for more close cooperation between Hungary and Italy. After the audience I heard a great deal of discussion between my elders, most of whom were in leading positions in Hungary. The general impression of Mussolini was very negative.

We had several memorable trips to Greece, mostly through visiting professorships at the Metaxas National Cancer Institute in Pyrheus. We took several groups of children at various times and usually spent a few days just touring Greece. One of our favorite places was Arachova, where they had wonderful archeological specimens for sale. We made acquaintance with a farmer, from whom we rented mules, and ascended to the Parnassus mountains. The farmer was telling us that no matter what happens in the world of politics, he is safe because one of his mules is called America and another mule is called Arrusia, so whether the Americans come or the Russians, they will be friendly to him. We used the same mules on several trips with several groups of children. On many of these trips our host was Dr. Denis Rezis who worked with us for many years at the Roswell Park Cancer Institute, as did his daughter, Evi. Later, Dr. Rezis became the head of a cancer unit in Greece where he worked together with his daughter. We spent many pleasant days together.

At one time we were asked to consult for a high official, who was very grateful and offered to arrange that we could have the Royal yacht for several days and tour the islands. Unfortunately, we were due on another assignment in Cairo and could not take advantage of this offer. When we went to Greece the next time the King was gone and so was his yacht. Nevertheless, we had friends who lent us their yacht. Together with an English captain and his wife, who turned out to be an excellent cook, we sailed and visited several islands including Santaorini, which was supposed to be the ancient site of Atlantis before a volcano blew up half of the island and created a large bay. We arrived in Crete very late in the evening. It was almost dark and I was sailing the ship while our Captain was asleep. I almost hit a wall, which later I was told was built recently, in one of the bays. Fortunately we managed to avoid it and arrived in Crete in good order. Everyone told us that we would have no difficulty on the trip South since the meltemi is blowing continuously from north to south, but we would have difficulties getting back, and we had to be back in time to deliver our papers at a medical meeting. We divided the family into several watches and we tagged into the wind for several days, sailing day and night, and arrived in Pyrheus just a few hours before one of our papers was due. We left the children to clean up the boat and rushed, soaked with water and smelling after several days of continuous sailing, to the meeting. We arrived just a few minutes before one of our papers was due. Everything went well and when we returned to Pyrheus the children had managed to clean up the boat together with our English crew. We visited the site of the ancient Olympics, and had a small, family, 200-yard race, starting from the starting groves presumably left over from Olympic times. We visited the family of our friend and colleague, Dr. Constantin Karakousis, in Kalamata, and went fishing with the local fishermen.

Some of the most remarkable trips we were taking at home were to the Grand Canyon. We went several times with several groups of children, always hired a pack of mules, and went down to the bottom of the Canyon. We usually slept at the bottom of the Canyon in the Phantom Ranch, and then ascended through another route taking us through an Indian village. The Indians put on a war dance which we were watching from the back of our mules. We also went on various mountain trips out West, either climbing or hiring mules or horses. At one time I was leading Linda, who was about five years old, on a lead line when my horse stumbled and fell down several hundred yards into the Canyon. I remained hanging on the lead line on Linda's horse's head and managed to climb up without injury. My horse was laying on the bottom and we were very worried about it. Through a circuitous route, I climbed down, quickly gave the horse a few strikes to the cardiac area and some quick artificial respirations, whereupon it shook itself and stood up apparently without much additional trouble. Through a circuitous route I managed to take it up again on the trail where my family was waiting and we continued on without much difficulty.

Another remarkable vacation I remember was during our student days in Switzerland when we were invited to a vacation ski camp at the university chalet on the Piz-Sol, not far from Arussia. In those days there were no ski lifts and we climbed up by attaching seal skins to our skis, which prevented sliding backwards. A climb to the top of the hill took several hours and a slide down only a few minutes. Three or four trips a day is all one could do. There was an interesting group of international students who had seen the war from various angles and we had some interesting exchanges of our experiences.

We did a visiting professorship in Nairobi, where the Dean of the Medical School was a former resident of mine in the Makerere University Hospital. On one of our vacation days we went on a hot air balloon trip. We could descend just a few yards on top of an elephant herd and we could see much wildlife from the air. Unfortunately, eventually a significant wind blew up and our guide was afraid that we may be blown over a great Rift Valley, crash there, and have difficulty getting out. For this reason, we decided to land rapidly. The balloon tipped on its side and was dragged along by the wind. I wound up on top of Clara and Cathy, our young daughter who was with us, and Clara's face became a great deal abraded. When we finally stopped in some bushes, we found that about one hundred yards away, there was a pride of lions dining on a recently bagged zebra. They didn't bother us and we didn't bother them. Traditionally, when one lands in a hot air balloon, there is a champagne lunch celebration. Fortunately the lunch and the champagne were packed so we had our meal not far from the lions who had their meal. We radioed to the balloon center and soon they sent a truck to pick us up and take us back to Nairobi. On this same trip, on another weekend, we went to the Tree Tops, which is a small "hotel room" built into the branches of a large banyan tree. In front of it there was a large watering hole to which herds of animals came all day and all night to drink, play, and fight. It was a wonderful view from a small balcony and a marvelous photography opportunity. The little tree top room we spent the night in was famous for the fact that it was visited by Queen Elizabeth when she was notified that her father died and she is now Queen of England.

One of our friends, who was an anesthesiologist at the General Hospital, recommended that we visit his sister and brother-in-law in

Nairobi. They actually owned the Kenyan safari club, where I spent some time during an earlier stay in Uganda. We spent several evenings together, went to various restaurants, and they told us to chew the betel nut from a special shop after a nice meal. They also lent us a car and driver for several trips around the country. One of the trips was to the "deadman's canyon," which was the nesting and breeding site for the European Condor, which is the largest bird in Europe and a relative of the American vulture and the European Golden Eagle. Our driver stayed at the top of the area with the car, and Clara and I descended and enjoyed the scenery and the magnificent fauna and flora. Suddenly, our driver came running and very excitedly said that we had to leave right away and that we had to hurry, hurry, hurry. He grabbed us by the hand and started driving us upwards. I didn't understand what was going on. He pointed out that at the upper part of the cliff there were a number of caves in which various groups of beggars lived. They were already assembling outside their caves, probably ready to capture us and hold us for ransom. We reached the top in good time and quickly sped away in the car.

We did a visiting professorship in Abidjan Medical School, the capital of Ivory Coast, in West Africa. This was at the time the only country whose President was an M.D. He was famous for building the largest cathedral in the world, larger than St. Peter's in Rome, at his birthplace in a small village not far from Abidjan. At one time, he invited us for dinner. We dined on the terrace of his palace. He spoke excellent French, was a graduate of a French medical school, and we had pleasant conversation about improving medical care in his country. He told us that as after dinner entertainment he ordered the orchestra of his bodyguards to march up and down in front of the terrace and play a concert to us. Pretty soon we noticed that at the entrance of the palace, the bodyguard orchestra arrived with small donkeys pulling carts with big drums, and they had to stop at the entrance where the French paratroopers examined them, shaking the drums – probably looking for hidden bombs; and after the French paratroopers passed them, the bodyguards could come to the President and his guests and play their concert.

We worked in Brazil several times. At one time we had a government contract to study health problems among the Indians in the Amazon rainforest. Another time, friends took us on a trip to the Pantanal, which has probably the world's most spectacular collection of birds. We had a small tent and did some fishing, at times beside a large collection of Caimans, the local relatives of crocodiles, which sun themselves on the shores. We left our camp with our guide to look for howler monkeys. At one point, we arrived at a large clearing in the middle of the jungle, which appeared to be easy going; but our guide became very excited and insisted that we run and get out of the area as soon as possible. He told us that this was a landing strip for the planes of cocaine of smugglers. If they catch somebody observing them, they cut them down with machinegun-fire without asking any questions. Our guide apologized that we got lost in the jungle and wound up at this spot. We waded through some small rivers with caimans swimming around and arrived back to our camp very late after dark. All of our friends were up looking for us and greeted us with much joy and relief. Our children, who were with us, had another interesting experience.

Hungary

We visited Hungary several times, always with different groups of children as part of visiting professorships, lectureships, and at the time when I had to give my inaugural address after being elected as a foreign member of the Hungarian Academy of Science. Clara was elected as a member some years later – she still owes them an inaugural address. During each visit we made a point to spend a few days at the Hungarian Pampas near the eastern city of Debrecen. The Hungarian Olympic Equestrian Team was stationed there and we were good friends with the head trainer. We borrowed Olympic horses and rode out into the Pampas observing the herds of Hungarian long-horn cattle, sheep, and horses. The local cowboys always put on nice show for us including trick riding and precision roping. They showed that the horses were trained as in the old days to lay down on command and serve as a base for guns from which attacking brigands could be shot. They cracked their whips to imitate the sound of guns and showed that their horses laid there motionless. We also rode down to the surrounding marshes and stood in water up to the chests of our horses. At one time, the migration of peregrine falcons just came flying over our heads. I also wanted to show my children our old farm. In communist days, we were advised not to go there. We were told that some of the old workers of our farm would recognize us and make a big scene of welcome. They would then be reported by the communist observers and would be severely punished after we left. The farm was nationalized and distributed between all the people who worked there earlier; but soon thereafter, they were all nationalized again into a large cooperative farm. After communism ended, we could go and visit the farm. It was a great disappointment. Our houses, barns, and all buildings were gone. We were told that first the people came and chiseled out the plumbing and electric wires, but later they actually took the bricks and used it for their own buildings. Interestingly enough, the only thing left from all of these buildings was a small marble mounting block, which was put in front of the stables. This was all that was left from a large building complex. We photographed it and said a tearful goodbye.

During one of the visiting professorships, the International Falconry Meeting and Competition was held in Hungary. I participated with a peregrine falcon and a golden eagle. We won some prizes and were surprised by the tremendous richness of game for the competitive events. At the end of the day, we piled up about 300 pheasants, many rabbits, and a couple of deer, and listened as our trumpeters blew taps honoring the fallen game. When we traveled to Hungary, we stopped overnight in London and flew on to Budapest the next morning. When we entered the hotel with a falcon and an eagle on our gloves, they appeared not to be surprised at all. They politely asked whether we wanted a separate room for our birds. We did not bring our birds back, partly because of the lengthy and expensive quarantine required, but left them as breeding stock for the Hungarian Falconry Center. I understand that they had many first-rate offspring in subsequent years.

At the Falconry competition, I also participated in the mounted falconry division. A local stallion station lent me a thoroughbred stallion that was the great-great-grandson of Kincsem, one of the best-ever Hungarian race horses. It was a descendent of a stallion that the Hungarian troops captured while attacking Napoleon's army retreating from Russia. The stallion I received was most excellent; it jumped large, wide ditches without any difficulty at all. The only problem with him was that he didn't like to stop and stand still. During lunch breaks I had to keep circling around our little camp while munching on my sandwich, rather than stopping or dismounting. Dr. Aradi, Professor of Biochemistry at the University of Debrecen Medical School, paired up with me and we flew our falcons together.

Munich

We were invited to do a visiting professorship in Munich. We had to make rounds with the medical students, residents and fellows. It turned out that half of the fellows in the group were from Hungary. I asked, "Do we conduct these rounds in Hungarian, German, or in English?" We finally agreed on German. Our host was the Associate Dean of the medical school, Helmuth Gastpar. Helmuth and his wife, Trudy, took us to an event of the Octoberfest which went on just at that time. They had arranged that at one point the orchestra leader asked me to come up to the stage and conduct the orchestra. I remembered some old German folk songs and conducted them with gusto. We later developed a great deal of scientific research collaboration with Dr. Gastpar. He visited us many times during the Summer vacation, and worked with us in the laboratory. He usually stayed with us at the farm and enjoyed riding with us. A couple of times I took Helmuth to the foxhunt in Geneseo. We were worried that one of these days the Russian army would invade West Germany, and in a very short time they could be in Munich. They asked us to sell them a small segment of our farm. If anything happened, they said, they could go to the American embassy and say that they were farmers in Buffalo and to take them with the next evacuation flight. I actually introduced them to a close friend who was head of the Voice of America in Munich, and reassured them that he would help them if anything went wrong. Fortunately, it never came to that.

Israel

We were invited to give lectures at an international medical meeting in Jerusalem, and also do some lectures and teaching rounds at the Hadassa University Hospital. We were surprised to see that a large number of patients in the hospital were Arabs from the West Bank. They came over at that time without much difficulty and were given free medical care. We met several of our colleagues and former students who immigrated to Israel and played leading roles in the medical community. We also had many Arab friends who showed us different aspects of the country. Michael Sabah, the Archbishop of Jerusalem, was also the patriarch of our order, the Knighthood of the Equestrian Order of the Holy Sepulchre. He lent us a car, a driver, and a young seminarian to take us around and show us most parts of the country and the West Bank. He told us that one of the goals of our Knighthood is to free Jerusalem from the heathen and re-establish the Latin kingdom. My duty, therefore — he said — was to get rid of myself. One interesting episode was at a lunch on the rooftop, which we were told was the best Arab restaurant in the country. We enjoyed the view, and suddenly our driver appeared was very excited and asked us how much more time we needed to finish our meal. He begged us to finish quickly so we could go as fast as we could. We got back in the car; and the driver, who was a good careful driver, suddenly started speeding like a maniac, rushed us through all the checkpoints, and got us back to our hotel in Jerusalem. We didn't understand what had happened. We went up to the room and turned on the television to watch the news. We heard that just where we were dining, a bomb went off producing some damage. Apparently our driver knew about it and got us out in the nick of time.

Japan

I did visiting professorships in Japan at various universities five times. At one time, we had our two daughters, Madeline and Linda, with us. Faculty members were nice in showing them around while we were working. At one time our host offered to take us to Mt. Fuji and climbed with us to the top. It was very late in the season, and the various rest stops where they usually burned a sign into your walking stick showing how far you managed to climb were about to close; we were probably their last customers. On the way down, we did a great deal of sliding on the lava crumbles while sitting on our climbing sticks and arrived to the Mt. Fuji hotel pretty much exhausted. As we went up the stairs, a metal rod which held down the red carpet jumped up and slit open the leg of my wife. It needed several stitches to fix up. This made us very sad because we were going from there to India and we were supposed to join friends and climb Mt. Everest, at least part way. Nothing came of it, of course, since the India-Pakistan war broke out and our hosts telephoned saying that we should stay in Japan a little longer – the war couldn't last more than a few days, and we should then join them. They also said that they would take us out on their elephants, and guaranteed that we could shoot a tiger. Nothing came of it, however, since the war dragged on and we had another appointment in Thailand and in Cairo, so we had to go there.

Vacations with Children

We made sure that our children got a great deal of learning experiences in foreign countries. They traveled with us on various trips, whoever happened to have time from their studies. We also arranged for some of them to stay and do some work in foreign countries. Julian Jr. worked for a summer vacation with my friend, Weatherley Main, the Head of Medicine and the Hematology Section at St. Thomas Hospital in London. When I came to visit, Dr. Main told me, "I have a great deal of trouble with your son. He is a third-year medical student, but he knows too much and I can't run him with my medical students; I have to run him with the registrars – the equivalent of residents." I made rounds with the residents and kept them going for a long time. They became restless because it was tea time. I took them to the Professor's Lounge to have a snack and continued our discussion. The head waiter came and said, "Sir, you don't seem to know our customs. This lounge is for the senior Professors only. You are not supposed to bring registrars here." I said, "I'm sorry. I invited them. They are my guests. I want to continue my discussions with them. They are staying." The head waiter, murmuring something about uncivilized behavior, did nevertheless serve us.

Peter was sent to South Africa to work with some of my friends. He was training at the Baragrava Hospital, and then sent around to various missionary hospitals where he did a great deal of surgery. As a third-year medical student, this was a great learning experience for him. Steven was sent to do a year abroad in Dublin. I saw him when I did a brief visiting professorship at the medical school. We rented a car and did the round of Kilarney and visited many other parts of Ireland. Steven was much interested in fishing, so we rented a boat and engaged a fishing guide. At the time, a shark fishing contest was on, and Steven landed a nice shark. Our guide told us that there is a bounty on these sharks, so he would have it measured for a possible prize, collect the bounty, and send it to Steven. We never heard from him again. Kathy was with us on trips to East and West Africa, the Brazilian Amazon, and to Hungary. She stayed in Hungary on a research fellowship with the National Agricultural Research Institute of Hungary, which was part of the University of Budapest. She wrote a thesis and obtained an additional doctorate. Charlie and Kathy were both with us during our trip to the Amazon in Brazil. We also visited Peru, including a trip to the Machu-Pitchu. All seven children, and three of our oldest grandchildren, visited Hungary at various times. A colleague of mine was Professor of Hematology in Abidjan, Ivory Coast. He was French, and a refugee from Algeria. His son stayed with us for one year and studied with us in the Graduate School. In return, Charlie stayed with his family, both in France and in Spain, where they had Summer homes.

Fiftieth Anniversary of Graduation

I graduated from the Evangelic Gymnasium, the equivalent of our high school, in 1942; and when invited to the 50th graduation anniversary, I took along some of my children. We toured the old high school together. One of my classmates, Sir Peter Abeles, donated a computer laboratory and a Physics Laboratory, which were very well equipped. He was the owner of one of the Australian airlines; and when we visited Australia, he hosted us, including first class air tickets to the various universities where we had to lecture and the various trips to other parts of Australia. We found out that about half of our classmates were dead, partly because of the War. One of our classmates, we were told, was severely ill and hospitalized in one of the university hospitals. We decided to interrupt the festive dinner, and some of us, including some of my classmates who became physicians, went there after calling the professor of medicine on the telephone. We actually got him out of bed, but nevertheless he met us there and we had a quick bedside consultation about our ill classmate.

As a youngster I often visited the farm of a neighbor and good friends, the Elek family. I remember once we went out with my friend Peter, early in the morning, hid in the haystacks by the river, and shot a number of ducks and geese which were flying between the small local lakes and rivers early in the morning. We were proud of our trophies and entered the house with a number of birds hanging from our belt while the families and their distinguished guests from England were having breakfast. Peter's mother, without any word, got up and gave him a huge slap in the face, saying to him, "I told you, never come to the dining room unless you first wash up, change your clothes, and get rid of your trophies." Somehow I never forgot that. Peter later became Professor of Economics in Philadelphia and we often visited each other. We became Godparents to one of his daughters.

Tropical Medicine

In trying to run tropical medicine teaching clinics in many parts of the world, we always faced the problem that the local population first looked at us with distrust. My approach was to always find the local Saman and try to establish a working relationship. I tried to convince him that we are not trying to denigrate him or to make the people lose confidence in him. In fact, I proposed that we should collaborate. If he had seriously ill patients who may die and may decrease his reputation, he should refer them to us. On the other hand, if we had patients whom we believed he might cure better than we could (including possibly psychosomatic problems) we would refer them to him. One of the things I also learned in West Africa was that children who had a large number of amulets hanging from their necks and on their wristband should never be asked to take these off. They had wristbands protecting them against all kinds of diseases, including one that had a picture of knife painted on it, which presumably protected against attacks with knives. We assured the parents that we would not interfere with the power of these amulets, and that our medicine would simply add to their power.

I remember at one time we pulled into a small jungle village in Uganda and requested the village elders for permission to establish a clinic. At this time, we usually sat in a circle, made an agreement, and to seal it, a gourd with banana wine was passed around and everybody had to drink from it. As the gourd went around, I usually made additional diagnoses – framboesia, possibly syphilis, and others. Nevertheless, when the gourd arrived to me, I had to drink from it – otherwise there was no agreement. Meanwhile, I quickly went to my camp which my boys had erected, and shot myself full of penicillin and washed my mouth with antiseptics. At this particular village, I was told that our clinic was not needed because everyone was healthy. However, we could help with the problem of some rogue elephants. They came and raided the maize fields, and the population then went out with pots and pans, made a lot of noise, and chased the elephants away. However, there is a rogue bull elephant which would turn around and attack, and had already killed about half a dozen people. Maybe, they said, I should operate on him. I did go out with some of my assistants dutifully and shot him as he charged. In my excitement, I missed hitting him in the right point, and hit him in his jaw. The elephant tusks, which now hang over my fireplace, still have a large hole on the backside. The elephant kept charging and I screamed, "Karibu bumdugi," to my gun bearer to give me my second gun. I hit him in the forehead and he collapsed a few yards in front of me. It was a close call.

Dracunculosis is a tropical disease due to a parasite which is acquired by drinking water which contains the pinhead-sized intermediary stage of the parasite. One would think that in a semi-desert area, this wouldn't be a problem. However, we found that women could fetch water only by actually stepping into the small drinking holes; and while fetching water, they would also release the eggs of the parasite, which in the meantime, had grown to about a yard long and would stick its uterus out from under the skin, releasing the eggs. We tried to convince the people that instead of doing that, they should remove the water by buckets and ropes. They should also either filter or boil the water before drinking it. They should introduce tilapia fish into the water holes, which eat the intermediary stage of the parasite. We showed them that putting fish into a bowl of water doesn't make the water bad, and demonstrated that I could drink water from the bowl with a tilapia swimming in it. We told them that they should not catch the tilapia for food, but let them multiply in the water. They all seemed to agree, but I am not sure whether the tilapia survived after we left. Dracuncolosis may be the second disease, after smallpox, to be eliminated from our planet if some simple, inexpensive precautions are instituted as outlined above.

Surgical Stories

I kept telling my medical students that a gastroduodenal ulcer patient has only two chances of significant bleeding; after the second, the patient needs surgery. This was before the days of modern anti-ulcer medications. I myself had three bleeding episodes and the third one just did not stop. I admitted myself to the General Hospital just after finishing a teaching session there. A gastroenterostomy was performed by my friend, Dr. Winn Butsch, and a day after surgery my residents came around and said what a pity it is that I am here as a patient when they have a few very interesting cases in the neighboring rooms. I said to bring me a lab coat and I made rounds with my residents and students on my neighbors. Dr. Butsch said, "I can't keep you down." and sent me home after a few days. Unfortunately, after awhile I developed a benign tumor on the suture line and required re-operation. This was performed by another friend, Dr. Jim Upson.

I was scheduled to give a paper at an international meeting in Vienna a few days after surgery, and Clara and I were picked to be the opening pair for the waltz after the opening dinner in the Esterhazy Palace. I left the hospital a few days following surgery, and dutifully did the opening waltz with Clara. Having something to do seems to decrease post-operative problems and suppresses post-operative pain.

When Linda was about five years old, I was teaching her how to ride. At one time we were cantaloring while her horse was on a lead line held by me; she fell off the horse and my horse stepped on her belly. It appeared that there was a major bleeding problem and I took her immediately to the Children's Hospital, requesting immediate surgery. My old friend, Dr. Winn Butsch, did the surgery and I scrubbed in and excitedly kept telling him what to do. He didn't know how to shut me off and started to tell me a story of President McKinley when he was shot in the belly during his visit in Buffalo. He told me that Roswell Park, who was head of surgery at the time, was unavailable because he took some visitors on a special train to Niagara Falls. Surgery on President McKinley was performed by the Chairman of Obstetrics/Gynecology, who unfortunately neglected to explore the pancreatic area. There was some bleeding in that area, a pseudocyst formed, and the President died. "We are not going to make the same mistake," said Dr. Butsch. He carefully explored the pancreatic area. It kept me spellbound; I was quiet, and let him operate. Unfortunately, a short time later a pancreatic pseudocyst formed and required a second surgery. At that time, we found that after the previous splenectomy and ligation of the splenic artery, a few small accessory spleens grew to significant size, which was probably effective in fighting certain infections. This observation gave me the idea that the adult spleen probably produces population-size, feedback control mechanism-related substances which prevent auxiliary splenic tissue from growing. When the spleen is removed, it no longer produces this inhibitor and auxiliary spleens start to grow. We proved this in some animal experiments, which were published, and started a study on isolating and identifying the growth regulatory factor. This study is still in progress.

Evolution

I was asked to participate in a symposium on Evolution by the Catholic Academy of Sciences in Washington, D.C. An Archbishop from the Vatican was scheduled to discuss the Pope's new book on evolution and his own studies with the Vatican group. I was supposed to discuss these issues after his paper. I was planning to start my presentation with a short excerpt recording of Darius Milhoud's *Le creation du monde* (the creation of the world) octet. This was a very new type of work at its time, combining classical music and American jazz patterns. It shows that if different factors are mixed, new, interesting phenomena will result. I did point out that there are five major theories on evolution:

1. *Creation, as described in Genesis.* There are two sources, the J (Jehovah's) and the P (Priestly). The first simply states that God created the universe and all there is in it. The second, which is best known, describes a six-day creation where the more primitive forms are created first, and the more complex ones last. Some interpreters pointed out that a day here may mean a "cosmic day," which may be many millions of our years.
2. *Intelligent Design.* Some authors pointed out that some of the structures in biology, for example the human eye, are so complicated that they couldn't have developed with the aid of natural selection. They must have been designed intelligently.
3. *The new Darwinism.* Most readily accepted by the scientific community, pointing out that we are surrounded by mutagenic factors (e.g., cosmic radiation) which continuously produce mutations. The bad ones are eliminated by natural selection, the good ones persist and multiply.
4. *Evo-Devo.* It was pointed out that some apparently new characteristics do not develop by new mutations but the appropriate genes have already existed for a long time in inactive form. Then they become activated by environmental factors. For example, the genes necessary to form limbs are already present in certain fishes but are suppressed. The reversal of suppression by various factors may result in new land animals.

5. *Creation of evolutionary mechanisms including co-evolution.* Investigators subscribing to this theory believe that God created the universe with the basic rules of physics, chemistry, and biology. One of the rules of biology is evolution, which then proceeded as described by modern science. Co-evolutions means that as we evolve, so do, for example, some of our parasites. While we develop defenses against bacteria, bacteria develops defenses against our defenses. One example is the development of activity by many viruses to induce four interferon inhibitors against our protective interferon mechanisms as described by our group in a series of publications.

I will point out that during the past millennia, there was little physical change in the human species; however, there was a great deal of cultural, ethical, and mental evolution. These resulted, for example, in advances in medicine, agriculture, nutrition, architecture, and energy uses, all acting together to increase the human life span in the last centuries, from a few decades to close to 80 years, depending on the geographic area. There is a definite delay between scientific discoveries and widespread applications with the general benefits. For example, the first table below shows some preventable diseases in the USA where current action is needed. The second table shows some preventable or curable tropical diseases. Institution of some of the methods outlined would save many lives and reduce much suffering throughout the world.

One example is the recent story of MRSA (methicillin-resistant staphylococcus aureus). It was said that this infection probably originated from inappropriate use of antibiotics, which selected out antibiotic-resistant bacteria. On the other hand, this explanation doesn't tell us how the resistance originated. It is likely that actual antibiotic use wasn't the major reason for initiating this epidemic. MRSA organisms existed for a long time in the soil and were probably contaminants of skin wounds. Antibiotic use, of course, eliminated susceptible organisms and allowed resistant organisms to persist.

Some Preventable Diseases in the USA (Responsible for about 50% of Outpatient Visits)

Disorder	*Some Consequences*	*Some Causes*	*Prevention*
Obesity Hypercholesterolemia	Diabetes Mellitus – Type 2; Cardiovascular Disorders	Genetics; Habituation; Maternal malnutrition	Diet; Exercise; Education; Antilipidemic agents; Research on new anti-taste and anti-appetite agents (hormones) in progress
Smoking	Lung and bladder cancers; Cardiovascular disease	Habituation	Education
Alcoholism	Hepatic cirrhosis and cancer; Mental disorders; Car accidents	Genetics; Habituation	Education
Drug addictions	Mental disorders; Car accidents	Genetics; Habituation	Education
Lung cancers (including mesotheliomas)	Metastatic disease	Smoking; Industrial exposure	Education; Industrial hygiene
Hypovitaminosis D (70% of the normal population in the USA)	Osteoporosis; Immunologic dysfunction	Lack of exposure to sunshine; Diet	Dietary supplementary medication

Infantile respiratory distress syndrome (hyaline membrane disease)	High death rate	Prematurity; Inadequate pregnancy care; Diabetes; OB/GYN problems	Adequate pregnancy care; Surfactant therapy; Plasminogen therapy (experimental); Respiratory care
Lead poisoning in children	Mental retardation	Household factors; Toys; Cribs	Education; Care in buying

Some Preventable or Curable Tropical Diseases

Disorder	**Some Consequences**	Causes	**Prevention or Treatment**
Schistosomiasis	Urogenital disease, intestinal and liver fibrosis, growth retardation	Schistosoma mansoni, Sch. Japonicum, and Sch. Hematobium	Life style changes, single dose praziquantel
Lymphatic filiariasis	Lymphedema and hydrocele	Wurcheria bancrofti, Burgia malayi and Burgia timori	Life style changes, single dose ivermectin
Trachoma	Blindness	Chlamydia trachomatis	Fly control, azithromycin, ophthalmic drops into newborn
Onchocercasis	Blindness	Onchocerca volvulus	Single dose ivermectin, annual ivermectin
Dracunculiasis	Secondary bacterial infection	Dracunculus medinensis (guinea worm)	Filtered water, trilapia into wells, larvicides

Chagas Disease	Cardiomyopathy, mega colon, and mega esophagus	Trypanosoma Cruzi	Vector control including housing modifications, benzimidazole
Leishimaniasis	Kala-azar	Leishmania donovani, L. Chagasi, L. infantum	Vector control, pentamidine, miltefosine

Medical War Stories

During World War II, there was a great deal of concern about burn injuries induced by flame throwers and the potential of radiation injury induced by various weapons, including atomic bombs. Working in a research laboratory as a volunteer medical student, I was involved in a planning session on what to do about them. I remembered that during high school I used to assist our biology teacher, who was also an Assistant Professor of Biology at the University, in his research on plant hormones, including the auxins, particularly heteroauxin which he isolated. I had to develop screening methods to assay auxin isolates and preparation. I was wondering that if auxins have growth affects in plants, they may also have some effect in animals and may help in healing burn wounds. I developed a method to develop standard burn wounds in rats, working with the animal colony of one of the teaching hospitals which was left empty during the War. I tried local application of auxins and came up with largely negative results. I continued some of this work much later at the medical school in Buffalo, which resulted in equally negative results. This was in contrast to some of the research publications by Japanese investigators who reported activity in human cell lines by some of the auxin derivatives. After much delay, I put together some of our data and submitted it for publication. It contained some of the data generated over 60 years ago as a high school student.

We later studied several Vitamin D analogs which appeared to have differentiation-inducing effect and may be useful in promoting the healing of burn injuries. Some of them are now used in the treatment of psoriasis. A study on burn wounds is still to be undertaken. Several Vitamin D analogs were supplied to our studies by the Hoffman LaRouche Company and some by the Wisconsin Research Foundation through Dr. Hector DeLuca.

We also did research on potential radiation protective agents. Much more sophisticated work was performed in the meantime by the US Army. They came up with some compounds (e.g., AET) which metabolizes into MEG which has a very high protective effect in rodents but is very toxic in primates, including man, and for this reason was discarded. We have found that this agent does not absorb from the gastrointestinal or urinary tract; but it develops local radiation protection. In animal experiments, when loops of the bowel were filled with this material or when the urinary bladder was filled with this, local radiation injury to these normal tissues was largely prevented. We thus thought that this may be useful when tumor radiation involves segments of the bowel or the bladder and may result in significant injury, thus presenting an important limiting factor in radiation therapy. This proved to be correct in animal experiments. Clinical studies are still to be undertaken.

Infant Mortality

Over all, mortality in some advanced countries is relatively high. An important factor appeared to be a high rate of infant mortality, which in turn was due in a large degree to respiratory distress syndrome — Hyaline membrane disease (HMD). At the time my wife, Clara, was working at the Children's Hospital of Buffalo and we teamed up to study factors involved. We studied major factors in HMD and possibly related pathophysiologic mechanisms.

1. Prematurity is possibly the most important factor. A defense mechanism against fibrin deposition in the lungs during birth trauma – plasminogen – was found by our group to develop slowly during embryonic life, and develops largely during the last weeks of pregnancy and to some degree after birth. Lack of plasminogen, the basis of an important defense mechanism, may

be an important factor. Plasminogen is activated by activators in the lungs to plasmin which dissolves fibrin deposition.

2. The incidence of HMD is high in diabetic mothers. We found that in these patients, antiplasmin levels were very high, related to an inhibition of the protective fibrinolysin system.
3. Many of the mothers of these patients had bleeding complications of pregnancy. We found that probably as a compensatory mechanism, these patients developed high levels of fibrin stabilizing factor (FSF, factor XIII), also resulting in relative inhibition of the protective fibrinolysin system.

We studied protective mechanisms of which the application of plasminogen as a preventive agent, and urokinase-activated plasmin as a therapeutic agent, were most effective in a study of 500 infants. These agents were produced in our laboratory at the time. We hope eventually someone will take over large-scale production and, following confirmatory studies by other groups, these agents will be available for general use. Others at the Children's Hospital developed surfactant. Maybe it should be combined with our plasminogen preparation.

Myocardial infarction

Our studies on the fibrinolysin system resulted in the preparation of, or obtained from various sources, several enzyme preparations to dissolve blood clots. We did the first comparative clinical study together with our associates at Buffalo General Hospital, Millard Fillmore Hospital, and the Roswell Park Cancer Institute. We compared streptokinase (which later became standard therapy, even though it proved to be allergenic), streptokinase-activated plasmin, urokinase (which also became available for general use), and urokinase-activated plasmin. We found the latter to be most effective. Unfortunately, this preparation is still not available for general use. Tissue plasminogen activator has become available since then. We also explored some of these preparations in blood-clot related strokes with moderate success. Our main collaborators were Dr. Larry Golden of the Millard Fillmore Hospital, Dr. Eugene Lipschutz of the Buffalo General Hospital, and Dr. Joseph Sokal from Roswell Park Cancer Institute. Most of our data were published, although a few still await publication.

More War Stories

During the war, at the dinner table, I heard my elders discuss rumors about the so-called T4 program by the Nazis in Germany. It was run by Dr. Werner Heyde and Dr. Paul Nitsche. It was a procedure to kill the mentally ill and the severely handicapped. There were also notices of Dr. Karl Brandt, who performed perverse medical experiments on people in concentration camps. I heard a great deal of discussion of how one could possibly help. One idea I heard discussed was that the Hungarian government should be requested to present a proposition to the German government. That is, that we will take handicapped people and people in concentration camps and keep them in our facilities. After the war, if the Germans win they can deport them to Madagascar or other areas they were talking about; but they should not be killed, and medical personnel should not participate in activities opposed to the Hippocratic oath. In return, we would open up vacation spots on the Balaton Lake where families of German leaders could avoid bombing raids. I learned that these proposals got nowhere and that governmental officials were afraid to approach the Germans with such proposals.

Arthur Kornberg

I was asked by one of the medical groups to say a few words on the death of Arthur Kornberg. This outstanding scientist won the Nobel Prize for discovering DNA polymerase, an enzyme needed for the synthesis of DNA. I briefly reviewed his life story and emphasized what we can learn from it. I knew Dr. Kornberg superficially from some medical meetings. I also knew his son, Roger, who also received the Nobel Prize some years after his father. Arthur Kornberg graduated from the City College in New York, together with Dr. Herbert Hauptmann, of Buffalo, who also received the Nobel Prize and whom I knew well. Dr. Kornberg received his medical degree from the University of

Rochester in 1941, and interned at the Strong Memorial Hospital in Rochester. Even though he spent his entire life in basic science, the fact that he graduated and was trained in medicine helped him a great deal in his work. We probably should do more to encourage those who want to enter research to first train in all aspects of medicine. After graduation, Dr. Kornberg applied for several research training grants from the Federal government and private organizations, but all turned him down. He wound up in the Navy and was eventually assigned to the National Institutes of Health, where he worked in a research laboratory. My son, Julian Jr., had a similar assignment. After completing his residency in Internal Medicine, Julian did a fellowship at NIH while serving in the Navy. I often pointed out that although he was a naval officer, the biggest boat he ever sat in was the small rowboat called "Tex" (named after Mary Jane Tex Bardos who presented it to us) on the small lake in our farm. Dr. Kornberg later became Chairman of Microbiology at Washington University in St. Louis, and then Chairman of Biochemistry at Stanford University. He also founded a small research company which later became part of the Schering-Plough Company. Dr. Kornberg's pioneering work, for which he eventually received the Nobel Prize, was described in two papers submitted to the Journal of Biologic Chemistry. They were rejected with a sarcastic letter from Dr. Irvin Chargaff. Dr. Kornberg rewrote the papers and when a new editor, Dr. John Edsall, came to the journal, they were finally accepted. They were published with a delay of over one year. This again shows problems with our medical publications. I do serve as Editor-in-Chief of the Journal of Medicine, and on the Editorial Board of several other publications, together with my wife Clara. We are committed to help authors to get their papers in print as fast as possible, after necessary corrections are made, but not to hold back anything for significant periods of time. Dr. Kornberg's work laid the basis for production of a number of anti-cancer and anti-viral drugs. Interestingly enough, my group has studied DNA polymerases from biopsies of tumors and normal tissue surrounding the tumors of our patients. We found significant differences, and published these in a series of papers. We are still working on attempts to develop agents that would attack one type of polymerase and not the other. Dr. Kornberg and his group were also the first to synthesize the active inner core of a virus. This raised the question of whether it would be possible to "synthesize life."

Personalized Medicine

I have discussed with my students that there is a "revolution" coming in medicine – the various aspects of personalized medicine.

1. Genomic analysis makes it possible to predict susceptibility and possible prognosis to certain diseases, e.g., BRCA1 and BRCA2 genes may indicate susceptibility to breast and ovarian cancer and in some cases may suggest preventive therapy or surgery.
2. Genomic analysis may indicate responsiveness to certain drugs, e.g., proper dosage of Coumadin (which has a very narrow therapeutic index) can be predicted by genomic analysis. Analysis of certain genetic mutations will predict whether a patient will respond to certain epidermal growth factor inhibitors. While up-to-date medical practice would require such tests, generally insurance companies do not pay for them and they are rather expensive.
3. We have worked on studies in which tumor biopsies were put in culture and incubated with the patient's own white cells and certain stimulating factors (interferons, interleukin 2). We have shown in vitro that these "educated" white cells can kill the patient's cultured tumor cells. Active defensive cells were then injected into the patients. Clinical studies – partly during visiting professorships abroad – were at times spectacularly successful and at times ineffective. The reasons for this are still under study.

Local Custom

I learned that it is most important to study the local customs and behave accordingly when in foreign countries.

When lecturing in Saudi Arabia, I was told that before each lecture, we have to say: "Bissm Illah el Raman el Rahim," which means: "In the name of Allah, the merciful, the compassionate." I had no difficulty with that. After all, we are all the children of the same God, by whatever name we call Him.

I remember at one time I had to examine a patient who came with an interpreter and complained about a bellyache. I was wondering about a possible gastroduodenal ulcer, and asked him whether he had melena – black stool. He got red in the face and started swearing at me in Arabic. "You have asked the wrong question," said the interpreter. "He feels that it is his private business and none of yours to ask him about the color of his stool." I said, "I understand that you are a very famous falconer. Falconers have to look at the castings of their falcons, break it open, smell it, to tell whether the falcon is healthy. Just like you had to look at the castings of your falcon, I have to know about the color of your stool." "Oh, you know all about Falcons? You are my brother." He embraced me and from then on we got along very well. He actually invited me to come and falcon with him in the desert. We had a small argument before we set out about Arabic vs. European/American methods. It turned out that after three days of intensive falconry, we only caught about one hubara – an Arabian bustard – it was caught by my falcon. I said, "Maybe American methods aren't quite so bad." He said, "But three days is nothing. If you stayed with me for three weeks I could really show you the superiority of Arabic methods. After all, you all learned falconry from us after the Crusades."

When conducting a traveling medical clinic in Uganda, we did not have room in our Landrovers to carry any food because it was packed with equipment, students, and helpers. I had to go early in the morning every day to hunt, and whatever I shot we ate, and so did our patients who sometimes walked long distances to come to the clinic. I had a gun bearer who was Muslim. He told me he was not allowed to eat any of the meat unless it was prepared the right way. He asked me to shoot antelopes by just wounding them with a shoulder shot but not killing them. He then took his handjar between his teeth and ran hell for leather to catch the antelope, sling rope on its hind legs, pull it up on a tree branch, cut its neck, and bleed it out. Once it was bled, it was alright for him to eat. I remembered that even in our Old Testament, there was a paragraph saying that blood and meat should never be mixed.

More Gypsy Stories

The barber at the Saturn Club was an ex-violinist of the Buffalo Philharmonic Orchestra, who retired and then returned to his father's profession – barbering. At one point, he told me that a new Hungarian restaurant opened on the lakefront and they were advertising that they were looking for a gypsy violinist. He wanted to apply for the job but he really didn't know what to play. So, while he was cutting my hair I was whistling and singing to him various Hungarian tunes. We had several sessions, and he then went and applied for the job successfully. He eventually had a small "gypsy orchestra," and often invited us to listen to him play. We never had the time, and by the time we did decide to have dinner there, the restaurant went bankrupt and closed.

Falcons

It is believed that falcons are difficult to breed in captivity. They require a "freedom flight," when they chase each other over long distances and finally settle down and mate. We developed a technique that seemed to work very well. We kept males and females separately in individual horse stalls. At feeding time, I put on a cowboy hat and put one or more dead mice from the laboratory on top of it. The falcons came, sat on the hat, and ate the mouse. Eventually they fell in love with the hat. The males would crouch down after a meal and ejaculate on the hat. I could pick the sperm up with an eyedropper. I then went to the cage of the female, who was also in love with the hat, and after the meal would crouch down, assume the lordotic position, and I would pick her up, stroke her back, and inject the sperm into her vagina. In this way it was actually possible, not only to breed purebred falcons, but also to generate hybrids. Most of the hybrids, or at least their next generation, were sterile. On the other hand, hybrids between Gyr falcons and Saker falcons, remained fertile. This proved to be an excellent breed since they could function well both in very cold and very hot weather. Gyr falcons alone we found quite inadequate in Saudi Arabia, where it was too hot for them. My Saudi hosts only carried them on their gloves in their sitting room as a prestige item but couldn't hunt with them. They were called falcons of "Mayalis." I recommended to the Saudi Arabian breeders to try to concentrate on this hybrid. One of my plans was to try to establish a hybrid between the Berkut eagle from **Kyrgisistan** and the quail eagle from Spain. So far, I couldn't get hold of appropriate breeders. I thought that these would be a magnificent bird which would also readily "wait on."

I remember as boy, back on the family farm, I used to have Uhu's (eagle owls) – European relatives of the great horned owl. I would have them sit tethered to a T-shaped perch, and build a blind some 30 feet away. When an owl unexpectedly appeared during the daytime, all kinds of birds, including crows and magpies, came to attack it and they could be shot or captured. Occasionally the Uhu would jump off the perch, lay on his back, and point his talons skyward. This was a sign that an eagle is coming to attack him. The eagle could then be captured with a net, and eventually be included in our colony of raptorial birds.

Our House

Our house on Windsor Avenue was originally part of the Rumsey farms. Interestingly enough, our farm in Boston, New York, originally also was a Rumsey farm. Our house was built in 1917 and, of course, when we bought it there was a great deal of repair to be done. At one point we called for a plumber to fix some problems. He said, "I do know this house. I worked here many years ago. Whom did you buy it from?" I told him. He said, "Oh, Mr. X from the Cosa Nostra." The plumbing continued to give us problems. One day I came home from the hospital very late and heard patterns of rain, which was strange since it wasn't raining outside. When I went to the living room it was raining from the ceiling. While I stood there trying to figure out what to do, the whole ceiling came down. It required major repairs. Old houses with high ceilings are lovely to live in, but they need continuous repairs.

Madáme Curie

When Madáme Curie and her husband discovered radium and some of its biological effects, they were interested to explore whether it would be suitable to treat cancer. In France, they did not allow them to do any clinical studies since they were not MDs. They came to the Roswell Park Memorial Institute in Buffalo, New York, where they were received cordially and allowed to do the first clinical treatments. A small room was assigned to them in the basement, where they compounded the radium which they had brought with them from France. After they returned to Paris, it turned out that the room in which they were working was thoroughly contaminated with radium dust. It appeared almost impossible to clean it up and therefore a decision was made to simply wall in the entire room and forget about it. Many, many years later somebody, probably an employee, chiseled his way into the walled-off room and stole the radioactive gold which was there. He sold it to a jeweler who in turn made it into rings and sold it to several customers. Nobody knew that this contained radioactive material. Some of the people who bought it developed skin or bone cancer, and when the cause was uncovered they sued Roswell Park Memorial Institute because they had not guarded the radioactive material well enough. Eventually the suit was dismissed. A picture of Madáme Curie still hangs in the foyer of the auditorium. We often discuss this story with visitors as we were told about these affairs.

Calasanctius School and Some Church and Health Affairs

In Hungary, the two best, private-church high schools were those of the Piarist Fathers, which excelled in the Liberal Arts, and the Evangelic gymnasium, whose strength was in the sciences (several alumni won Nobel Prizes). After the War, a group of the Piarist Fathers came to the United States and established a school in Buffalo,

New York; Martin, Kentucky; Devon, Pennsylvania; Washington, D.C.; Ft. Lauderdale, Florida; and Miami, Florida. The head of the Buffalo school was Father Stephen Gerencser, an old friend. The school was established in 1957, and I served on the Board of Trustees. The principle of the school was that all those who are talented and met the stiff admission criteria should be taught, regardless of their ability to pay tuition. This, of course, was a problem. The majority of the students paid partial tuition or no tuition at all. This, together with the fact that most of the European faculty gradually became old, retired, or died, and teachers had to be hired who required proper salaries – in contrast to the Fathers who were not paid at all. This essentially resulted in the inability to maintain the school, and in spite of all efforts and private donations, the school had to be closed in 1992. The Piarist Order and the original school were founded by Father José de Calasanz in Rome, Italy, in the late 1500s. Its alumni included Mozart, Goya, Schubert, Victor Hugo, Johann Mendel, and a host of astronomers, kings, emperors, presidents, and a pope. In the last few decades, most of the schools were in Hungary, Poland, and Spain. The Fathers who came to the Buffalo school, and with whom I had the most contact, included Father Michael Palotai from Hungary; Father Benjamin Cobos from Catalan, Spain; Father Peter Marsdeval, also from Spain; and Father Bela Kiegler, also from Hungary. The school curriculum emphasized languages, and courses were available in Spanish, German, French, Japanese, Chinese, Russian, and Hungarian. The school was located two houses away from our house on Windsor Avenue. They also owned a dormitory facility a couple of blocks away and a retirement home on the seashore, which was originally built by one of the outstanding American architects, Frank Lloyd Wright. We shared a cook, Betsy Perez, who worked part-time for us and part-time for the Piarist Fathers. Betsy came from Indonesia, but was of Chinese origin. She could cook Chinese, Indonesian, French, and Hungarian dishes. My mother and Father Gerencser taught her Hungarian cooking. She was also sent to the father of one of the school alumni, who owned the Four Season Restaurant in New York City, for an internship in American and French cooking. Betsy and Father Gerencser arranged occasional gourmet dinners and wine tasting events, which turned out to be great fundraisers for the school. When Betsy and her husband arrived as refugees in Buffalo, they had a hard time finding a job since they spoke very little English. We employed her as a cook and her husband as a house painter. Unfortunately, her husband died very soon and Betsy was left with her children to earn a living. We arranged that she could also work part-time for the Piarist Fathers a couple of blocks away, and she turned out to be a great success. After the school closed, Betsy became a chef of several restaurants in Buffalo. She eventually retired and joined one of her children, a successful businessman, in Ohio.

One of the interesting small episodes I remember was some years ago, when early in the morning I was flying my falcons in the backyard and a small kestrel came by. My falcon devoured the mouse I had for her on my glove, chased the kestrel, and came down with it on the roof of the Calasanctius school. I didn't want the kestrel to be injured, so I ran over there, held up a mouse with my glove, and started making falcon sounds. The children were just arriving to school, and they saw me in tattered clothes, with a dead mouse, making strange sounds in front of the school entrance. They stood around in awe, and when the falcon let the kestrel go and came down on my glove to devour the mouse, they all cheered. They then went to class with Father Kriegler and told him, "We have seen a real madman in front of the school today."

I was a member of the Wine and Food Society, and had to give occasional talks about French and Hungarian wineries, including one on our own farm and its production methods. The Society purchased outstanding wines occasionally, and many of them were donated to Calasanctius school for their fundraising wine-tasting events.

On Sundays we went to church at the Calasanctius chapel and enjoyed the old Latin masses and Gregorian music. The children, however, preferred mass at the Newman Center, State University of New York at Buffalo college chapel, also around the corner, where masses were celebrated in English with guitar-accompanied music.

Father Weimer preached up-to-date and maybe semi-revolutionary addresses. When I was made Chairman of the Catholic Physicians Guild Subcommittee to advise the Bishop's Conference about permissibility of genetic engineering, I used Father Weimer, Msgr. A.M. Caligiuri, and Father Gerencser as advisors. The report I wound up writing started with "Remember Galileo…." The report of the Bishops was forwarded to the Vatican and no prohibition was pursued against genetic engineering.

The Catholic Physicians Guild, Buffalo Chapter, charged the Executive Committee to appoint a Subcommittee to draft a position paper on the health care system reform proposals. I was Chair of this Subcommittee, and an extensive report was published in one of the medical journals. We are probably the only industrialized nation in the world where health care coverage is not extended to all citizens. It is unconscionable to have about 40 million in our country who are not properly covered with health care. Admittedly, some people are covered periodically and not covered at other periods of employment. It is true that we don't see people dying in the streets like in some under-developed countries, and all emergencies are taken care of one way or another. This is accomplished by doctors working many hours free of charge; hospitals devoting significant parts of their budget to charity, in spite of great financial difficulties; medical students, residents, and clinical fellows under the guidance of medical school teachers rendering care as part of their education;, and charitable contributions by many physicians. Nevertheless, the system needs to provide a great deal of feeling of security to all, particularly those who are not covered by health insurance. The present system is also very complicated. It is supposed to serve the ill, the elderly, and the very young, all of whom are confused by the intricacies of the system and are in no position to make proper decisions as to what type of insurance and which type of drug care assistance would be most advantageous to them. It is most important to simplify the system. The current health care system is fragmented, costly because of multiple layers of administrative responsibility, and involves a great deal of paperwork. To mention an example: one of the clinics where I was involved earlier had six physicians, three nurses, and one secretary. However, nine clerks and supervisors were involved in handling the paperwork. Innumerable clerks are involved at the insurance companies and various government agencies at the next level. It is estimated that at least 25% of the health care funds are spent on various levels of administration. This is simply one aspect that is open to savings. Politicians often say that "managed competition" is needed. This is an oxymoron: the more it is managed, the less it is competitive, and vice versa. Interposing health insurance purchasing cooperatives, regional health alliances, and a National Board between physicians and patients represent additional layers of beaurocracy and expenditures. Any system which would make employees of physicians (like certain HMOs) will result in decrease of the best patient/doctor relationships. The doctors will be under pressure to spend minimal time caring and listening to their patients, and patients will have the feeling that they are treated like numbers in a big, industrial organization. If we make employees out of physicians, they will then react by behaving as employees; instead of working 60-80 hours per week, as most physicians do today, they will work 40-hour weeks. They will be available for night calls only on assigned days and not seven days per week, as many physicians have been and still are. Consequently, the need for physician numbers will greatly increase.

The quality of health care in the United States is probably the highest of all times and areas. Unfortunately, a gap developed between those who can afford the most advanced, cutting-edge treatments, even if they are not yet approved by insurance companies, and those who depend for all payments by insurance companies or who are not insured at all. Maintaining a high quality of medical care will require continued emphasis and support for medical research and medical education at all levels for medical schools, residencies, and fellowships. Currently, there is an inadequate number of physicians in primary care and some specialties. We have to make primary care more attractive to those in training. Remunerations have to be brought closer between those of the various specialties and subspecialties. Positive incentives, including loan forgiveness, have to be introduced to those entering primary care. Professional liability reform is essential to reduce "defensive medicine" including ordering of excessive tests, and will thereby reduce healthcare costs. Liability insurance premiums are a major handicap for allowing elderly physicians to practice on a part-time basis, and they represent a major problem for all physicians – but particularly those young physicians starting out in practice.

Physicians have to be advocates for their patients. They must work for high-quality health care for all of those in need. For this reason, they must have a voice on issues relating to delivery and payment. Many decisions should not be left to administrators, particularly when they work for a strong profit motive. Today in business circles it is often pointed out what excellent profits many health insurance companies make. Many of the insurance company executives receive seven figure salaries, with additional bonuses and perks (Table). These individuals should not be in a position to make important decisions for the life and death of patients, and should not be in a position to dictate procedures to physicians.

Total honoraria of chief executives of some managed care companies in 1994

CEO	Company	Pay (millions)
Norman C. Payson	Healthsource, Inc.	$14.28
Daniels D. Crowley	Foundation Health Corp.	$12.99
William W. McGuire	United HealthCare Corp.	$6.07
George J. Jocum	Mid-Atlantic Medical Services	$4.78
Leonard Abramson	U.S. Healthcare Inc.	$3.87
Stephen P. Wiggins	Oxford Health Plans	$2.79
David A. Jones	Humana, Inc.	$2.30

Methods have to be found to pay for emergency treatment of uninsured travelers and illegal immigrants. Leaving them untreated is not only inhuman, but it also endangers public health. Maybe travelers and temporary foreign employees have to obtain and provide adequate insurance before obtaining a visa. A fund has to be established to pay for other emergencies. including the care of illegal immigrants. Thorough medical examinations of immigrants have to be established. Diseases dangerous to public health (including AIDS) have to be kept out. Each AIDS patient admitted may cost nearly $100,000 to the health care system and many times much more. "Our globe is shrinking." This is a threat. We have to intensify research even on "tropical diseases" and export the technological "know-how" and medical help. Otherwise, "new" epidemics may show up sooner or later in our own country.

We perceive a great deal of anxiety among our patients from the eventual rationing of health care. There is a fear that we will return to the long-discarded two-tier system of medical care: one level for the wealthy who can afford using their own funds above what the insurance system provides and for those in powerful positions.

It is often pointed out that taking care of all of those who are in need is an obligation for all of us. For this reason, a single payer option supported by general taxes, should be seriously considered. Employer-mandated systems may be a hardship to many small, fledgling businesses.

Another subcommittee I chaired for the Guild dealt with general church reform. It was preparing to write a position letter to the Vatican; however, this was never a completed project. When my term as President of the Catholic Physicians Guild expired, the Subcommittee stopped its work. Our ecclesiastical advisor, Msgr. A.M. Caligiuri, was transferred from the Bishop's office to a parish. Nevertheless, a few of us continued to work on this issue and maybe eventually a report will develop. It will deal with such issues as admission of women to the priesthood, marriage of priests, the use of contraceptive methods that do not involve killing embryos, and others. Reforms may be needed in view of the declining church attendance, particularly in Europe. On trips to Europe, we observed that at morning masses in large cathedrals which seat many thousands of people, only a few dozen are present, mostly old women and a few ancient men. Recent scandals of priestly pedophilia probably contributed to all of this.

More about Tropical Medicine

Obesity in Underdeveloped Countries: When we worked in Africa in the early 1950s we saw a great deal of malnourishment. When we returned many years later, we saw both malnourishment and obesity side by side in the same hospitals. We were also impressed by some of the childhood obesities we had seen. When we investigated this issue carefully, we found that often mothers are relatively malnourished while pregnant, and it appears that embryos develop mechanisms to metabolize nutrients more efficiently. When they are born and receive relatively normal nutrition as infants and young children, these adaptive mechanisms result in childhood obesity. We were wondering whether this may be a problem in our country when pregnant women afraid of gestational diabetes and being overweight go on relatively restrictive diets. Could this be a factor of childhood obesity in our country?

Sickle cell disease: In early visits to Africa we had seen virtually no sickle cell (SS) crises in the hospitals we worked at. However, in visits during the last several years, we have seen this problem. It appears that in the early days, most SS genotype children died of early problems, particularly auto-splenectomy, due to occlusion of the splenic blood vessel, resulting in increased susceptibility to infections and infectious death. In later years, however, early SS disease was properly treated and many of these children survived but came back later to the hospitals with a serious SS crisis.

Pox Viruses: We have seen several cases of monkey pox during visiting professorships in Africa. Most are children, some with visible vaccination scars, and their parents indicated they were vaccinated within the last few years. They had only a light course of the disease. It appears that smallpox vaccination offers only partial protection against monkey pox. It was thought that this is a disease not prevalent in Western countries. However, a few years ago a pet store in Wisconsin imported some giant gambian rats from Ghana which were apparently infected with this virus. The infection spread to prairie dogs also kept in the same pet store and infected a pet store employee, several veterinarians, and a number of customers who bought these rats. A total of 104 cases of monkey pox were reported. Smallpox is, of course, the first disease which was eliminated from the world with an intensive vaccination program. However, there are a large number of pox and related viruses in animals, many of whom are not pathogenic to humans, including elephant pox, camel pox, buffalo pox, canary pox, fibroma and myxoma of rabbits. The danger exists that some of these viruses may hybridize under natural conditions by infecting the same host, or else that biowarfare laboratories will produce hybrids which may turn out to be highly pathogenic to man and may spread rapidly in a non-immune population. There is a large cooperative study going on in our medical school to develop therapies against pox viruses.

We have studied another pox virus in Africa, yaba virus, which we found to be possibly involved in Burkitt's lymphoma. While working with this virus, one of our technicians infected himself and developed a tumor, which was promptly resected. When ground up and re-infected into monkeys, it produced a certain type of tumor in them. This was the first case when Koch's criteria were fulfilled to prove that a virus can produce tumors in man. Infiltrates of the tumor were able to produce more tumors in susceptible hosts. We also thought that our studies showed that in order to produce a cancer, such as Burkitt's lymphoma, several factors have to work together, one of which may be the EB virus and others, maybe malaria, and possibly Yaboe's virus.

AIDS: AIDS is widespread throughout the world, but presumably it originated in Africa by mutation of viruses relatively common in the great apes. We had seen a patient in the Hemophilia Center who received a transfusion with apparently infected blood. We had samples of the infectious blood saved in the freezer and saw the patient monthly, and blood was drawn at each visit. We found that after about one year, 18 mutations of the original virus were present. Whether these small mutations were clinically significant, of course, we never found out since nobody volunteered to be inoculated with them. Nevertheless it showed that the AIDS virus is a highly mutagenic virus. This explains why at the time when the epidemic started in our country, it was chiefly homosexually transmitted, but later the virus changed and it became easily transmitted heterosexually. The danger, of course, exists that one of these days the virus may mutate to be transmitted not only sexually but also through the respiratory system by droplets, as for example, smallpox. A great many experiments are in progress on the treatment of AIDS in our laboratory. Some preliminary papers have been published of initially promising data.

Students

From 1972 to 1992 I was Professor and Chairman of the Department of Experimental Pathology, State University of New York at Buffalo, Roswell Park Division. During that time, over 100 students received graduate degrees from this department, and for about one third of these students, I was the direct thesis advisor. They worked in my laboratory and my clinic. A number of them were advised by Clara Ambrus. We had two special programs: in one, students received a graduate degree (usually MA) and then continued on in medical school. For a while we had a special grant to support this program. The purpose was to graduate individuals who will go on to medical research pursuits being trained both in clinical medicine and basic research. It was thought that more of these double-trained individuals were needed. In the second program, physicians who were enrolled in oncology fellowship training at Roswell Park Cancer Institute were also enrolled in the graduate school. They were to complete their medical specialty training and at the same time obtain a degree in a basic research program. Blocks of time were set aside in their fellowship schedule for research training, which was both in the basic and the clinical research sciences. They were also asked to attend certain graduate courses. I was teaching a course in Hematology, another one in Tropical Medicine with special emphasis on Tropical Oncology and Hematology, and a course in Pathophysiology. The latter ran four semesters a year, including both summer semesters, and was open to medical students and residents from all programs. For awhile, we also accepted graduate students from Niagara University. The program for physicians was highly successful in attracting first-class applicants to our oncology fellowship program. The applicants were highly-qualified individuals with an interest to enter academic medicine. The following table lists graduates from these programs, the topics of their thesis, the name of their thesis advisor, and the first position they received after graduation.

102 Graduates of the Experimental Pathology Department
(22 were in the MD-MA-PhD Program)
SUNY Buffalo/Roswell Park Memorial Institute
Graduate School Division
Julian L. Ambrus, MD, PhD, Chairman
(37 directly advised by J.L. Ambrus and 3 by C.M. Ambrus)
1973 - 1988

Name	Degree Conferred	Res. Advisor	Title of Dissertation	1st Position after Graduation
Timothy Burke	PhD, 1973	Dr. G. Moore	Characterization of cultured lymphoid cells derived from mouse thymus	Cancer Research Scientist, Radiation Dept., RPMI
Peter S. Ambrus	MA, 1975	Drs. E. Klein & J.L. Ambrus	Endocrine influence on the synthesis of cholinesterases	MD, SUNY Buffalo; Fellow, Peter Bent Brigham Hosp.; Asst. Prof., Head & Neck Surg. Othorhinolaryngology, Harvard Med. School, Boston (special MD-MA program)
Ayada El-Shirbiny	MD, PhD, 1975	Dr. J.L. Ambrus	Immunization with common antigen in protection against infectious problems in cancer patients	Resident, RPMI Dept. of Pathology. Asst.-Assoc. Prof. of Pathology, Kuwait Univ. Med. School, Kuwait
David B. Lillie	MA, 1975	Drs. E. Klein & J.L. Ambrus	Effect of common gram negative enterobacterial antigen on experimental pyelonephritis	MD, Wayne State Univ.; Resident, Urology Dept., Temple Univ., Phaladelphia, PA; Asst. Prof. of Urology, SUNY Buffalo (MD-PhD program)

Name	Degree Conferred	**Res. Advisor**	**Title of Dissertation**	**1st Position after Graduation**
Madeline A. Lillie	PhD, 1975	Drs. E. Klein & J.L. Ambrus	Systemic side effects of oral contraceptive agents	MD, Wayne State Univ.; Fellow, Univ. of Penn.; Asst. Prof. of Pediatrics & Clin. Immunol., SUNY Buffalo (MD-PhD program)
Michael Gillette	MA, 1976	Dr. J.L. Ambrus	The synthesis of members of the fibrinolysin system in an isolated perfused rat liver preparation	MD, SUNY Buffalo; Res. Assoc., Univ. of Penn.
Elias G. Elias	MD, PhD, 1976	Dr. J.L. Ambrus	The transfer of delayed hypersensitivity by thymic extract	Prof. Surg. Oncol., Univ. Maryland, Baltimore, MD
Vera Papermaster	PhD, 1976	Dr. J.L. Ambrus	Desensitization: Effects on cutaneous and peritoneal manifestations of delayed hypersensitivity in relation to release of mediatrs or inhibitory serum factors	Postdoctoral Fellow, Univ. Texas, Houston, Texas.
Petrina Genco	MS, PhD, 1976	Drs. S. Cohen, J.L. Ambrus and R. Bettigole	A study of a procoagulant lymphokine produced by stimulated lymphocytes	Res. Assoc., Rome, New York
David Sokal	MA, 1976	Dr. H. Stoltz	Effect of mumps vaccine on the age specific incidence rates of childhood diabetes mellitus	MD, SUNY Buffalo; Staff Member at CDC, Atlanta, GA (MD-PhD program)
James Hipkens	MA, 1977	Dr. J.L. Ambrus	Studies on the induction of hexobarbital hydroxylase in mice	MD, Emory Univ., Atlanta, GA

Name	Degree Conferred	Res. Advisor	Title of Dissertation	1st Position after Graduation
Carl Killian	MA, 1977	Dr. T.M. Chu	Serum alkaline phosphatase isoenzymes as quantitative markers for bone nad liver metastasis in prostatic cancer	Cancer Research Scientist, Roswell Park, Dept. Diagn. Immuno. Research & Biochemistry
John Ritter	MA, 1977	Dr. C.M. Ambrus	Pancreatic alterations seen with Phenobarbital administration	MD, Cambridge Univ., London, England; Res. Orthopedic Surgery & Clinical Instructor of Orthopedics, Tufts Univ. School of Medicine, Boston, MA (MD-PhD program)
Frederick J. Weber	PhD, 1978	Dr. J.L. Ambrus	Studies on thrombolysis using fibrinolytic enzymes	MD, SUNY Buffalo; Resident in Medicine, Philadelphia, PA (MD-PhD program)
Babu Bhaswar	MA, 1978	Dr. J.L. Ambrus	Role of fibrinectin in reticuloendothelial function	Director, Clinical Laboratories, MDS, Olean, NY
Charles J. Gomer	PhD, 1978	Dr. T. Dougherty	Evaluation of in vivo tissue localization and photosensitization reactions of hematoporphyrin derivatives	Res. Associate, Children's Hospital, Los Angeles, CA; Asst. Prof. Pediatrics & Radiation Oncol., Univ. Southern California School of Med, Los Angeles, CA
David Cooper	PhD, 1978	Dr. J.L. Ambrus	Differences between inbred rat strains in catecholamine synthesizing enzyme activity after immobilization stress	Res. Associate, Tennessee Neuropsychiatric Inst., Nashville, TN; Executive Director, Myotonia Foundation
Lawrence Papsidero	PhD, 1978	Dr. T.M. Chu	Immune complexes and tumor associated proteins in human breast cancer	Cancer Res. Scientist, Dept. Diagn. Immunol. & Biochemistry; Vice President for Research, Cellular Products, Buffalo, NY

Name	Degree Conferred	Res. Advisor	Title of Dissertation	1st Position after Graduation
Beata Kereszti	MS, 1978	Dr. J.L. Ambrus	Studies on cellular membrane fluidity	Medical student (MD-PhD program)
Anthony J. Russo	PhD, 1979	Dr. M. Goldrosen	Mechanism of the microleukocyte adherence inhibition assay	Staff fellow NIH, Gerontology Research Center, Baltimore City Hospital, Baltimore, MD
John J. Black	PhD, 1979	Dr. C. Wenner	Carcinogenic hazards in aquatic ecosystems	Cancer Res. Scientist, Dept. of Experimental Biology, Roswell Park, Buffalo, NY
Samuel R. Sirianni	PhD, 1979	Dr. C. Huang	Modified host-mediated assay using human and Chinese hamster cells cultured in diffusion chambers in mice	MD, SUNY Buffalo; Resident in Medicine, Millard Fillmore Hospital, Buffalo, NY (MD-PhD program)
Sandra Gordon -Hollander	MA, 1979	Dr. J.L. Ambrus	A study of platelet aggregation inhibitors on nephroblastoma in Wistar-Furth strain rats	MD, New York Univ.; Resident and Fellow, Hematology-Oncology, New York Univ., New York, NY (MD-PhD program)
James Hipkens	PhD, 1979	Dr. H. Gurtoo and Dr. J.L. Ambrus	Studies on the role of metabolism in the toxicity and chemotherapy of cyclophosphamide	MD, Emory University, Atlanta, GA (MD-PhD program)
George L. Carlo	PhD, 1979	Dr. S. Graham	Organic drinking water contaminants and the incidence of selected gastrointestinal and urinary tract cancers	Clinical Instructor, SUNY Buffalo School of Med., Dept. of Social & Preventive Med., Buffalo, NY; Carlo & Associates, Buffalo, NY
John W. Wojcieszyn	PhD, 1979	Dr. T.M. Chu	The purification and characterization of a female urinary acid phosphatase	Cancer Res. Scientist, Dept. Exper. Pathology, Roswell Park, Buffalo, NY

Name	Degree Conferred	**Res. Advisor**	**Title of Dissertation**	**1st Position after Graduation**
David Cooper	PhD, 1978	Dr. J.L. Ambrus	Differences between inbred rat strains in catecholamine synthesizing enzyme activity after immobilization stress	Res. Associate, Tennessee Neuropsychiatric Inst., Nashville, TN; Executive Director, Myotonia Foundation
Veronica Nwobi	MS, 1979	Dr. J.L. Ambrus	The effect of tripeptides 166 and 451 on the release of lipoprotein lipase in vivo	MD, SUNY Buffalo, Buffalo, NY (MD-PhD program)
Susan Leong	PhD, 1979 (joint with Dept. Physiology)	Dr. J. Sokol and Dr. J.L. Ambrus	Sensitivity of malignant cells in CML to various chemotherapeutic agents	Professor of Pathophysiology, Roswell Park; also owns two restaurants
John C. Robin	MS, 1979; PhD, 1981	Dr. J.L. Ambrus	Osteoporosis: Its induction and measurement in an animal model	Fellow, Dept. Exper. Pathology, Roswell Park, Buffalo, NY
Judith Walker	MS, 1979	Dr. J.L. Ambrus	Blood coagulation parameters in oral contraceptive users	Director, MDS Clinical Laboratory, Buffalo, NY
Peter Bugelski	PhD, 1980	Dr. T. Dougherty	Morphologic aspects of the photosensitizing effects and distribution of hematoprophyrin derivatives in experimental tumors and cultured cells	Principal Cancer Res. Scientist, Dept. Exper. Pathol., Roswell Park, Buffalo, NY; Senior Investigator, Smith, Kline & French, Philadelphia, PA
Richard L. Kirsh	PhD, 1980	Dr. G. Poste	The role of macrophage activation in host defense against neoplasia	Res. Assistant, Dept. Exper. Pathol., Roswell Park, Buffalo, NY

Name	Degree Conferred	Res. Advisor	Title of Dissertation	1st Position after Graduation
John Korzelius	PhD, 1980	Dr. Bealmear	Suppressor substance in the culture supernatant of the L562 cell line inhibits Mitogen and MLR responses	MD and Residency, Dept. of Surgery, Univ. of California at Los Angeles, Los Angeles, CA
Arthur Michalek	PhD, 1980	Dr. C. Mettlin	Cancer mortality patterns in the Catholic clergy	Cancer Res. Scientist, Roswell Park, Buffalo, NY
Mong H. Tan	PhD, 1980	Dr. M. Goldrosen	Pathogenesis of metastasis in colorectal and cutaneous tumors: Studies in two syngenic murine tumor model systems	Research Affiliate, Dept. of Diag. Immunology Research & Biochemistry, Roswell Park, Buffalo, NY
John Vena	PhD, 1980	Dr. S. Graham	Air pollution and lung cancer in Erie County, Buffalo, NY	Res. Associate & Asst. Professor, Dept. of Social & Preventive Med., SUNY Buffalo; Res. Asst. Professor of Exper. Pathol., SUNY Buffalo, Roswell Park
Bertram M. Maidment, Jr.	PhD, 1980	Dr. T.M. Chu	The analysis and isolation of the antigen and antibody components from immune complexes by isoelectric focusing	Senior Analyst for Central Intelligence Agency, Washington, D.C.
Ahmad A. Attallah	PhD, 1981	Dr. J. Lee and Dr. J.L. Ambrus	Prostaglandins, renin and salt and water hemostasis	Research Assistant, Dept. of Medicine, SUNY Buffalo; Dean, Graduate School, Univ. of Jeddah, Saudi Arabia
Frederic I. Preffer	PhD, 1981	Dr. P. Bealmear	Immune evaluation of patients with selected malignant diseases: Laboratory and clinical studies of subcellular factors	Research Fellow at Massachusetts General Hospital, Dept. Pathology, Boston, MA

Name	Degree Conferred	**Res. Advisor**	**Title of Dissertation**	**1st Position after Graduation**
Michelle J. Marinello	PhD, 1981	Dr. J.L. Ambrus	Double minute chromosomes in human	Res. Asst. Prof., Dept. of Medicine, Buffalo General Hospital, Buffalo, NY
John L. Wilson	PhD, 1981	Dr. S. Graham	The incidence of cancer in Blacks and Whites: The influence of socio-economic status Buffalo, NY 1971-85	Corporate epidemiologist, Exxon Corporation
Satya D. Sharma	PhD, 1981	Dr. C.M. Ambrus	Immobilized phenylalanine ammonia lyase for the depletion of phenylalanine in phenylketonuric patients	Associate, Clinical Pathology Dept., Buffalo General Hospital, Buffalo, NY
Gail P. Scott	PhD, 1981	Dr. J.L. Ambrus	The effects of feiba on platelet function: Interaction between plasma coagulation factors and platelet coagulant activity	Head, Medical Laboratory, Toronto, Ontario, Canada
Thomas P. Koestler	PhD, 1981	Dr. T.M. Chu	Detection, isolation and characterization of antigen component(s) obtained from immune complexes in human breast cancer	
Carl Killion	PhD, 1981	Dr. T.M. Chu	The usefulness of the phosphates and the polyamines as tumor markers in prostate cancer	Asst. Cancer Res. Scientist, Dept. Diag. Immunology & Biochemistry, Roswell Park, Buffalo, NY

Name	Degree Conferred	Res. Advisor	Title of Dissertation	1st Position after Graduation
Philip C. Nasca	PhD, 1982	Dr. P. Greenwald	An epidemiologic case control study of ovarian cancer	Director, Cancer Control Section, Bureau of Chronic Disease Prevention, NYS Dept. Health, Albany, NY; Res. Assoc. Professor Exper. Pathol., SUNY Buffalo, Roswell Park, Buffalo, NY
Nefissa Meky	PhD, 1982	Dr. J.L. Ambrus	Studies on sickle cell anemia	Asst. Professor, Ain Shams University, Cairo, Egypt; Assoc. Professor, Univ. of Yemen
Okhee Suh-Gray	PhD, 1982	Dr. L. Weiss	The development of a technique for the morphometric analysis of invasion of cancer	Cancer Res. Scientist, Biomathematics Dept., SUNY Buffalo, Roswell Park, Buffalo, NY
David A. Bellnier	PhD, 1982	Dr. T. Dougherty	In vitro photoradiation, hematoporphyrin derivative accumulation, sensitization and interaction with ionizing radiation	Fellow, Radiation Biology, Baylor Research Foundation,; Advanced Laser Research Facility, Dallas, TX
David B. Jacobs	PhD, 1982	Dr. C. Wenner and Dr. J.L. Ambrus	TPA-induced stimulation of adhesion in mouse spleen leukocytes	Postdoctoral Fellow, Biophysics Dept., Buffalo VA Med. Center, SUNY Buffalo, Buffalo, NY
Stephen Nelson	MA, 1982	Dr. R. Hefner	A clinico-pathologic study of malignant fibrous histiocytoma of the central nervous system	MD, Albert Einstein School of Medicine, New York, NY (MD-PhD program)

Name	Degree Conferred	**Res. Advisor**	**Title of Dissertation**	**1st Position after Graduation**
Ming F. Lin	PhD, 1983	Dr. T.M. Chu	Purification & Characterization of new human prostatic isoenzyme and of a prostatic acid phosphatase acid phosphatase like glycoprotein	Postdoctoral Fellow, Dept. Diag. Immunogy Res. & Biochemistry, SUNY Buffalo, Roswell Park, Buffalo, NY
Brian Schepart	PhD, 1983	Dr. R. Bankert	Idiotype-specific regulation of the Balb/c mouse (1-8) dextran antibodies	Damon Runyon-Walter Winchell Postdoctoral Fellowship, Univ. of North Carolina, Chapel Hill (Dr. Jeffrey Frelinger)
Patrick Capone	PhD, 1983	Dr. T.M. Chu	Passive immunotherapy of human breast tumors with monoclonal antibodies	Postdoctoral fellow, Dept. Diag. Immunology & Biochemistry, SUNY Buffalo, Roswell Park, Buffalo, NY; MD, SUNY Buffalo, 1986
Gary A. Croghan	PhD, 1983	Dr. T.M. Chu	An epithelial and tumor associated antigen recognized by monoclonal antibody F36/22	Postdoctoral Fellow, Dept. Diag. Immunology & Biochemistry, SUNY Buffalo; medical student, 1988
Debra Jenkins	PhD, 1983	Dr. M. Goldrosen	Role of t-cells detected by the microplate leukocyte adherence inhibition test	Professor, Erie Community College, Buffalo, NY
Helena Gabor	PhD, 1983	Dr. L. Weiss and Dr. J.L. Ambrus	Cancer cell destruction in micropores: A model for mechanical trauma in passing through the microcirculation as part of the metastatic process	Asst. Research Pathologist, John Muir Cancer and Aging Institute, Walnut Creed, CA (Deceased, 1987)

Name	Degree Conferred	Res. Advisor	Title of Dissertation	1st Position after Graduation
Daniel Melewski	PhD, 1983	Dr. D. Higby	Assessing the value of chemotaxis complement and c-reactive protein assays as prognostic indicators for determining outcome of infectious episodes in patients with severe granulocytopenia	Postdoctoral Fellow, Dept. of Pathophysiology, SUNY Buffalo, Roswell Park, Buffalo, NY
James Sciandra	PhD, 1983	Dr. J. Subject	Stress induced protein synthesis: Correlations with thermosensitivity	Res. Fellow, Dept. of Exper. Therapeutics, Univ. of Rochester Cancer Center, Rochester, NY
Elizabeth de la Pava-Barren	MS, 1983 (Natural Sciences)	Dr. C. Ambrus		Research Assistant, Children's Hospital, Obstetrics-Gynecology Dept. Buffalo, NY
Robert E. Heinl	MS, 1983 (Natural Sciences)	Dr. J.L. Ambrus	Spleen metastasis: Analysis of autopsy data	Medical student, University of Warsaw, Warsaw, Poland
Dona Upson	MA, 1983 (Pathology)	Dr. J.L. Ambrus	The role of branched chain amino acids in clinical stress	MD, Med. Coll. Of Wisconsin, Resident, Dept. of Int. Medicine, Jefferson Univ. Hospital, Philadelphia, PA; Director, Family Practice Dept., Tucson, AZ (MD-PhD program)
Kimberly Witkowski	MS, 1983 (Natural Sciences)	Dr. J.L. Ambrus		
Annlouise Assaf	PhD, 1983	Dr. S. Graham	A randomized clinical trial of three methods of training women how to perform breast self examination	Epidemiologist, Memorial Hospital, Pawtucket, Rhode Island

Name	Degree Conferred	**Res. Advisor**	**Title of Dissertation**	**1st Position after Graduation**
Glenn Miller	PhD, 1984	Dr. M. Goldrosen	Characterization of the IgG response on renal cell carcinoma patients receiving specific active immunotherapy	Research Fellow, Sloan-Kettering Cancer Center, New York, NY
Frank LaDuca	PhD, 1984	Dr. R. Bettigole	The interaction of von Willebrand factor, platelets and collagen in platelet agglutination and aggregation	Postdoctoral Fellow, Johns Hopkins, Baltimore, MD
John J. Doll	PhD, 1984	Dr. J.L. Ambrus and Dr. G. Poste	Interactions among clonal population in B16 melanoma	Research Scientist, Smith, Kline & French, Philadelphia, PA
David Kennedy	PhD, 1984	Dr. P. Bealmear	Prevention of lethal graft vs. host disease following bone marrow transplantation. Pre-treatment of the inoculum with purine metabolic enzyme inhibitors	Postdoctoral Research Fellow, Dept. of Medicine, Division of Geriatrics & Gerontology, Cornell Univ. Medical Center
Lydia Wingate	PhD, 1984	Dr. M. Zielezny	A prospective study to determine the efficacy of physical therapy for the post-mastectomy patient	Coordinator, Rehabilitation Medicine, Buffalo General Hospital, Buffalo, NY
Anthony A. Campagnari	PhD, 1984	Dr. M. Goldrosen	Isolation and immunological characterization of an unusual acid protein found in the effusion fluids of patients	Res. Assistant, Departments of Medicine & Microbiology, Erie County Medical Center, Buffalo, NY
Paul Niswander	MS, 1984 (Natural Sciences)	Dr. G. Tritsh, Dr. J.L. Ambrus, and Dr. W. Greco	Control by purine catabolism of superoxide secretion during macrophage membrane perturbation	PhD Candidate, Computer Science Dept., Univ. of California at Davis, Sacramento, CA; JD, Univ. of California

Name	Degree Conferred	Res. Advisor	Title of Dissertation	1st Position after Graduation
Sylvia Dlugokinski	MS, 1984 (Natural Sciences)	Dr. J.L. Ambrus	A study of red blood cell deformability and platelet aggregation in patients with bronchogenic carcinoma compared to normal subjects	Nurse, Urologic Oncology Department, SUNY Buffalo, Roswell Park, Buffalo, NY
Steven M. Waldow	PhD, 1985	Dr. T. Dougherty	Evaluation of hyperthermia as an adjuvant modality to photodynamic therapy of cancer: studies at the animal and cellular level	Res. Scientist, Wenske Laser Center, Ravenwood Hospital Center, Chicago, IL
Cynthia B. Rodgers	PhD, 1985	Dr. M. Goldrosen	Characterization of a reticulum cell sarcoma tumor and the role of liver non parenchymal cells in the development of hepatic metastases	Postdoctoral Fellow, Department of Microbiology & Immunology, Univ. of Illinois, Chicago, IL
Maria G.Ikossi-O'Connor	MD,PhD, 1985	Dr. K.C. Chadha, and Dr. J.L. Ambrus	The interferon system in patients with malignant disease: Possible modulation of interferon production and biological activity	Clinical Staff, MD Anderson Hospital & Tumor Institute, Houston, TX (MD-PhD program)
Thung Tai-Shyy	PhD, 1985	Dr. J. Subject	Functional analysis of the mammalian heat shock response	
Donna A. Volpe	MA, 1985	Dr. F. Orsini	Modulation of murine megakaryocyte precursor cells (CFU-MEG) by vinca alkaloids and anthracycline antibiotics	PhD candidate, Physiology Dept., SUNY Buffalo, Roswell Park, Buffalo, NY

Name	Degree Conferred	Res. Advisor	Title of Dissertation	1st Position after Graduation
Noma B. Roberson	PhD, 1986	Dr. C. Mettlin	A community cancer control intervention for Black Americans in Buffalo, New York: A case study	Research Assistant, Minority Education Program, SUNY Buffalo, Roswell Park, Buffalo, NY
Norma J. Nowak	PhD, 1986	Dr. L. Papsidero	Biological studies of oncogene transformed cells in immunocompetent mice	Postdoctoral Res. Associate, Department of Human Genetics, SUNY Buffalo, Roswell Park, Buffalo, NY
Constantine P. Karakousis	MD-PhD, 1986	Dr. J.L. Ambrus	Explorations in regional chemotherapy (role of limb salvage and infusion of other organs)	Assoc. Chief, Department of Surgical Oncology, SUNY Buffalo, Roswell Park; Professor of Surgery, SUNY Buffalo, Millard Fillmore Hospital (MD-PhD program)
Steven P. Corwin	MS, 1986 (Pathology)	Dr. J.L. Ambrus and Dr. G. Poste		PhD candidate, Exper. Pathology Dept., SUNY Buffalo, Roswell Park, Buffalo, NY
Mark S. Baptiste	PhD, 1986	Dr. P. Nasca	The relationship of serum cholesterol with cancer incidence and mortality	Director, Cancer Etiology Program, NYS Department of Health, Albany, NY
Randall Loftus	MA, 1986 (Pathology)	Dr. M. Goldrosen	The evaluation of spent media from an established pancreatic cancer cell line as a source of antigen in the microplate LAI assay	PhD candidate, Experimental Pathology Dept., SUNY Buffalo, Roswell Park, Buffalo, NY

Name	Degree Conferred	**Res. Advisor**	**Title of Dissertation**	**1st Position after Graduation**
Peter J. Fung	MA, 1986 (Pathology)	Dr. H. Gurtoo	c-DNA cloning of PAH-inducible cytochrome P-450 from a human lymphoblastoid cell line	Medical student, Univ. of Rochester Med. School, Rochester, NY (MD-PhD program)
Denise A. Scala	PhD, 1986	Dr. M. Ip	Characterization of a two component estrogen-receptor complex in the MTW-9B transplantable rat mammary tumor	Postdoctoral Fellow, Fox Chase Cancer Center, Boston, MA
Alexandra C. Miller	PhD, 1986	Dr. B. Henderson	The influence of chemical effectors of reactive oxygen species and GSH depletion on cell survival following photodynamic treatment and ionizing radiation	Postdoctoral Fellow, National Institutes of Health, Radiation Biology Department, Bethesda, MD
Mahmoud K. Mahafzah	MD-PhD, 1986	Dr. J.L. Ambrus	Radiation biologic, immunologic and hemorrhagic effects of a prostaglandin-leukotriene inhibitor	Resident, Department of Internal Medicine, Sister's Hospital, Buffalo, NY (MD-PhD program)
Michael Herrman	MD-PhD, 1986	Dr. P. Bealmear	The use of purine metabolic pathway inhibitors as modulators of graft vs. host disease	Resident, Dept. of Surgery, Case Western Reserve Univ. Hospital, Cleveland, OH (MD-PhD program)
Brian N. Bundy	PhD, 1986	Dr. M. Zielezny	A mathematical model of the effects of exogenous estrogens on endometrial cancer	Associate Group Statistician, SUNY Buffalo, Roswell Park, Buffalo, NY
Stephen Radel	PhD, 1987	Dr. E. Mayhew	The effect of calcium antagonists and metabolic inhibitors on the retention of adriamycin, in both free and liposòmal form, in a number of tumor cell lines	Postdoctoral Fellow, Dept. of Molecular Medicine & Immunology, SUNY Buffalo, Roswell Park, Buffalo, NY

Name	Degree Conferred	**Res. Advisor**	**Title of Dissertation**	**1st Position after Graduation**
Elias A. Lianos	MD-PhD, 1987	Dr. J.L. Ambrus	Experimental glomerular immune injury: Glomerular prostaglandin and thromboxane synthesis and effects on renal hemodynamics	Assistant Professor of Medicine, Medical College of Wisconsin
Lemuel Herrera	MD-MA, 1987 (Pathology)	Dr. E.D. Holyoke	Ornithine decarboxylase activity in normal colonic mucosa adenomatous polyps, primary and metastases from colorectal cancer	Surgical Oncologist, Department of Surgical Oncology, SUNY Buffalo, Roswell Park, Buffalo, NY
Gary A. Giovino	PhD, 1987	Dr. C. Mettlin	Eval. of a training program to teach physicians counseling and behavioral strategies to aid smokers in quitting	Project Manager, Smoking Research Program, Univ. of Rochester, Rochester, NY
Ivana T. Croghan	PhD, 1987	Dr. K.M. Cummings		Postdoctoral Research Affiliate, Cancer Control & Epidemiology Dept., SUNY Buffalo, Roswell Park, Buffalo, NY
Germaine M. Buck	PhD, 1987	Dr. D.L. Cookfair	Sudden infant death syndrome (SIDS) in Upstate New York, 1984	Postdoctoral Research Associate, Dept. of Social & Preventive Med., SUNY Buffalo, Roswell Park, Buffalo, NY
Timothy R. Batt	MA, 1987	Dr. C. Huang		
Sandra Selenskas	PhD, 1987	Dr. C. Mettlin	The effects of dietary fat as a risk factor in the epidemiology of prostate cancer: A case control study	Postdoctoral Fellow, Yale University, New Haven, CT

Name	Degree Conferred	Res. Advisor	Title of Dissertation	1st Position after Graduation
Anthony Jankowski	MD-MS, 1987 (Natural Sciences)	Dr. J.L. Ambrus	Effect of etiocholandione & homo- logous bone marrow on hemopoietic recovery in irradiated mice	Research Affiliate, Dept. of Pathophysiology, SUNY Buffalo, Roswell Park, Buffalo, NY
Elinor R. Schoenfeld	PhD, 1987	Dr. C. Mettlin	Applications of diffusion theory to cancer care in the United States, 1972-1981	
Martin C. Mahoney	PhD, 1987	Dr. A. Michalek	Patterns of mortality and cancer incidence among the Seneca Nation of Indians, 1955-1984	Postdoctoral Fellow, Bureau of Cancer Epidemiology, NYS Dept. of Health, Albany, NY
William C. Biddle	PhD, 1987	Dr. E. Sarcione and Dr. J.L. Ambrus	A critical evaluation of monoclonal antibody – Anthracycline immunoconjugates specific for human breast carcinoma and acute lymphoblastic leukemia	Postdoctoral Research Fellow, Department of Clinical Immunology, SUNY Buffalo, Roswell Park, Buffalo, NY
Frank N. Konstantinides	MS, 1988 (Natural Sciences)	Dr. J.L. Ambrus	Effects of total parenteral nutrition solutions on measurements of mixed venous blood gases, calculated oxygen content and oxygen consumption	Director, Surgical Metabolic Research Facility, Department of Surgery, St. Paul Ramsey Medical Center, St. Paul, MN 55101 (612-221-3537)

We also had a Summer Program for junior high school and college students. They were assigned to research laboratories to develop interest in graduate and professional school training, and medical research. I was a member of the committee that ran the program, and in 1989 I was the Director of the program. The following list and table show students in the program for that year. We were not always successful. The son of a prominent scientist came at the end of the program and said, "Thank you. I learned a lot." "What did you learn?" I asked. He replied, "That this is not what I like." He later became a prominent politician.

Summer Students 1989
State University of New York at Buffalo/Roswell Park Memorial Institute
Dr. J. L. Ambrus, Director
(159 students, 5 directly assigned to J.L. Ambrus)

Madeline L. Bryant (JLA advisor)
Insulin receptors in normal and neoplastic tissues:
Role in the growth of neoplastic cells.
June 26-August 18, 1989
RPMI Summer Research Program

Dominic Smiraglia
257 Idlewood
Tonawanda, NY 14150
692-6159
Jr. at SUNY Buffalo/Biology
(Friend of Dr. Jacobs)
Clinical Biology

Zahra Ghorishi
193 Springville
Amherst, NY 14226
838-6252, ex. 3279 – Dr. T. Tomasi lab
Clinical Biology

Asha Subramanian (JLA advisor)
57 Old Spring Lane
Williamsville, NY 14221
689-9560
RPMI Summer Research Program
Jr. at Buffalo Seminary

Neera Gulati
36 Mar-Del Way
Williamsville, NY
631-0966
Albany Medical School
RPMI Summer Research Program

Kurt Venator (JLA advisor)
65-C Oakbrook Drive Williamsville, NY 14221
689-8721
Jr. at Nichols
RPMI Summer Res. Prog.

Larry Jacobs, Jr.
24 Middlesex Avenue
Buffalo, NY 14216
(at Nichols)

Jeff Kaczorowski
66 Maria Lane
Cheektowaga, NY 14227
2nd yr. Medical student at University of Rochester
RPMI Summer Research Program

Scott M. Miloro (JLA advisor)
152 Soldiers Place
Buffalo, NY 14222
Platelet factor 3 release and platelet aggregation in cancer.
RPMI Summer Research Program

Student Name	**Address**
Francis P. Alcedo	78 Snug Haven Court Tonawanda, NY 14150
Patricia E. Allen	78 Langfield Drive Buffalo, NY 14215
Robin Jo Arent	75 Betty Lou Lane Cheektowaga, NY 14225
Kenneth J. Baker	550 LaSalle Avenue Buffalo, NY 14215
Daniel J. Barbero	90 East Summerset Amherst, NY 14228
Chad L. Beatty	4B Kenville Road Buffalo, NY 14215
Martha I. Bennett	524 Winspear Avenue Buffalo, NY 14215
Paula A. Bennett	199B Kenville Road Cheektowaga, NY 14215
Student Name	**Address**
Jennifer J. Bergoine	204 Hodge Avenue Buffalo, NY 14222
Antonio M. Bird	301 Linwood Avenue, #2 Buffalo, NY 14209
Joel S. Brenner	255A Niagara Falls Blvd. Amherst, NY 14226
Brian P. Brett	14 Godfrey Street Buffalo, NY 14215
Tracy Lynn Brobyn	393 Winspear Avenue Buffalo, NY 14215
Daphine A. Brown	130 Sanders Road, Apt. E Buffalo, NY 14216
Gregory M. Bugaj	197 Cable Street Buffalo, NY 14206
Thomas Burnette	300 Parkridge Avenue, #C-1 Buffalo, NY 14215

Student Name	Address
Enrico Caiola	316 Sunrise Blvd. Williamsville, NY 14221
Maria Cartagena	10 West Klein Road Williamsville, NY 14221
William L. Cecere	250 Montrose Kenmore, NY 14223
James F. Chmiel	1921 Northwood Drive Amherst, NY 14221
Scott P. Cholewinski	3901 Main Street #11A Buffalo, NY 14226
Dennis B. Chugh	30 Waterford Park Williamsville, NY 14221
Lynn M. Cieslak	27 Montbleu Drive Getzville, NY 14068
Kelli Ann Cooney	770 Maple Road, Apt. 11B Williamsville, NY 14221
Devin A. Coppola	132 Concord Drive Buffalo, NY 14215
Edwared J. Cosgrove	1394 Amherst Street Buffalo, NY 14214
Joseph P. Cronin	781 West Ferry Buffalo, NY 14222
John L. D'Souza	63 Richmond Ave., Apt. C1 Buffalo, NY 14222
Ketan C. Dave	195 Koenig Road Tonawanda, NY 14150
Maria L. Davis	1394 Amherst Street, Apt. #19 Buffalo, NY 14216
Christian R. DeFazio	4389 Chestnut Ridge Road, A7 Amherst, NY 14228
Deborah L. DeLozier	400 LaFayette Ave., Apt. 3 Buffalo, NY 14213

Student Name	Address
Tracy I. Demino	4545 Chestnut Ridge Rd., #207 Amherst, NY 14228
Todd A. Dorfman	314 Crestwood Avenue Buffalo, NY 14216
Winston G. Douglas	1469 Hertel Avenue Buffalo, NY 14216
Brian C. Dowdell	340 Campus Drive, #3 Snyder, NY 14226
Darlene A. Durkin	3541 Bullis Road Elma, NY 14059
Joseph M. Falsone	452 Normal Buffalo, NY 14213
Maureen A. Fay	221 Rounds Ave., Upper Buffalo, NY 14215
Glen T. Feltham	210 Buckeye Road Amherst, NY 14226
Amy E. Ferry	73-3 W. Summerset Lane W. Amherst, NY 14228
Sarah Finnegan-Sloan	19 Robie Street Buffalo, NY 14214
Mark D. Fisher	57 Euclid Avenue Kenmore, NY 14216
Lorna K. Fitzpatrick	82 Russell Avenue Buffalo, NY 14214
David S. Foley	950 Tacoma Avenue Buffalo, NY 14214
Maura P. Foley	139 Princeton Avenue, Apt. 3 Amherst, NY 14226
Patricia A. Geil	73-3 West Summerset Lane W. Amherst, NY 14228
Petros Ghermay	14 Godfrey Buffalo, NY 14215

Student Name	**Address**
Michael T. Giovanniello	4545 Chestnut Ridge Rd. Amherst, NY 14228
Gloria Gladkowski-del Valle	135 Dellwood Amherst, NY 14226
Douglas J.Golding	73 Lincoln Blvd. Kenmore, NY 14217
Mabel P. Gong	44 Merrimac St., G/F Buffalo, NY 14214
Idalia M. Gonzalez	131 Kenville Road Buffalo, NY 14215
James D. Gould	113 Hitchcock Drive Depew, NY 14043
Theodore S. Grabow	225 Summer Street, Apt. #1 Buffalo, NY 14222
Kim Griswold	39 Lexington Avenue Buffalo, NY 14222
Geoffrey M. Gullo	443 Stockbridge Avenue Buffalo, NY 14215
Horacio Gutierrez	340 Crescent, Apt. 5 Buffalo, NY 14214
Sandra Gutierrez	528 Highgate Avenue Buffalo, NY 14215
George E. Haddad	486 Emerson Drive Amherst, NY 14226
Tegest F. Hailu	121 Loring Avenue Buffalo, NY 14208
Steven D. Hammel	66 Old Colony Drive Tonawanda, NY 14150
Christian H. Hansen	3901 Main Street, #11A Amherst, NY 14226
George J. Hatsios	4545 Chestnut Ridge Rd.207A Amherst, NY 14226

Student Name	Address
Diane R. Heimback-Morrison	139 Creekside Drive, #2 Amherst, NY 14228
Geoffrey G. Hobika	76 Chasewood Lane East Amherst, NY 14051
Karen L. Houck	1 Lakewood Parkway Snyder, NY 14226
Carline T. Hyppolite	409 Eggert Road, Upper Buffalo, NY 14215
Gregory T. Jehrio	194 Wellingwood Drive East Amherst, NY 14051
Andrew D. Jenis	25 Lawrence Lane Williamsville, NY 14221
Jeffrey W. Kanski	3901 Main Street, Apt. 5C Eggertsville, NY 14226
Joseph D. Kay	97 Sunrise Blvd. Amherst, NY 14221
Barbara P. Kearney	60 Mitchell Drive Tonawanda, NY 14150
Glen E. Kershen	95 Old Lyme Road, Apt. 2 Williamsville, NY 14221
Carol Ann Killian	430 Highgate Avenue Buffalo, NY 14215
Richard J. Kozak	225 Summer Street, #1 Buffalo, NY 14222
Michael J. Krabak	100 Ashland Avenue Buffalo, NY 14222
David G. Kupkowski	95 Inwood Place Buffalo, NY 14209
Timothy J. LaRosa	4 St. John's Ave., Apt. 1 Buffalo, NY 14223
Michael K. Landi	685 Auburn Avenue Buffalo, NY 14222

Student Name	**Address**
Christian D. Lates	644 Marilla Street Buffalo, NY 14220
Janet M. Lawrence	770 Maple Road, Apt. 11B Williamsville, NY 14221
Kirsta Leale	726 Amherst Street Buffalo, NY 14216
Paul J. Lee	225 Summer Street, Apt. 1 Buffalo, NY 14222
Wendy L. Leffel	111 Midland Avenue Buffalo, NY 14223
Chien H. Lin	1400 Millersport, #210 Williamsville, NY 14221
Stephen C. Machnicki	4389 Chestnut Ridge Rd., Apt. 7 Amherst, NY 14228
Andres M. Madissoo	4393 Chestnut Ridge Rd., Apt. 6 Amherst, NY 14228
Stacey A. Madoff	204 Hodge Avenue Buffalo, NY 14222
Rita M. Malvaso	22 Jewett Parkway, #2 Buffalo, NY 14214
Frank J. Mascaro	2814 South Park Ave. Lackawanna, NY 14218
John R. McArdle	210 Campbell Blvd. Getzville, NY 14068
Elizabeth A. McClintick	48 Highview Road Buffalo, NY 14215
Lisa L. Miller	156 Callodine Avenue Amherst, NY 14226
Christina G. Miller-Weston	770 West Ferry, #1A Buffalo, NY 14222
Stephanie C. Mitchell	126C Kenville Road Buffalo, NY 14215

Student Name	**Address**
Paul J. Mustacchia	496 Elmwood Avenue, Apt. 3 Buffalo, NY 142222
Michael A. Nasiak	163 Surrey Run Amherst, NY 14221
Tung V. Nguyen	788 Potomac Avenue, #4 Buffalo, NY 14209
Michael P. O'Neill	580 Wyoming Avenue Buffalo, NY 14215
Juliana S. Paik	54 Addison Avenue Amherst, NY 14226
Michael J. Pelechaty, Jr.	7613 Behm Road West Falls, NY 14170
Michaelle D. Penque	5555 East River Rd. Grand Island, NY 14072
Sean Perini	401 Kinsey Avenue Kenmore, NY 14217
Richard G. Pinckney	971 Beach Road Cheektowaga, NY 14225
John Pollina, Jr.	Bidwell Parkway, Apt. 9 Buffalo, NY 14222
Ulka Prakash	120 Meyer Road, #406 Amherst, NY 14226
John P. Pryor	140 Linwood Avenue, Apt. B5 Buffalo, NY 14209
Nita K. Ram-Divan	4595 Chestnut Ridge, #4 Amherst, NY 14228
Nasser Razack	345 Meadowview Lane Williamsville, NY 14221
Edward D. Reidy	37 Hodge Avenue, #5 Buffalo, NY 14222
Cindy D. Repicci	120 Deer Run Williamsville, NY 14221

Student Name	Address
Charles A. Rocci	107 Cunard Avenue Buffalo, NY 14216
Thomas M. Romanelli	230 North Street, Apt. A26 Buffalo, NY 14201
Paul J. Sagerman	275 Scamridge Curve, B4 Williamsville, NY 14221
Diana R. Sanderson	39 Fuller Avenue Tonawanda, NY 14150
Pina C. Sanelli	400 Lafayette Avenue Buffalo, NY 14213
Paul Sansone	6695 E. Quaker Street Orchard Park, NY 14127
Todd E. Schlesinger	439 Burroughs Dr., #8 Snyder, NY 14226
Mark W. Sheldon	198 Tacoma Avenue Buffalo, NY 14216
John T. Sherwood	950 Tacoma Avenue Buffalo, NY 14214
Donna G. Sinensky	248 Callodine Amherst, NY 14226
Donald M. Slate, II	17C Kenville Road Cheektowaga, NY 14215
Paul Slavenas	220 Crosby Blvd. Amherst, NY 14226
Wendy I. Snyder	144 Winspear Ave., Apt. #3 Buffalo, NY 14214
Kenneth A. Sobel	340 Crescent Ave., Apt. 12 Buffalo, NY 14216
James W. Spain	22 Meadowbrook Road Williamsville, NY 14221
Maya D. Srivastava (JLA advisor)	23 Ascot Circle East Amherst, NY 14051

Student Name	Address
Michael Stanton	44 Bidwell Parkway Buffalo, NY 14222
Donna M. Stawasz	27 Nassau Lane Cheektowaga, NY 14225
Gregory H. Stiller	415 Dartmouth Avenue Buffalo, NY 14215
Mary E. Stock	1525 Amherst Manor, #502 Williamsville, NY 14221
Thaddeus E. Szarzanowicz	1263 Borden Road Depew, NY 14043
Sharon A. Szukala	82 Russell Avenue Buffalo, NY 14214
Behzad Tabibian	50 Florence Avenue, Apt. 5 Buffalo, NY 14214
Debra R. Tarantino	789 W. Ferry, Apt. A5 Buffalo, NY 14222
Jennifer M. Thompson	85 Paradise Lane, Apt. 15 Tonawanda, NY 14150
Gregory V. Tobias	66 Gilbert Avenue Blasdell, NY 14219
Madonna R. Tomani	4520 Clinton Street West Seneca, NY 14224
Jennifer M. Tufariello	257 Hunter's Lane Williamsville, NY 14221
Joseph S. Valenti	615 Linwood Avenue, #2 Buffalo, NY 14209
Yvette M. Vinson	14 Jewett Parkway, Rear Buffalo, NY 14214`
Lauren J. Vriesenga	450 Winspear Avenue Buffalo, NY 14215
Jennifer C. Wargula	657 Auburn Avenue Buffalo, NY 14222

Student Name	**Address**
Amy L.White	393 Winspear Avenue, Upper Buffalo, NY 14215
Andrea M. Williams	409 Eggert Road Buffalo, NY 14215
Douglas W. Wisor	107 Cunard Road Buffalo, NY 14216
Christopher Wood	486 Emerson Drive Amherst, NY 14226
Theodros Yohannes	1525 Amherst Manor, # 412 Williamsville, NY 14221
Atif Zafar	64 Northington Drive East Amherst, NY 14051

Leo Szilard

Leo Szilard was probably the single most important factor causing the initiation of the Manhattan Project, which led to the development and use of the atomic bomb. He was born in Hungary, educated at the Berlin Technical University in the early 1920's, and was a student of Albert Einstein. His fellow students included John Von Neuman and Denis Gabor, who all played an important role in American scientific life. Dr. Szilard worked in Vienna, London, and Princeton. He gained knowledge of the German plans to develop an atomic bomb and wanted to make sure that the United States got there first. In 1934 he obtained a patent on nuclear chain reactions and the building of an atomic reactor. In 1937 he was invited by New York University and settled in this country. He was relatively unknown and thought that he best persuade his most prestigious former teacher to approach the President of the United States requesting the establishment of a project to build an atomic bomb. He didn't have a car and was driven first by Eugene Wigner (a past schoolmate of mine who also became an important contributor to the Manhattan Project and won the Nobel Prize in Physics) to discuss this matter with Einstein. For a second meeting he was driven there by Dr. Teller, the father of the hydrogen bomb. Dr. Teller mentioned later that his most important contribution to the atomic bomb in the new atomic age was to be a chauffeur for Leo Szilard. Einstein finally wrote the critical letter to President Roosevelt and the Manhattan Project was initiated. Szilard, Von Neuman, Wigner and Teller, together with Fermi, were the key scientists participating in this project. After the war many of these individuals became much concerned about the oncoming atomic age. They did a great deal to discourage further use of nuclear technique in warfare. Szilard gave up physics research and trained himself to become a biologist involved in phage research. He developed a friendship with David Pressman, a prominent biologist who was Director of Scientific Affairs at Roswell Park Memorial Cancer Institute. Later on, Szilard developed urologic cancer. He consulted a large number of his colleagues, including George Klein and his associates at the Institute of Cancer Biology in Stockholm. He also asked David Pressman to recommend more consultants, and David sent him to me. All of the consultants agreed on a course of treatment and Szilard did very well. Many years later he died of cardiovascular problems. An autopsy revealed that his urologic cancer had been basically cured. Szilard was one of the those scientists who published relatively little, did not take credit for much, but was most instrumental in inspiring others, scattering ideas around, and being responsible for the initiation of many projects throughout the world. Many colleagues often said that without Szilard, our world would look different, for better or worse.

More on Teaching

Medical students at SUNY at Buffalo could graduate with honors if they presented an acceptable thesis. I had many students work with me on this program. We also had Ph.D. students who were advised jointly by several groups. For example, Kenneth Bilat wrote a thesis on breast cancer and was advised by our groups (both Medicine and Pathophysiology) and by the Department of Biology. He graduated in 1975 and became an official of the National Cancer Institute, National Institutes of Health.

I was teaching a course in Pathophysiology for medical and graduate students, which ran for two Winter semesters and two Summer semesters, all year round. I also taught a two-semester course in tropical medicine. Later, when selective courses were introduced for third-year medical students, I also taught a short course in tropical medicine and another in hematology. As a member of the Internal Medicine faculty, I was assigned periodically to be in charge of hospital wards for teaching medical students and residents. At one point, I was in charge of Internal Medical consultations for pregnant and recently delivered women at the Children's Hospital. I was in charge of a weekly seminar for graduate students at the Roswell Park Cancer Institute. For several years, I was also Chairman of weekly staff seminars at Roswell Park and later at the Buffalo General Hospital.

For over 20 years, I was Chairman of the Department of Experimental Pathology of the State University of New York at Buffalo, Roswell Park Division. My colleagues who participated in teaching these courses included Clara M. Ambrus, M.D., Ph.D., Abdul Islam, M.D., Ph.D., Selena Akhter, M.D., M.A., Richard Lee, M.D., Madeline Lillie, M.D., Ph.D., David Lillie, M.D., M.A., Julian L. Ambrus, Jr., M.D., and many others. Assistants in the laboratory exercises included Dr. George Fejer, Irvine Mink, BA, and Richard Schilds, BA.

Hypnosis

The Director of Roswell Park Cancer Institute decided at one point to enroll the senior staff in a course on hypnosis, in order to reduce the amount of analgesics, hypnotics, and anti-obesity agents we were prescribing. It was an intensive one-semester course which I religiously attended and became quite good at it. I practiced for a while on our patients, but largely abandoned it later since it was extremely time consuming. I also engaged in some related research. With the aid of my colleague, Werner Noel, a German scientist (he was brought over to this country after the war with the rocket engineering group under Dr. Braun, but was later allowed to take positions anywhere in the country). He was an excellent biophysicist. He constructed a galvanic skin response recorder which indicated the slightest electronic changes in the skin, including depolarization of the sweat gland membrane under sympathetic nerve influence. The slightest degree of anxiety could be recorded. For example, a strong unexpected clap of the hands produced a slight reaction and was recorded. We combined the instrument with electrodes which produced small, slightly painful electric stimuli to the skin. When we told the patient that a painful stimulus was coming, the patient immediately recorded a slight fear reaction. This appeared to be a suitable procedure to evaluate ataractic agents as well as analgesics. Using this method we demonstrated that ataractics, such as chlorpromazine, potentiated the effect of analgesics such as morphine. We developed very low dose morphine and chlorpromazine combinations for the treatment of our cancer patients. Using this instrument we also demonstrated that hypnosis in susceptible subjects produced similar effects to ataractic drugs. It also potentiated the effect of low doses of analgesics. We presented our instrument and its effect at a medical meeting with great success.

Childhood Infections in the Tropics

When touring the bush with our traveling clinic, we were often asked to see children who were close to death and could not be brought to the clinic. We entered the huts with thatched roofs, where there appeared to be smoke coming from the roof. We initially had a hard time seeing because our eyes were tearing from the smoke-filled hut. There was a fire in the middle of the hut and the whole hut was filled with smoke. This continuous smoke appeared to keep mosquitoes and diseases borne by them away from newborn children, who spent virtually all their time in the hut. However, my colleagues often pointed out that continuous smoke inhalation may be responsible for respiratory diseases and even neoplasms in the adults. We found that newborn infants went through several stages of dangers from infectious disorders. There was a great deal of homozygous sickle cell disease, which resulted in vascular occlusion in various areas, often resulting in autosplenectomy with increased susceptibility to infections at a very early age, resulting in high mortality. This was probably the reason that we seldom saw adults in sickle cell crisis; the homozygous patients died in early childhood. When the children became older they no longer received mother's milk. They still spent all their life in the hut, away from sunshine, and Vitamin D deficiency became common. Newer data from our laboratories and elsewhere seems to indicate that Vitamin D plays an important role in immunologic competence, and this may be a problem with the high incidence of infectious diseases in these children. Once they became older and started to crawl around, they often ventured out of the hut to crawl around outside. This resulted in more exposure to sunshine and relieved the Vitamin D deficiency. On the other hand, it resulted in exposure to mosquito bites, and this was the time when they acquired malaria. There was a relative shortage of meats, and "jungle meat" became widely used. Monkeys were cut up and cooked in the hut. Hungry children often stole half-cooked bits of meat and licked blood, which was spattered all over the place. This was probably the time when they picked up simian immune deficiency viruses (SIV), EB virus, and possibly Yaba virus. Simultaneous exposure to these viruses and malaria was probably responsible for Burkitt's lymphoma in para-equatorial Africa.

Malaria was ubiquitous. Tribal leaders who taught young warriors instructed them that if they want to kill their enemy with a lance, they shouldn't try to thrust into the heart because it is small and easily missed, but rather the spleen which is huge since almost all of these people are infected with malaria and have an enlarged spleen, and its injury results in rapid bleeding to death. It is an organ that is hard to miss.

Eventually, most natives developed partial immunity to several strains of malaria. Whenever young girls became pregnant, and as part of pregnancy their immunologic resistance somewhat decreased (probably as a protection of the fetus against rejection), malaria symptoms again became manifest and often resulted in abortion. In fact, recurrent malaria appeared to be the single most common cause of abortion in para-equatorial Africa.

Several decades after our first sojourns in Africa, treatment of malaria and sickle cell disease became more prevalent, at least in the cities with medical centers. Accordingly, less children died of autosplenectomy in early infancy, and more young children and adults survived and came to the emergency rooms of the university hospitals in sickle cell crisis which, as mentioned earlier, was barely seen earlier.

Several charitable organizations constructed and distributed new heaters which resulted in less smoke in huts. This probably will reduce respiratory disorders, but the question is, will it eliminate the protection against malaria? Spraying the walls and the thatched roofs with insect killers and the use of insect killer impregnated netting on the entrances may solve this problem. There is an argument about which insect killer sprays would be allowable, and there is the problem of making available adequate personnel for patient education.

Programs which send young volunteers to Africa provide fair numbers of individuals to teach English, but only a few well-qualified individuals who could engage in health care education – or even more importantly, in health care procedures, agriculture, or some useful trades.

More Ugandan Stories

Our traveling clinic pulled into a small village, and the locals told us that there is a Peace Corps volunteer in the village from the United States whom we may want to meet. We found her in a small thatched roof hut, very much depressed and almost crying. She said, "Look what they have done to me during the night," and she took us to the other side of the white-painted walls of her cottage and there written in chicken blood was: "White girl go home." She said, "Look at me, I am Black, look at my hands. I came to Africa to see my heritage and to help the local people. I was assigned to this village to teach English." I discussed with her that even though she may be Black, she is much lighter than the inhabitants of the village, she is dressed more in American style, she speaks only English, and her attitudes and her behavior is clearly American rather than African. To the Africans, she is White, which to them simply means foreign. She was assigned to come to this village to teach English, in which apparently the local population is not much interested. The locals need many things, including better agricultural methods, educators, and providers of health care, medicine, improved methods of communication, and many other things. Our volunteers sent over here by the Peace Corps are largely individuals with no specific skills useful to the community. Their American lifestyle and their small possessions and facilities generate envy, and their only skill, to teach English, doesn't yet seem to be valuable in the bush. We may have to consider whether in the future we want to send volunteers with useful skill and facility, some knowledge of the local languages, habits and culture, and definite leadership qualities. Unfortunately, it may be more difficult to find this type of volunteer.

Assistantships Post Graduation

After we completed our medical education and our doctorates at the University of Zurich, we received several requests for assistantship positions. Clara was of interest to Dr. Bleuler in Psychiatry (his father is of early schizophrenia studies fame), Dr. Fanconi, Chairman of Pediatrics (of the Fanconi syndromes fame), and Dr. Amsler in Ophthalmology. I was approached by Dr. Loefler (of the Loefler's syndrome fame) and Dr. Frommell, Chairman of Pharmacology in Geneva. The latter offered the position of chef de travoux, second in command after the professor, an unusually high position for a new graduate. However, he said that while this is a well-paid position, he expected Clara to also work in the department as a volunteer without salary. At the same time, we had an invitation from Madame Trefuel, the wife of the Director of the Pasteur Institute, to work with Dr. Jacob and Dr. Luc Montagnier in Virology. We were also to work in the hospital of the Institute Pasteur (which at that time was concentrating on Tropical Medicine), as well as associated programs at the Hotel Dieue; we chose the latter opportunity. After close to a year in France, we received a fellowship to the Jefferson Medical College in Philadelphia, PA, to work with Dr. Leonardo Tocantius in Hematology-Oncology and Dr. Charles Gruber in Pharmacology. Since at the time fellows received no salary, we were given a paid teaching position at the associated Philadelphia College of Pharmacy and Science to teach pharmacology. Thus we were simultaneously fellows, the lowest rank in the medical facility, and professors in the graduate school of the College of Pharmacy.

Equestrian Stories

We participated in an annual three-day event, organized by the Genesee Valley Hunt Club. Julian Jr. won first prize on our 17-hand Chestnut thoroughbred, Impending Storm, whom we used to call Stormy. Peter was second on Red Fox. Julian Jr. was also third on Angel

Dark, a black thoroughbred mare who was a great-granddaughter of Man of War (presumably the best race horse this country ever had). Julian, however, said that he couldn't accept this prize. When he came to a river to be jumped, his horse stopped and he had to make a circle and re-take it. The jump judge, however, was a lady who was chatting with a spectator and never noticed it. She should have reported it and disqualified him. Therefore, the next in line should get the prize. This honesty became legendary in the Genesee Valley. Pony Club children were told about it and we heard it discussed for a long time. Stormy became a champion jumper in many jumping and three-day events, including the Cleveland Championships. One of the judges wanted to borrow him for the Olympic team but we declined since Julian Jr. continued to ride him in many events.

Warburg

When we worked at the Pharmacology Research Laboratory of the University of Budapest, we learned to use the Warburg apparatus, which at that time was considered to be a most up-to-date research instrument suitable for a number of biochemical studies. We continued to use this technique and this apparatus when we became student assistants in the Department of Pharmacology of the University of Zurich in Switzerland. Before they entrusted us to use this apparatus, they asked Professor Almasy, a fellow Hungarian from the Veterinary School, and an expert on this technique, to spend the day with us on a Sunday and watch us use the apparatus. He reported to our Chief, Professor Fisher, that we were indeed competent and he could entrust the apparatus to us. We received a large laboratory, fully equipped, including the Warburg apparatus, and we were given part-time services of the Professor's own technician/secretary, Madame Regli. Many years later, we spent Summers as guests of Professor Szent-Györgyi, at the Woods Hole Biologic Laboratory, and among others we wanted to use a Warburg apparatus. There was only one in the institute, which they let us have. It had a big sign on it: "This is Professor Warburg's Warburg. Please handle with care." Dr. Warburg, the Nobel prize winning biochemist, spent several summers in Woods Hole, and used the apparatus he invented. We were careful indeed using it, and published several papers based on techniques using this apparatus.

Education and Creativity

One of the problems that appears in our education system is that it over-emphasizes "factual minutia," as opposed to emphasis on critical thinking and professional skills. This is reflected on the examinations, including the national examinations such as the medical college admission test (MCAT) and the graduate record examination (GRE). Teachers in high school, and sometimes even in college, teach primarily for the exam and do not lay the foundation for continuous self-education. They stress more rote memorization and acquisition of factual knowledge and recall. There is less emphasis on knowledge-comprehension, application, analysis, and evaluation. It appears that the MCAT examination is a good predictor of success in medical school, where again there is a great deal of emphasis on factual knowledge, memorization, and recall. On the other hand, even though exact studies are not available, it is my observation that they are less good predictors of eventual quality of medical practice and research accomplishments. Overall, all of our educational systems and our examinations are based heavily on content knowledge, and courses focus more on facts than on skills, analysis of quantitative evidence, and creativity. This is somewhat in contrast to the education system I have experienced in the top high schools in Europe (Hungary and Switzerland) where individuality, creativity, and even the tendency to argue with the professors was honored, and "memorization and regurgitation" was emphasized to a lesser degree. In addition to regular class work, there were after-hours meetings of literary clubs chaired by senior professors, where students presented their own poems, short stories, and essays, as well as reading and discussing modern contemporary literature which wasn't yet in the official study plan. Musicians presented their own compositions. Painters and sculptors presented their work. In history class, for example, high grades were given to those who showed good understanding of cultural, sociological, and even anthropological diversity, and they were forgiven if they don't memorize all the dates of major battles as well as the dates of coronation and birthdates of all the kings and top leaders in history.

I believe we have some of the top educational systems in our country, but we do have to emphasize and encourage creativity more. Some of our children find that their time is completely booked with organized activities, after-school sports, music lessons, and others, and they have relatively little time to dispose of at their own interests, to engage in individual, creative activities. There are, for example, far fewer children who write diaries, poems, and short stories than there were in the old days before all this regimentation was introduced. Parents think that by providing all the regimented activities, they do the best for the development of their children. They also expect discipline, respect for their elders, and hard work. They do little to emphasize creativity. One of the problems we have in many schools is that most examinations are multiple choice. This makes it easy for the teacher to just let the computer correct the examination. However, the students learn to put check marks in the right boxes, and not to write intelligent sentences. There are virtually no more oral examinations, and students don't learn the importance of expressing themselves correctly, even in a stimulating way. Writing and taking exam questions that test memorization is much faster and easier for both students and teachers than writing and taking exam questions that test higher-order thinking. Advanced placement (AP), GRE and MCAT exams are nationally standardized, and therefore it may be more difficult to introduce emphasis on creative thinking. The same goes for the dental admission test, nursing entrance examination, pharmacy college admission test, and many others.

Ecumenism

When I was in the Netherlands for a second visiting professorship, they again invited me for an ecumenical evening meeting. They might have liked my earlier presentation and asked me to speak again. This time I had advance notice and had some time to look up a few things in the library in my spare time. I said that one of our basic tenements, the "golden rule," was set down by Matthew (7:1-2) and Luke (6:27-36): "And as you would that men should do to you, do you also to them likewise". Interestingly enough, the same theme is found in many other religious opuses – it occurs several times in the Old Testament: Kings 6:8-23, Psalm 109:5, Proverbs 21:13, 24-29, Obadiah 15, Leviticus 19:18, and the following:

- Hinduism (c. 13th century B.C.): "Do not do to others what ye do not wish done to yourself....this is the whole Dharma. Heed it well." The Mahabharata.
- Judaism (c. 13th century B.C.): "What is hateful to you, do not do to your neighbor; that is the entire Torah; the rest is commentary; go learn it." The Babylonian Talmud.
- Zoroastrianism (c. 12th century B.C.): "Human nature is good only when it does not do unto another whatever is not good for its own self." The Dadistan-i-Dinik.
- Buddhism (c. 6th century B.C.): "Hurt not others in ways that you yourself would find hurtful." The Tibetan Dhammapada.
- Confucianism (c. 6th century B.C.): "Do not do to others what you do not want done to yourself." Confucius, Analects.

But, G.B. Shaw rewrote the golden rule: "Do not do unto others as you would have others do unto you – they may have different taste."

In a new book on Neuroscience, Donald W. Pfeff discussed the "golden rule," and suggested that this is universally embedded in the human brain and that we have an instinct for "fair play" by learning our own identity with the identity of another person. For example, if we attack another person we instinctively envision the fear that the other person would experience. Scanning studies show the anterior cinanate cortex in the insular area (a site of emotional quality and activity) lights up in these areas in response to perceiving someone else's pain.

Dengue Hemorrhagic Fever

A distinguished member of our medical community and a Professor in our Medical School traveled to India. On his way back, he fainted on the airplane and started massive bleeding from the nose and the oral cavity. The pilot radioed and asked what to do. Since I was in charge of the Tropical Medicine course, this was referred to me. We asked the pilot just to proceed to Buffalo and sent an ambulance to pick him up and bring him to the General Hospital. Meanwhile, I called the Centers for Disease Control in Atlanta and asked about recent epidemiologic information of the areas which he had visited. It appeared that there was a major epidemic of Dengue fever going on at that time. Originally, Dengue was a relatively mild flu-like disease, but it became deadly over time, probably due to a series of mutations. On arrival, the patient's blood pressure was low. He bled from all orifices, including showing blood in his urine. He had a modest maculo-papular rash and he appeared to be in the Dengue shock syndrome. Laboratory studies indicated that he may also have disseminated intravascular coagulation syndrome. Physical exam revealed that he had some pleural and pericardial effusion probably due to the capillary leak syndrome. I prescribed intravascular fluids, electrolytes, and treatment for disseminated intravascular coagulation. The residents were somewhat afraid of the latter, but I assured them that everything would be all right. He also received blood transfusion and rapidly improved. Diagnostic workup confirmed that he suffered from Dengue hemorrhagic fever. One of the considerations for differential diagnosis was a Zika virus infection. This relatively newly described disease I had first encountered in Uganda, and it appeared to have spread rapidly throughout the world. Outbreaks were reported in Nigeria, Indonesia, and Malaysia, and it was on its way to spread throughout the world; but no cases had yet been reported in India. The patient rapidly improved; and from then, on whenever we met in the hospital or at faculty meetings, he always expressed his gratitude for saving his life. Dengue appears to be more serious in patients who had previous episodes of this disease, including any of its subtypes, but our patient was unaware of any previous episodes. Of course, sometimes the disease presents itself as only a small, flu-like situation and remains undiagnosed. I understand that currently research is in progress at NIH on developing Dengue vaccine. The question arises whether antibodies produced by an effective vaccine do not actually increase the severity of the disease. Complex research is required to find out what type of immunity is safe and protective, and what type of vaccine should be developed. This is becoming an increasing problem with vaccine development in many other diseases.

Medical Diplomacy

In the post World War II period, I was invited to give a keynote address in one of the first international medical meetings in Germany. I was the only American invited and initially my colleagues looked at me somewhat hesitantly. They didn't know that I understand German and I heard them behind my back saying such things as: "We need newly developed specialized knowledge from America, but we don't really need an American; they are basically boorish and uncivilized." At one point my wife and I were standing at a bus stop waiting for a bus chartered by the meeting to take us from one meeting place to another. A couple of chartered busses passed, but they were full and we couldn't get on. We stood among a group of distinguished colleagues, and as one of the busses passed, I said in German, "When does the next swan come?" This sentence has a complex background. One of the finest German operatic tenors was Otto Schlezak; he wrote a very humorous book about his career, which was widely read in German intellectual circles. He described in his book that when he was singing Lohengrin, at the end of the opera a swan is supposed to come and pick him up and take him back to his castle. Something went wrong with the machinery; the swan boat was pulled on stage and rapidly pulled off again. This happened two times. Meanwhile, Schlezak was supposed to sing the good-bye aria. When the swan was rapidly pulled off the stage again, he said, "When does the next swan come?" A small sentence immediately put me in as a brother to German intellectuals who read selected German books. My colleagues immediately warmed up, cheered me on, and from then on we had excellent relationships. We were invited to dinner to the Rector magnificus (equivalent to our University President), who happened to be a hematologist, and developed several close contacts in collaborative projects with other colleagues. Sometimes a well-placed sentence may break the ice and helps in long-term diplomacy.

More War Stories – The Bartok Family

When the Germans invaded Hungary, they started to build fortifications against an upcoming Russian invasion. They drafted Jews into labor camps and worked them to death, starving them and at times treating them cruelly. At the time, they also included into these labor camps Christians whose religion they felt was similar to Judaism. This included Jehovah's Witnesses, the Nazarenes, and the Saturnalists. The Unitarians were much afraid that they would also be included, but eventually they were left alone. We heard from one family among our friends who were Unitarians, and this was the family of Bela Bartok, the well-known music composer. He managed to escape, however, and come to the United States. Eventually, he also brought along his wife, Gitta Pasztori, a famous piano artist, and much later his son Peter, who was a classmate of mine. The Bartok's had a hard time making ends meet and eventually Bela Bartok died of leukemia. Peter became a sound engineer and eventually published most of his father's work on disks. At one point, he asked me to see his fiancé and cure her from impending schizophrenia. I told him that, unfortunately, there is no established cure for this disease and I am no psychiatrist, and there is no reason for me to see her. However, I was happy to recommend a first-class psychiatrist if he so wished. He probably never forgave me for not curing his fiancé.

Medical Education

One of the medical groups asked me to talk about the need of teaching tropical medicine in medical school and some aspects of education in our country in general. I thought that it all starts in early education. Together with Dr. Dembinski, we reviewed the International Student Assessment (PISA) reports of the Organization for Economic Cooperation and Development (OECD) reports, the Digest of Education statistics, the United Nations Population Division (UNPD), and the World Health Organization statistics for 2006. Preliminary statistics indicated that in a random test of 400,000 15-year-old students, U.S. students scored lower in science literacy than their peers in 16 of 29 OCED jurisdictions, and 6 of 27 none OCED jurisdictions. Results of the reading and mathematics test are listed in order of rank in the following tables. The U.S. was not listed under the reading test because of a printing error in the test booklets. In mathematics, we are way down, toward the end of the list, just below Azerbaijan and Russia. Good preparation in high school and college is important for medical school.

Program for International Student Assessment (PISA)
International Rankings (in order)
15-year-old pupils – 2006

Reading	Mathematics
South Korea	Taiwan
Finland	Finland
Hong Kong-China	Hong Kong-China
Canada	South Korea
New Zealand	Netherlands
Ireland	Switzerland
Australia	Canada
Liechtenstein	Macao-China
Poland	Liechtenstein
Sweden	Japan
Netherlands	New Zealand
Belgium	Belgium
Estonia	Australia
Switzerland	Estonia
Japan	Denmark
Taiwan	Czech Republic
United Kingdom	Iceland
Germany	Austria
Denmark	Slovenia
Slovenia	Germany
Macao-China	Sweden

Austria	Ireland
France	France
Iceland	United Kingdom
Norway	Poland
Czech Republic	Slovak Republic
Hungary	Hungary
Latvia	Luxenbourg
Luxemborg	Norway
Croatia	Lithuania
Portugal	Latvia
Lithuania	Spain
Italy	Azerbaijan
Slovak Republic	Russian Federation
Spain	United States
Greece	Croatia
Turkey	Portugal
Chile	Italy
Russian Federation	Greece
Israel	Israel
Thailand	Serbia
Uruguay	Uruguay
Mexico	Turkey
Bulgaria	Thailand
Serbia	Romania
Jordan	Bulgaria
Romania	Chile
Indonesia	Mexico
Brazil	Montenegro
Montenegro	Indonesia
Columbia	Jordan
Tunisia	Argentina
Argentina	Columbia

Azerbaijan	Brazil
Qatar	Tunisia
Kyrgyzstan	Qatar
	Kyrgyzstan

Note: In the U.S., a printing error in the test booklets for reading meant some items had incorrect instructions, so the mean performance could not be accurately estimated and therefore no results were reported.

One of the problems in the U.S.A. is the heterogeneity of the population, e.g., 15% of 15-year-olds are recent immigrants, mostly from Mexico. Some of these, and even second generation immigrant students, lag considerably behind. While the U.S. performs below average overall, it has an average level of top performers.

The second problem in pre-medical studies comes in at the college level. All of those who wish to enter medical school have to take a course in biology, general and inorganic chemistry, organic chemistry, and physics. It is also recommended, but not required, that they take a course in advanced mathematics and psychology. Besides taking all of these courses, which are usually hard and time-consuming, they tend to take easy courses in which it is not difficult to get good grades, rather than taking courses in which they are really interested, because they have to have a good record for a chance to be admitted to medical school. In most European universities, biology, chemistry and physics are actually courses in the first year of medical school. There is no college; students enter medical school after completing high school. In most countries, it is easier to be admitted to medical school than in our country; but it is also easier to flunk out if they don't perform well at any level. In most European medical schools there are systemic lectures in all of the clinical subjects as well, rather than mostly clinical practice-type education as in our country. I am much concerned about increasing emphasis on computer-type training and the decreasing emphasis on lectures and direct contact with the most senior professors. Many of the department chairmen and senior professors are busy with administration, fund raising, grant writing and research, on which their careers depend, rather than direct student contact and lectures. The latter is mostly delegated to the more junior staff and even to the residents and fellows who are still in training. In most European medical schools, almost all of the senior professors, including those who teach the basic medical sciences, are primarily medically trained. In our country, the majority of the basic science professors are PhDs.

One of the subjects missing from our medical school curriculum is tropical medicine, including preparation for possible bioterrorism. A description of my presentation on this topic follows.

With "globe shrinking," increasing travel and increasing opportunity to volunteer for shorter or longer assignments in developing countries, the study of tropical medicine is becoming more important. Some problems related to tropical medicine are discussed in microbiology and pathophysiology, but rarely in internal medicine, pediatrics, and family practice. There is, however, no concentrated course on this topic in most medical schools. We feel that study of emerging, new, infectious disease mutants and their possible use in bioterrorism also belongs in this area. After completing a visiting professorship in Uganda, I found myself frequently called for telephone consultations from my old colleagues. In our medical school, we have offered a course in tropical medicine for two semesters, which was also open to graduate students. Eventually, however, time restraints on courses resulted in changing this to an intensive one-week program under the category "Selected Courses System." This course started at 8:00 a.m. and was run until 5:00 p.m. for six days, and included clinical rounds and laboratory exercises. The course was open to third-year medical students. In laboratory exercises, the students were taught simple laboratory methods, which they could perform themselves and were aimed at stays in underdeveloped countries with minimal laboratory facilities. We also made contact with the student health office for referral of many students arriving from tropical countries who had to be evaluated for the possible presence of tropical diseases. We were also in contact with the travel clinic in town, which was advising travelers on preventive measures before embarking on travel in tropical countries and, of course, evaluated them when they returned. We received some referrals from these sources as well. Our clinical units had seen many patients for various reasons where tropical diseases also had to be considered. We had seen recent immigrants who arrived with tropical disease problems. We managed to present adequate patient material in our rounds and clinics for students in this course. We also involved faculty members, residents, and fellows who came from tropical countries and had ample experience which they could present to the students. The schedule of lectures in the 1996 selective course is enclosed. We believe that although tropical diseases are often discussed in the microbiology course, a clinically-oriented course in tropical medicine may be desirable in medical schools. We are currently considering developing an on-line course which could be made available to all medical schools and which would be helpful, particularly in those which have difficulty in finding adequate time and faculty.

A Selective Course: Introduction to Tropical Medicine

And Geographic Pathology

For 3rd Year Medical Students, State University of New York at Buffalo, School of Medicine, and the Buffalo General Hospital

Instructors:
Julian L. Ambrus, Sr., MD, PhD, FACP (Internal Medicine)
Philip T. Loverde, PhD (Microbiology)1:00
Clara M. Ambrus, MD, PhD, FACP (Pediatrics, OB/GYN)
Madeline A. Lillie, MD, PhD (Pediatrics)
Robert Berke, MD (Internal Medicine)
Steven Stadler, PhD (Internal Medicine)
Abul Islam, MD, PhD, FACP (Internal Medicine)
Selina Akhter, MD, MA (Internal Medicine)
Mohamed Kulylat, MD (Surgery)
Richard Lee, MD (Internal Medicine)
David Lillie, MD (Urology)
Julian L. Ambrus, Jr., MD (Internal Medicine)

Sample Schedule:
Day 1:
9:00 AM to 12:00 PM: Introduction, Geographic Pathology, Neoplastic Disease in the Tropics, Burkitt's Lymphoma, Nutritional Problems in the Tropics, Sickle Cell Disease, Genetics and Epdemiological Aspects.

1:00 PM to 5:00 PM: Inpatient Rounds, Outpatient Visits

Day 2:
9:00 AM to 12:00 PM: AIDS, Multi-drug Resistant Tuberculosis, Respiratory disorders, Trypanosomal Diseases, Chagas' Disease, Leishmanial Diseases

Travel Medicine, Vaccination and other Preventive Programs, Public Health Aspects

Tissue-inhabiting parasites, Dracunculosis

1:00 PM to 5:00 PM: Clinical Demonstrations, review of specimens

Day 3:
9:00 AM to 1:00 PM: Hemorrhagic Fevers: Dengue, Congo-Crimean, Chikungunya, Ebola-Marburg. Hanta viruses (HFRS): Korean Hemorrhagic Fever, Navajo Disease

Lassa Fever, Malaria, Schistosomiasis, Plague, Yellow Fever

Diarrheal Diseases of Travelers, Gastrointestinal Diseases in the Tropics, Intestinal Parasites

New Therapeutic and Preventive Measures and Ongoing Research in Tropical Medicine

2:30 PM to 6:00 PM: SUNY at Buffalo Medical School Campus, Microbiology Laboratory: Laboratory diagnosis of blood, urine, and stool specimens

Day 4:
9:00 AM to 12:00 PM: Tropical Skin Disorders, Leprosy, Neuromuscular Disorders: Lyme Disease, Poliomyelitis in the Tropics

CNS Disorders: Rabies, Tetanus, Cryptococcosis. Ophthalmic Disorders of the Tropics: Trachoma, Toxocariasis

1:00 PM to 5:00 PM: Clinical visits. Recapitulation.

Day 5:
9:00 AM to 3:00 PM: Written and Practical Examinations

Day 6:
9:00 AM to 3:00 PM: Recapitulation. Discussion of Examinations

Oral re-examinations

Required Texts:

- S.B. Halstead and K.S. Warren: Diseases of Travelers and Immigrants. 1987, Scope Publishers.

Other Recommended Texts:

- B.G. Maegraith and H.M. Gilles: Management and Treatment of Tropical Diseases. 1987.
- G.W. Hunter: Tropical Medicine. 1980, W.B. Saunders Co.
- R. Desolvitz: New Guinea Tapeworms and Jewish Grandmothers. Tale of Parasites and People. 1987, Norton and Company, paperback.

O. P. Jones

O.P. Jones, Ph.D., was Chairman of Anatomy and the Dean of our medical school. At one point, he decided that if he is to run a medical school, he should have a medical degree as well. He registered as a student in his own medical school, appointing substitutes for his major administrative duties. One of the courses for first-year medical students at the time was "Introduction to Medicine." First-year medical students were assigned in small groups to a clinician, made rounds with them, and observed what medicine is all about while studying the basic medical sciences in class and laboratory. This also made them feel that they are medical students rather than being involved in a continuation of college work. We also tried to emphasize the connection between the patients' problems and basic science aspects, showing them that, for example, what they are studying in biochemistry is really important knowledge at the bedside. I was asked to run one of these small groups of students and it so happened that O.P. Jones was part of my student group. So he was on one hand my Dean and Chief, but on the other hand my student. He came with his laboratory coat to the Roswell Park Hospital for the afternoon schedule, made rounds with me, and took occasional oral and written examinations. I made a point to not only show these students my own patients, but also took them to attend surgery and to visit the State Psychiatric Hospital to see psychiatric problems, of course always making arrangements with the local specialists to participate in this program. The students were also taken to my research laboratory and were shown how clinical observations grew into laboratory research programs and then back again into clinical trials. O.P. Jones participated in all of these programs and at one time, as a parting shot, he mentioned, "I will see you again next week; and by the way, your promotion is just on my desk – I will sign it."

Publications

Paul Erdos, a Hungarian-trained mathematician, and an acquaintance, died not long ago, and at his funeral one of the speakers mentioned that he published 1,500 papers in mathematics, physics, biology, and linguistics. Indeed in our country in academics, number of publications are a badge of honor and an important step in promotions. It was jokingly said of Dr. Gallo, at the time Director of the National Cancer Institute - NIH, that he not only was the author or co-author of more than one thousand publications, but in fact he even read some of them. The only more important factor in academic promotions than number of publications was the amount of grant money, particularly with high overhead costs. Grants with low overhead costs added were considered less favorably by promotion committees since they did not contribute as well to the coffers at the University. I often heard from my colleagues, "Why do I spend so much time on teaching, when my promotions really depend on research grants?"

Old School Days

Sometimes I think about long-ago school days.......in the first and second grades of elementary school, I was taught at home. My main teacher was Miss Flora. Although I already spoke four languages, my parents wanted me to maintain my language skills; and for this reason, twice a week, I had language lessons with separate teachers with an English tutor, a German Fraulein, and a French lady who was a pied noir, the daughter of French farmers in Algeria. I also had a separate mathematics teacher, since my parents thought this was most important, and I wound up doing mathematics at the high school level. In the third grade I was enrolled in the elementary school called Sajo (which is the same name as my Comondor shepherd dog on the farm). I did all right, except I refused in geography to learn the names of all the stations through which the main railroad lines run to various parts of the country. I thought that this was unnecessary rote memorization. My teachers took revenge on me. At the end of the school year, there was a theatrical performance at which folk songs, folk dances, and folk festivals of various parts of the country with various ethnic groups were shown. I was made the announcer, dressed as a railroad conductor, and I had to call out all the places to which our imaginary railroad was going, with all the stops in between, memorizing all of those long lists of the stations which I had refused to memorize during the school year. I was most interested in joining the varsity hockey team; but I was told that, before that, I had to learn figure skating and dancing on the ice. I had a teacher for this purpose and I really hated it. Eventually, however, I graduated and made the team. In high school one of my favorite subjects was Biology. My Biology teacher was also an Assistant Professor of Biology at the university. He was working on isolating heteroauxin, a plant hormone. He took me along to work in the late afternoons in his laboratory at the university. I developed a technique to measure the activity of his extracts. I planted beans under an umbrella so that the beans had to flex and grow in an L-shape towards the sun. When heteroauxin ointment was smeared on the opposite side it elongated and caused the plant to bend backward. The degree of deviation was proportionate to the amount of heteroauxin in the ointment. Much later, Japanese investigators reported that some of the auxins have proliferation inducing effect on human cells as well. Much later we have obtained many different auxins from collaborators, but none of the ones we found had an important effect on human cells. We are still playing with this approach in tissue culture studies. At the time of the war, this topic was of great interest since we had seen many injuries due to flame throwers, and superficial wound healing was an important problem in our hospital. As a young medical student, I was assigned to one of the university-associated hospitals for a course in clinical pathology. They had a large research laboratory and animal colony, which was largely empty since all of the workers in these sections were called to the military. I was given the run of the place, together with all of the rats I could use. I developed a technique to produce a measured burn wound on the depilated skin of rats by pressing a heated lead saddle on them, and applied some of the auxin ointments to it in the hope of finding one which would accelerate wound healing. I completely failed; none of them had any effect.

It is interesting that a topic I had started working on as a high school student accompanied me into medical school and much later; in fact, some experiments are still continuing.

My other favorite subject in high school was literature. My teacher was a well-known poet, under the pen name of Vathy Elek. At one point he received a national prize for his poetry. There was a celebration at the school and I presented him with a small album of my poems. This teacher was in charge of a small, after-school literary circle where we read each other's poetry and short stories, and presented musical composition. We had a great deal of fun. We also read poetry and short stories of modern authors who were not yet included in our regular teaching program; and in fact, some of them were of somewhat dubious reputation since they were "too modern" or else antagonistic to the government of those times.

Nutritional Supplements

We often hear questions from our patients as well as our medical students about the use of nutritional supplements. There is a standard lecture I presented several times to the medical students; the text is listed below. These may be useful for the lay reader. I understand that today some people spend large amounts of money in health food stores buying preparations of dubious usefulness. Even if they have some active ingredients, these are not adequately checked; and some preparations may contain very small, almost insignificant, amounts of the active ingredients, while others may contain too much. Some of these supplements are quite harmless, although their usefulness is highly questionable.

NOTE TO MEDICAL STUDENTS ON NUTRITIONAL SUPPLEMENT

Julian L. Ambrus, MD, PhD, FACP, and Clara M. Ambrus, MD, PhD, FACP

WE OFTEN HEAR QUESTIONS FROM OUR PATIENTS REGARDING THE USE OF NUTRITIONAL SUPPLEMENTS

Calcium, Vitamin D and Multivitamins. I believe everybody should have a multivitamin preparation with minerals. Most of these preparations have calcium in them, but not enough. I believe everybody should have 1,200mg of calcium QD mostly available in two 600 mg tablets. Pregnant women should have at least three tablets QD. Recent suggestions that excessive calcium may contribute to arteriosclerosis are not well founded. Vitamin D is needed to absorb calcium, and recent data indicate that it plays an important role in immunology and differentiation. Lack of Vitamin D may play a role in autoimmune and neoplastic diseases. Vitamin D is present in multivitamin tablets, mostly 400 IU. However, recent studies indicate that particularly older and pregnant individuals may need at least 800 to 1,000 IU or more. Most calcium tablet preparations also contain 200 IU Vitamin D. Thus, a multivitamin plus two calcium tablets of this type should be close to adequate. Pregnant women should have three to four tablets. Recent data indicate that up to 3,000 IU/day no side effects are to be concerned with. For many individuals I recommend an additional 1,000 IU Vitamin D_3 tablet per day. A recent study found that 70% of normal Americans have low Vitamin D levels. To test: 25 hydroxy-Vitamin D levels should be evaluated as the best measure of adequate status; it should be at least 30-60 ng/ml of blood. Vitamin D preparations have a half-life of 3½ weeks. Fresh preparations should be used.

Vitamin A. High levels of Vitamin A are toxic. I mentioned in the lecture that all Eskimos know that polar bear liver should be discarded.

If fed to sled dogs, it may kill them through Vitamin A poisoning. Adequate doses are present in most multivitamin preparations.

Homocysteine. Vitamin B6, B12, Folic Acid. High homocysteine levels are major factors in the development of atherosclerosis. Recent data suggest that it may also contribute to osteoporosis. Testing for homocysteine levels is quite expensive at the present time, and for the price of one test one can supply the three vitamins which decrease this effect for one year. Homocysteine is metabolized through three different pathways. One depends on folic acid, one on Vitamin B6, and one on Vitamin B12. Accordingly, I recommend that everybody should have an additional 800 μg of folic acid, 50 mg of Vitamin B6, and 1000 μg of Vitamin B12, the latter preferably as a sublingual tablet. Many patients, and the elderly, often produce inadequate quantities of intrinsic factor or inadequately absorb Vitamin B12 for other reasons. These large doses allow absorption by "mass action" even when intrinsic factor levels are inadequate. Sublingual administration also helps.

Vitamin C. There is a controversy whether additional Vitamin C is useful. Five hundred (500) mg QD should be adequate, but not more. Some faddists go up to several grams. This may cause kidney stones.

Vitamin E. Vitamin E is deposited in adipose tissue reservoirs and is a powerful antioxidant. Four hundred IU is usually recommended. This is mostly present in multivitamin preparations.

Acetylsalicylic Acid (aspirin). The optimal platelet aggregation inhibitor/thromboembolic disease preventive agent is 81 mg acetylsalicylic acid (aspirin) daily. I usually recommend chewable baby aspirin which should be chewed and swallowed as a suspension so as to avoid a tablet sitting on the gastric mucosa generating local high concentration-related erosions. Rarely aspirin resistance develops. It may be worthwhile to test platelet aggregation factors. Many resistant patients respond to Plavix 75 mg QD.

Acidophilus. Many patients also take acidophilus tablets containing 100 million bacteria each. This is advisable after a course of oral antibiotics, but I have no objection against its daily use.

Bee Pollen. Many patients take one or two tablets of bee pollen concentrate. I am not sure about its value, but have no objection to its use.

Cranberry. Many patients take 140 mg cranberry tablets daily which presumable are concentrated in the bladder and act as a urinary antibacterial factor. I have no objection against its use.

Isoflavinoids. Many patients take additional so-called antioxidant preparations such as lycopen or lutein. While their scientific value is not adequately proven, I have no objection to the use of these or other isoflavinoid preparations. Black tea is rich in polyphenoles.

Lipid Pattern: Nicotinic Acid and Oat Bran. Lipid pattern tests usually include cholesterol, triglycerides, HDL, and LDL. These studies should be performed annually. However, we should consider looking periodically at lipoprotein (a) which is a risk factor even in patients in whom the other members of the lipid pattern test are in the normal range. Even when lipid patterns are normal, I recommend, particularly for older individuals, a 500 mg nicotinic acid/140 mg inositol QHS, "the no-flush niacin preparation." Study of the effect of this preparation is still under way. Nicotinic acid has significant effect even on lipoprotein (a) (reducing it), and HDL (increasing it). I also recommend two 500 mg oat bran tablets BID which binds cholesterol and improves gastrointestinal motility.

Omega-3 Fatty Acids. Many patients take an EPA tablet containing Omega-3 fatty acids. Again, I am not sure about its value but have no objection to its use. Presumably it acts as a competitive inhibitor to harmful lipids.

Diuretics: Potassium. Those on diuretics should have their potassium level checked regularly, and as a preventive I suggest a potassium 20 mEq tablet QD.

Selenium. Many patients take one 50 µg or 100 µg selenium tablet daily, which is an antioxidant adjunct and has been advertised as a "prostate hypertrophy and cancer preventive agent." There is no scientific proof available to all of these claims. I have no objection to its use.

Slicium, Silikon. Western New York products are reported to be deficient in this agent. Veterinarians use it particularly in Western New York as a feed supplement in sheep and cow herds where abortion is common. Many multi-vitamin mineral preparations contain small amounts of this agent, which is most likely adequate.

Taurine. Taurine is an amino acid widely distributed and present in significant quantities in the myocardium and brain. There are suggestions that a 500 mg tablet has "cardioprotective," anti-arrhythmic, and positive inotropic and chronotropic effects. It was also reported to be an anti-osteoporotic, anti-oxidant, and a modest platelet aggregation inhibitor. Taurine has been reported to help with alcohol abuse. Even though adequate scientific data are missing, I have no objection against this supplement.

Carnitine and α lipoic acid. These are presumably required for proper mitochondrial function. Deficiencies are rare. I have no objection to their use.

CoQ10. This is widely advertised and expensive. There are no established scientific data to suggest that supplementary intake is needed by any group of patients.

NOTE: I usually tell patients that if they take all of these preparations, there is no need for any other more expensive preparations from a health food store or other herbal outlet; an exception would be the existence of a special problem for which a colleague has made recommendations.

Selected references:

1. Ambrus JL, Hoffman M, Ambrus CM, Hreshchyshyn MM, Moore D, Munschauer FE: Prevention and treatment of osteoporosis. One of the most frequent disorders in American women. A Review. J Med 23(6):369-388, 1992.
2. Krauss RM, Deckelbaum RJ, Ernst N, et al: Dietary guidelines for healthy American adults. A statement for health professionals from the Nutrition Committee. American Heart Association. Circulation 94:1795-1800, 1996.
3. Shils ME, Olson JA, Shike M, Ross AC: Modern Nutrition in Health and Disease, 9th Edition. Baltimore, MD, Williams & Wilkins, 1999.
4. Mahan LK, Escott-Stump S: Krause's Food, Nutrition & Diet Therapy. 9th Edition. Philadelphia, PA, WB Saunders, 1996.

5. National Research Council, Institute of Medicine. Recommended Daily Allowances, 10th Edition. Washington, DC, National Academy Press, 1989.
6. Lourenco R, Camilo ME: Taurine: a conditionally essential amino acid in humans? An overview in health and disease. Nutricion Hospitalaria 17(6):262-270, 2002.
7. Oliver MF: Interactions between taurine and ethanol in the central nervous system. Amino Acids 23(4):345-357, 2002.
8. Satoh H: Cardiac actions of a taurine as a modulator of the ion channels. Advances in Exp Med & Biol 442:121-128, 1998.

Fox Hunts

For a long time we went fox hunting in the Genesee Valley every Saturday. I had a number of my children on a series of ponies of various sizes behind me, and we had a great time. Once, we were on a run and jumped the coup and found a friend on the ground with his wife beside him crying. I dismounted and one of my children held the horses. We were told that the friend of ours, who was greatly allergic to bee stings, jumped the coup, stirred up a nest of wasps, was stung, fainted, and fell off the horse, and when his wife dismounted and listened to his heart there was no heart beat – he was dead. I always carried in my saddlebag a number of first aid items, including adrenaline and a syringe with a very long needle. I gave him an intracardiac injection of adrenaline, followed by an injection of Benedryl, gave him mouth to mouth resuscitation, and chest pressure-resuscitation; in a few minutes, he was up and around and feeling well but a bit dazed. We called in Roly, a hunt servant who usually followed the hunt in a jeep, and asked him to take this gentleman immediately to the Warsaw Hospital, the closest medical facility. One of my children, who held the horses, said, "Oh Dad, you always have to play doctor and here we were on a run after a fox." Nevertheless, we remounted and caught up with the hunt just when the fox was killed. Afterward, we went to our usual hunt breakfast at the Big Tree Inn. While we were there, the gentleman who had the accident appeared with his wife and said that the emergency room at the Warsaw Hospital examined him, found nothing wrong, and released him. He came by just to say "thank you."

Ours was one of the oldest fox hunts in the country, founded right after the Revolutionary War. In order to be distinguished from the red coats, our uniforms were dark blue rather than the customary red. However, our dress uniform was red. One day, my oldest daughter Madeline's coming out party was at the Waldorf Astoria in New York City. As usual, I was late leaving and in the hurry I didn't find my tuxedo. So, I grabbed my hunt dress uniform, which was red. When we came to our assigned table a number of people whom we did not know were already sitting there. One gentleman said, "Are you a waiter?"

One of our friends, who was the Director of the Kodak Company in Rochester, for whom I consulted, invited us at one time to take a flight on his small private plane, which he piloted to have a view from the air of our hunt country. He flew over the fences, which he pointed out to my children were ones where once I took a spill. It was said that when you take a fall from your horse you bought that part of the land. There were a few. It was a bit of an embarrassing trip.

Aging and Cancer Research

It appears that when cells divide and DNA is duplicated, part of the terminal nucleic acid becomes lost. These are partly rebuilt by telomerases. Nevertheless, gradual long-term loss of terminal nucleic acid components may be a reason for gradual loss of cell function in age-related death. It appears, however, that cancer cells have very high levels of telomerases, and thus they are immortal, grow rapidly, and suffocate surrounding tissues. For these reasons, we thought that telomerase inhibitors may be useful therapeutic agents against various types of cancer. Our chemical collaborators, Dr. Bardos and Dr. Aradi, synthesized a number of potential telomerase inhibitors, which we tested and selected a few for studies against cancer cells in vitro and in animal experiments. However, it appeared that some of these compounds are active not only against telomerases of cancer cells, but also telomerases of normal cells. Thus, the question arose whether they may not bring about premature aging. We continue to work on a search for selective anti-cancer telomerase inhibitors, if such can be found.

Behcet's disease

A patient came from South America with complex complaints. He had seen many doctors in several countries and no one made the right diagnosis. We found out that his major problem was Behcet's disease. This was somewhat strange since this disease occurs primarily in the Near East, including Turkey and the Arab countries, but is seldom seen elsewhere. This patient had no Near Eastern relationships and lived only in South America and Europe. He also suffered from ankylosing spondylitis, homocysteinemia, repeated episodes of thrombophlebitis, antiphospholipid antibody syndrome, and had a past history of rheumatoid arthritis with residual cardiac injuries. His HLA B27 antigen test was positive, supporting the diagnosis of ankylosing spondylitis. Detailed workup also showed that one of the problems, and the reason for his complications, was increased red cell membrane stiffness, causing periodic obstruction of small blood vessels. We became much interested in this, and during a visiting professorship in the Near East we managed to see 15 patients with Behcet's disease. They all had this newly discovered symptom of red cell membrane rigidity. We developed agents which decreased red cell rigidity and also inhibited platelet aggregation. Treatment with these agents, as well as Vitamin B12, B6, and folic acid to reduce homocysteinemia resulted in significant improvement. It seems that once in awhile we see very rare diseases in our country, and even a single case can lead to interesting new findings.

Hematology Teaching

For many years, I did run a course in Hematology-Oncology for medical students. I usually started out by saying, "As you know Hematology is the science of blood and the organs it perfuses, so that all of medicine is really a subsection of Hematology. Oncology is a science of neoplastic growth, and the diseases it causes. It involves abnormal regulation of growth, development, evolution, so that most of biology is really a part of Oncology." The course was first held at the Roswell Park Cancer Institute, and later at the Buffalo General Hospital. It included lectures, patient demonstrations, and inpatient and outpatient rounds. I emphasized and showed some examples how occasionally clinical observations can lead to ideas which are then followed up in laboratory studies, animal studies, and lead to clinical research. I suggested that all physicians should consider themselves as part of the medical research community, should contribute ideas, and should be willing to participate in clinical research programs. I discussed, among other things, the requirement of telling patients the truth but yet maintaining a glimmer of hope in keeping up the patients' spirits. One of my approaches was that if it was necessary to tell the patient that he has a terminal disease with a limited life expectancy, even by the best available treatments at that time, there were also new approaches. We, of course, would try to make sure that the patient would not suffer and not become depressed. However, I pointed out ongoing research in our group and elsewhere represented hope that significant results will become available during the patient's lifetime and will radically change the prognosis. This helped in maintaining hope, while at the same time often resulted in patients volunteering to participate in ongoing research here or in other institutions with which we collaborated. I also emphasized that it is our duty to spend all the time needed to discuss these factors with the patient and the family, to give them all data so that they can make proper plans. This is no place for a short-term visit, to which some of the institutions and insurance groups are trying to hold us. There is also no restriction desirable to call in consultants and subspecialist colleagues, or to refer patients out, if this is indicated. I included in the course laboratory exercises while trying to instruct students in at least the elements of reading bone marrows, evaluating blood coagulation factors, and using certain laboratory equipment, such as platelet aggregatometers. I also pointed out simple methods which the residents and medical students could actually do themselves at the bedside, not requiring laboratory studies with appropriate time delays. For example, I showed them our method to measure circulating platelet aggregates by a simple slide test at the bedside. I showed them methods of serial testing members of the blood coagulation and fibrinolysin systems in patients undergoing thrombolytic therapy. I was among the few who first emphasized that Coumadin therapy always had to be started under heparin anticoagulation and passed out a brochure outlining the mechanisms involved. I emphasized how important it is to collaborate with orthopedic surgeons to make sure that certain orthopedic procedures do not result in thromboembolic complications.

Fibrinolysin and Bureaucracy

For a long time we worked on the fibrinolysin system—the enzymes which dissolve blood clots—and developed methods of the preparation of various enzymes which we compared in vitro and in animal studies. We developed a technique to place radioactive-labeled blood clots into various blood vessels of monkeys and continuously register as they dissolved under treatment. Of the many enzymes that we compared, we found urokinase-activated plasmin to be the best. We tried urokinase-activated plasmin as well as some other plasmin preparations in patients with peripheral vascular disease and had a great deal of success. We then led one of the first clinical studies in the country on myocardial infarction, and the first one on stroke. These were cooperative studies between the Roswell Park Cancer Institute, Buffalo General Hospital, Millard Fillmore Hospital, and Erie County Medical Center. We produced urokinase from human urine, which we collected from volunteers; but later one of the pharmaceutical companies took over urokinse production for us. We made plasminogen from outdated blood bank blood and activated it with urokinase. When we started, no special permissions were needed. Later on, the hospital and the University Research Committee had to approve this project. This was a rapid, 24-hour, almost automatic procedure. Clinical studies could also be approved by the FDA, which was also fairly rapid. Today, this would be almost impossible. Animal studies have to be approved nowadays by the Animal Care Committees. This is usually lengthy and particularly difficult when the study deals with non-human primates. It would be almost impossible to get approval for clinical studies for a preparation made in our laboratory with ingredients isolated from human urine and human blood. The conflicts and time-consuming bureaucratic procedures required, including special certificates for all investigators, who have to take special courses on-line, makes the procedure more complex. These are probably the reasons why most investigators prefer to use in vitro samples working on cell lines and micro-organisims. Animal studies usually restrict themselves to small rodents and seldom progress to higher animals (cats, dogs, monkeys) for which the procedures are more complex. If you go to the animal colony nowadays, take a mouse and try to inject it with an agent for a preliminary study, a supervisor immediately appears and asks what is the approval number under which you are working. Clinical studies are most often sponsored by large pharmaceutical companies, which have special organizations to take care of the bureaucracy. During visiting professorships in Europe, it was much easier to do clinical research, even after bureaucracy became much developed. However, lately the European systems, under the United Europe guidelines, are becoming more complex as well. I still find that I can get a great deal done without delays and bureaucratic interference in Africa and parts of Asia. We also used fibrinolytic enzymes in the study of respiratory distress syndrome in premature infants and found excellent results in a series of 500 patients. This study was coordinated by my wife, Clara M. Ambrus, MD, PhD, FACP. Eventually, we concluded that the best result probably combines fibrinolytic therapy with surfactant, but at this point it still remains to be proven. We also found that this is a disease that can be prevented in most cases by injecting plasminogen immediately after birth.

Prevention of Radiation Injury

During World War II, the U.S. Army did a great deal of work to develop radiation protective agents to be used in warfare. The first agent developed was most effective in experimental animals but was too toxic to be used in man, and for this reason was abandoned. It was also found not to absorb when given orally, which also spoke against its use. We picked up this problem and found that, when given orally, it protects locally the gastrointestinal tract. Also, when inserted into the bladder, it protects locally the bladder but does not absorb. In radiation therapy of abdominal malignancies, injury to the intestinal tract and the bladder are the major limiting factors. We developed techniques to fill the intestinal tract and the bladder with locally-acting radiation protecting agents, and thus protected them against radiation injury during therapy of abdominal tumors. We also found another drug, which we explored extensively clinically, which acted against radiation injury. This agent, sodium meclofemamate, absorbs well when given orally and proved to be effective in radiation-induced intestinal and bladder injury. A combination of this agent with the above-mentioned radiation protective factor drug, AET (aminoethyl-iso-thiouronium) gave us the best results. We found that AET transforms in the body to the active ingredient MEG (methylethylguanidine). MEG, when given in ointment form, protects the skin from radiation injury. Systemically-given sodium meclofemamate was found to be effective in radiation-induced esophagitis and cystitis. This agent was also found to increase resistance to infection by activating the natural killer cells and increasing interferon production.

Medical Frustrations

Some research projects resulted in encouraging results but for various reasons it was difficult to turn them into practical use. One of our projects was described in an editorial in *Pediatric and Perinatal Epidemiology*. We had found in a study of 500 premature infants that one of the main causes of death, infantile respiratory distress syndrome—hyaline membrane disease, could be prevented by injecting plasminogen immediately after birth. In those children who developed respiratory distress in spite of this measure, the disorder could be cured in a large number of cases by the injection of urokinase-activated plasmin. The best results were obtained when the latter was combined with surfactant. Nevertheless, none of the pharmaceutical companies were interested in making these preparations commercially available, as they were afraid of viral contamination since plasminogen and plasmin were isolated from human blood. We also found that of the various fibrinolytic agents tested, urokinase-activated plasmin was most effective in treating thrombo-embolic disorders, including myocardial infarction and thrombo-embolic strokes. When tissue plasminogen activator produced by bioengineering became available, pharmaceutical companies were even less interested in making this preparation available. We also found that urokinase-activated plasmin is highly effective in myocardial infarction, thrombo-embolic strokes, and deep vein thrombophlebitis. A series of papers were published on these.

Classmates

I graduated in 1942 from the Evangelic Gymnasium, and with my classmates we decided that we will try to meet every 10 years. We also maintained a newsletter, and I was in touch with several of my classmates over the years. It may be of some interest to summarize what happened to this group. I can briefly report only about those with whom I remain in touch.

Sir Peter Abels wound up in Australia. He first drove a truck for a transportation company. He later took over the company and built it up to a large continental group. He also incorporated one of the major Australian airlines and became involved in Australian politics. He was knighted by the Queen. I visited him several times during visiting professorships in Australia. At one time, he gave a dinner for me, at which the Prime Minister of Australia also appeared. My neighbor at the dinner table quizzed me about tactics for his polo team and methods to handle difficult horses. Eventually, Peter developed pancreatic cancer and I was involved in his treatment. He died several years ago.

John Gyárfás also went to Australia and started a textile factory, which went bankrupt. With the help of Peter Abels, he opened a Hungarian restaurant which was considered to be one of the best eating places in Sidney. Several times I arranged meetings with my colleagues and students at his restaurant. Unfortunately he developed head and neck cancer (squamous cell type). I was also involved as a consultant in his treatment.

Ivan Beck wound up in Kingston, Ontario, and became Professor of Gastroenterology at Queens University. He retired a few years ago and a new medical school building was named after him. He invited me several times to lecture at his medical school.

The two Baron Bottliks wound up in Toronto, one of them got involved in some financial shenanigans and committed suicide. The other died a few years ago.

Francis Dán wound up in Minnesota. We visited him several times and he asked for help in the management of some of his maladies. I was just notified when writing these words about his untimely death.

Peter Engel was the smallest, weakest, and poorest gymnast in our class. After the war, he emigrated to Israel and I understand he became a soldier and a highly decorated war hero. He later emigrated to England and I understand he works as an engineer.

Francis Fűrst von Maroth became Professor of Architecture in Paris. I understand he retired officially but is still teaching.

Gustav Gűndish stayed in Hungary, and I was just notified of his death.

The two Novaks died during the war. Gabor Deckner was the best student in the class; he died during the war.

Laszlo Varga, a close friend, was probably the second best student of the class. He was shot by the Russians in front of my eyes; he never finished law school.

A classmate, Szadorf, also died on the Russian front. Another classmate, Egon Paris, I understand disappeared during the war.

Thomas Szemere emigrated to South America and became a successful businessman. He visited us several times in Buffalo during his business trips. He was an excellent engineer, very handy, and during one of his visits, he fixed our complicated heating system on Windsor Avenue.

Robert Frieder also wound up in South America and was involved in multiple business ventures. He lived a stressful life and died young, as did Szemere.

Two more classmates became physicians, Sommer and Polarecky. The latter came with his family to Hungary from Poland as refugees in 1939. His parents were managers of large agricultural estates and were given jobs in Hungary. Both Sommer and Polarecky became family practitioners.

My friend, Purgly, the nephew of the Regent of Hungary, also died not too long ago.

Paul Tomcsányi was the son of the Governor of Kárpitalja, a northern part of Hungary. He wound up with a Ph.D. in agriculture and became Professor of Agriculture in Budapest. He wrote several well-recognized books and became a member of the National Academy of Sciences in Hungary. He participated in the celebrations when my wife and I were elected to the Academy. Unfortunately, he developed multiple neoplastic diseases and a thrombo-embolic complication. I tried to contribute to his treatment, mostly by phone.

Gedeon Margitay became an economic consultant in New York City. He now divides his time between New York and his condominium in Florida. He visited us several times, including at the wedding of my daughter, Linda, held at our farm.

My classmate, Vári, married a well-to-do German lady and spent his time hunting in Africa, Hungary, and Germany.

Another classmate, Vas, became hospitalized while my wife and I were lecturing at the University in Budapest. We saw him in the hospital and consulted with the Professor who was in charge of his care; but he died shortly after we left.

Another classmate, Wertheimer, migrated to Uraguay, but we lost contact.

Another classmate, John Oláh, wound up in Canada. His cousin, Peter Oláh, died during the war, as did another classmate, Peter Messer.

Another classmate, Koltai, also emigrated to South America and became a businessman. At our last class reunion, he brought some semi-precious stone jewelry for my family.

Peter Bartok, the son of the composer, became a sound engineer. He was responsible for recording all of his father's compositions. Eventually he retired in Florida.

Kuszenda, who later changed his name to the more Hungarian-sounding Kökény, was the only one in the class who was pro-German. He died several years ago.

Polo

We used to have a first-rate local polo team in East Aurora. Our Captain was Norty Knox, and the team included his father Seymour "Shorty" Knox and his brother Seymour Knox. One of our members was Louie Smith, at one time the best player in the country. Unfortunately, in one game he collided with an opponent and killed him. From that point forward, he refused to play in competitive games. However, he remained manager of the polo stables, and he and the Knox's were marvelous teachers to all four of my sons. Franz

Stone, president of a local manufacturing company, and Henry Urban, editor of one of the local Buffalo newspapers, were regular players. The team included myself and my four sons. Peter and Julian became excellent players and followed each other as captains of the Yale team. While they were on the team, Yale always won the annual intercollegiate championship. At the time, I served on the intercollegiate polo committee and officiated at many games. One of my colleagues had his medical offices close to the polo fields. He often stitched up members of my family after minor injuries. At one time, he met me in the corridor of the hospital and said, "What is going on with your family? I didn't have anybody to stitch up for the last few weeks." We never managed to beat the Argentine team – they were the best in the world. At one time, Peter went with the team to Argentina and said, "We'll revenge you." They beat them too in Argentina. We taught the pony club children also to play polo. Our polo club team won the national championship and the reward given was a trip to England. They did very well against the British pony club teams, and as a reward they were asked to play the adult team of the guards (on which the Prince of Wales also played) on the last day. Since we couldn't afford to ship our ponies over, our team played the local mounts. Peter was captain of the team and was told that he could pick ponies for his team. He gave a good tip to a local groom who pointed out the best ponies, which Peter chose. The guard players said among themselves, "Let's be gentle with these colonial children – let's not push it too hard." The "colonial children" scored one goal after another, and by the time the guards decided to really play hard, it was too late. This episode was mentioned to me many times when we visited England in subsequent years.

Animal Breeding

On the farm, we bred Montadale sheep, who had some problems with frequent abortions. Our area was somewhat poor of silica content of the grass. We asked our local mill to mix some silica into the feed mixture which I designed, and from then on there were very few abortions. We also developed a hybrid cattle. We bred Charolais beef, which was the largest beef type available in this country, originally from France. Its meat is relatively poorly marbled; and for this reason it may be rather healthy, the type we should all have. However, the butchers for this reason did not classify it as prime beef. We then procured an angus bull and wound up with a Charolais-angus hybrid. It was a relatively small embryo in a large cow, with very few problems at birth. It was medium-well marbled, and still classified as prime beef. Eventually, these hybrids became well-recognized and we won several prizes at the various agricultural shows. We sold a large number of hybrids as breeders for Midwestern farmers. We also bred thoroughbred horses and developed a three-quarter thoroughbred, one-quarter quarter-horse hybrid, which turned out to be a most excellent polo pony. The intelligence, gentleness, and ability to make rapid turns of the quarter horse added a great deal to the speed and endurance of the thoroughbred. We gave away some of these hybrids as presents to our friends and also sold some. We also bred quail, pheasants, and wild turkeys, and released them into our hunting area. I was very much interested in a cattle breed I found in Uganda. This is a large, tropical disease-resistant breed, which is also very gentle and easy to train for farm labor. I thought it would be a species worthwhile to introduce to many tropical and semi-tropical areas. So far these are only plans. We were also interested in establishing colonies of the Beisa Oryx. Pyramid paintings in Egypt show the Oryx being herded by black slaves. It appears to be an animal highly suitable to areas of poor water supply, and another one worthwhile to consider for semi-desert areas. These are also in the plans. When falconing in Saudi Arabia, my hosts told me that a close relative of the Arabian Oryx is practically extinct. It mostly survives in zoos and wild animal parks. It should be bred-up and reintroduced into its native country. It's good sport.

I brought back from Uganda some Lord Derby Elands. This is the largest antelope, with large horns, able to defend itself even against lions. Yet, it was easily domesticated, got along well with our cattle and sheep in the pastures, and even protected them from coyotes and foxes. It had excellent meat and bred well in captivity.

We bred Hungarian vizslas, which are wonderful hunting dogs. They are all trained to work as upland pointers, water retrievers, as well as bloodhounds for big game. They were very gentle and nice with kids, but the only thing they were not good for was to use them as guard dogs. If a robber were to come into the house, they would jump up on him and lick his face. They were also trained to work as herding dogs. One of our puppies escaped and was hit by a car and lost a leg. Nevertheless, he functioned all right as a three-legged dog. At one point, my wife and I were at the hospital working, and the children were on summer vacation and were taking care of the dog. They were herding cattle and one of our bulls turned around and eviscerated the three-legged dog, who couldn't get away fast enough. His guts were hanging out and he was squealing in pain. One of my daughters found my service revolver and gave a coup de grace to the dog. When we came home the children told us they did not want to bury him because they thought I may want to examine him beforehand. Eventually, we buried him on the farm at a place where many of our former pets are buried. He was buried right beside Red Fox, our champion jumper, who had died of old age some time ago. I was proud of my daughter, who handled the situation well.

Airline Emergency

Traveling on an airline, I became aware of a sudden call from the captain, "Passenger in First Class appears very ill. If there is a doctor on the plane, please come urgently." I went and met there another gentleman, a very distinguished-looking white-haired physician. We introduced ourselves and I indicated that I worked at the SUNY at Buffalo Medical School. His immediate question, "What is your faculty rank?" I was surprised, but answered, "I am a Professor of Internal Medicine." He said, "Great, I am an Associate Professor of Cardiology at Harvard. You do out-rank me, so you run the procedure and I will assist you." He clearly wanted to make sure that whatever responsibility there was, it was mine. We took care of the patient, asked the pilot to land at the nearest airport, called for an ambulance, and the patient was taken to the hospital. Long-term follow-up by phone indicated that his myocardial infarction was taken care of adequately, and he recovered and was discharged.

Hyrax

In Uganda I had seen a great many rock hyraxes and a few tree hyraxes. They look like large rodents, maybe a big rabbit; but in fact they are ancestors of the elephant and have a somewhat similar denture, except of course for the tusk. They were probably the early small mammals from which eventually the elephants developed. I brought a few rock hyraxes back from Uganda and donated them to the Buffalo Zoo, together with a chart which we drew up showing how the elephant developed from the hyrax. As I suggested, the small cage with the animals and the large chart were displayed in the elephant house. Unfortunately, it didn't work out well. The elephants didn't like their ancient relatives and kept throwing dirt and dung at the hyrax cage. Eventually it had to be removed, together with the chart.

Internal Medicine at the Children's Hospital

The Children's Hospital always had one physician in charge of the internal medical problems of pregnant women who came to the hospital (which is now renamed Women's and Children's Hospital). When one colleague in this position left, I was put in charge of this office on a temporary basis, together with teaching medial students and residents at the Children's Hospital. I did this besides my regular duties at the Roswell Park Cancer Institute, working long hours in the evening, on weekends, and every day during a prolonged lunch hour. I realized that problems such as hypertension, diabetes, hematologic and neoplastic disorders, and many others represent major and special problems in pregnant women. I actually started to write a textbook on medical disorders during pregnancy. While I was part-way into compiling this text, an excellent book by W.M. Barron and M.D. Lindheimer came out on this same topic. With many other duties and plans on my hands, I quickly abandoned writing this textbook. Parts of the manuscript are laying around somewhere, and some of it is possibly outdated by now. I enjoyed my sojourn at the Children's Hospital, particularly since my wife was working there at the time, and ran a large laboratory as well as collaborative clinical studies in the neonatal unit. We had some joint teaching conferences for my students with my wife and Dr. Weintraub, Head of Neonatology. Some of the experiences at the Children's Hospital led to many basic and clinical research studies later on.

Bioterror, Agroterror and New Diseases

I was asked to present a paper (for a not purely medical audience) on Bioterror and Agroterror by the Catholic Academy of Sciences in Washington, DC. An outline is reproduced below. Later, I was asked to discuss this topic for medical audiences at the Erie County Medical Center, and again at Buffalo General Hospital:

New disease and modifications of old diseases continue to appear. Antibiotic-resistant tuberculosis and other strains are spreading rapidly throughout the world and produce a great deal of problems. Frequently, human activities are at the root of the appearance of new diseases, including the clearing of forests and cultivating of new land, which disturb the habitat of sequestered natural hosts, such as small rodents and blood-sucking insects, increasing their contact with humans and resulting in the transmission of new diseases. Increasing contact with forest animals, for example, hunting, preparing, and consuming "jungle meat," such as monkeys, results in new infections. It was thought that the AIDS epidemic originated in this way from chimpanzees that were carrying immune deficiency viruses, that in turn may have undergone further mutations in their new hosts. Today, increasing travel by ships, airplanes, and trucks have resulted in "shrinking of the globe" and rapid spread of new infections. Economic conditions in many parts of the world have encouraged the mass movement of workers to the city; thus, infections that may once have remained restricted to rural areas are likely to reach large populations.

In industrialized countries, high-density settings, such as daycare centers, can allow diseases to spread rapidly once they have gained foothold. The populations into which new infections are introduced have no pre-existing immunity and are of high susceptibility. For this reason, some of the new infections are potentials for bioterrorism; one of the most infectious agents, the variola virus, the causative agent of smallpox, is supposed to be the first serious infectious agent eliminated from our planet by intensive vaccination processes. Presumably, small deposits remain only in a few laboratories in the United States and Russia. On the other hand, there are large numbers of related pox viruses throughout the world (see table), some of which may be infectious to man. For example, we have studied Yaba pox virus, which we isolated from monkeys in Africa, and found that it can be infectious to man, and may be one of the contributing causative agents of Burkitt's lymphoma. One of our technicians, who by accident infected himself with this virus, developed a tumor, thus showing for the first time that a virus can produce cancer in man. Reinjection of biopsy of the tumor to rhesus monkeys resulted in tumor and death, fulfilling Koch's postulate for the first time for a cancer-causing virus[1-8]. The technician was followed for several years after the tumor was excised, and there was no recurrence.

We also found that pox viruses can be relatively easily hybridized, and thus new viruses can be produced by genetically combining two related viruses. This indeed can be performed in a small laboratory by a single, well-trained scientist. By contrast, nuclear bioterrorism is a highly complex, expensive, and labor-intensive procedure, also requiring the availability of not easily obtainable materials.

The table below lists a number of pox viruses presently known. Standard vaccinia vaccination does not protect against most of them, and only protects partially against others. For example, there were 81 cases of monkey pox in the United States. Most of these people had contact with Gambian giant rats imported from Ghana, or prairie dogs in contact with these animals in pet shops, and then them purchased as cuddly pets. In our experience in Africa, vaccinia vaccination protects only partially against monkey pox. Most patients recover from monkey pox infection, but we are fearful of possible monkey pox hybrids presenting potentially more serious diseases.

Poxviruses that Infect Humans and Cause Diseases

Genus and Species (Disease)	Primary Reservoir	Geographic Region	Mode of Transmission	Protection Provided by vaccinia Vaccination
Orthopox Viruses				
Cowpox (udder disease)	Rodents	Europe, Africa, Central & Northern Asia	Direct Contact	Yes
Monkeypox (systemic)	Rodents	Central & West Africa, Sudan, a local epidemic in the USA	Direct contact; Respiratory droplets	Partial
Vaccina	Unknown	Some strains used for vaccination probably hybrids of vaccinia and variola	Direct Contact	Yes
Variola (smallpox) (Systemic)	Humans	USA, Russia (laboratories)	Direct contact; Respiratory droplets	Yes
Yabapox Viruses				
Tanapox (localized)	Nonhuman primates	Kenya, Zaire	Direct Contact	No
Yabapox (histiocytomas)	Nonhuman primates	Central Africa	Direct Contact	No
Parapox Viruses				
Pseudocowpox (milker's nodules and paravaccinia)	Ungulates	Worldwide	Direct Contact	No

Bovine popular stomatitis	Ungulates	USA, Canada, Africa, Australia, Europe, Great Britain, New Zealand	Direct Contact	No
Orf (Systemic)	Ungulates	North America, Europe, New Zealand	Direct Contact	No
Seal pox (Systemic)	Seals	North Sea, Pacific Ocean, Atlantic Ocean	Direct Contact	No
Molluscipox virus				
Molluscipox virus (molliscum contagiosum)	Humans	Worldwide	Direct Contact	No

Our preliminary studies also indicate that the various animal poxes which may be infectious to man produce the most serious diseases in those who are relatively malnourished and/or are of the lower social economic groups.[7,8] The following table below shows a number of diseases and disease-causing agents that may represent potentials for bioterrorism. They are grouped according to their potential danger into Category A through Category C. One of the problems of bioterrorism is that it may be directed not only against man but also against nutritionally-important agricultural animals.

Bioterrorism Diseases/Agents

Category A

- Smallpox
- Anthrax
- Botulinum Toxin
- Plague
- Tularemia
- Viral hemorrhagic fevers (Ebola, Marburg)

- Arenaviruses (Lassa, Junin)

Category B

- Brucellosis
- Glanders
- Q Fever
- Alphaviruses (EEE, WEE, VEE)
- Epsilon Toxin (Clostridium perfringens)
- Staphylococcal enterotoxin B
- Salmonella spp.
- Cholera
- E. coli 0157:H7
- Cryptosporidiosis
- Shigellosis

Category C

- Nipah virus
- Hendra virus
- Yellow Fever
- Multidrug-resistant tuberculosis
- Tickborne hemorrhagic fever viruses
- Tickborne encephalitis viruses

The last table below shows a list of animal pathogens that may represent a danger in agroterrorism.

High-Risk Animal Pathogens

Disease/Pathogen	Mortality	Zoonotic
Foot and Mouth Disease	Less than 1% (morbidity near 100%)	No
Classical Swine Fever (hog cholera)	High	No
African Swine Fever (ASF) virus	60-100%, depending on isolate virulence	No
Rinderpest (RP) virus	High	No
Rift Valley Fever (RVF)	10-20% in adult animals; higher among lambs, kids and calves	Yes
Highly Pathogenic Avian Influenza (A1)	Near 100%	Yes

Exotic Newcastle Disease (END)	90-100%	Yes
Peste Des Petitid Ruminants	50-80%	No
Bluetongue (BT)	0-50%	No
Sheep Pox and Goat Pox (SGP)	Near 50%; can approach 95% in animals less than one month old	No
Swine Vesicular Disease (SVD)	Less than 1% (morbidity high among pig)	No
Vesicular Stomatitis (VS)	Low (morbidity near 90%)	Yes
Lumpy Skin Disease (LSD)	Variable, depending on prevalence of insect vector	No
African Horse Sickness	70-95% (horses) 10-50% (mules)	No
Contagious Bovine Pleuropneumonia	10-70%	No
SARS (Corona virus)	High	Yes

We have taken two approaches to the possible prevention and/or treatment of bioterror danger with new, unknown, causative factors. On one hand, we are trying to develop agents that increase host defense, particularly through the increased production of antiviral interferons.[9] We are also developing a technique where we can isolate gammaglobulins from infected patients, or even those who have died, and immobilize these antibodies in an instrument which can be inserted into the bloodstream and can be used to remove these otherwise unknown infectious agents. This may result in decreasing the infectious agent load in the patients, and at the same time concentrate these agents in the instrument, resulting in a concentration suitable for further study, including the rapid productions of vaccines. This method was also suitable to remove toxic chemicals and to re-introduce missing enzymes in certain metabolic disease cases. Preliminary experiments showed the ability of immobilized immune γ-globulin preparations to remove HIV from blood (but not the intracellular forms).[10-14] It is thought that these new methods will help in fighting new, previously unknown, infectious diseases, and will represent a reservoir for the treatment of bioterror and agroterror agents, which hopefully will never have to be used.

We have recently reviewed infectious disease problems in developing countries, including AIDS and the relationship to malnutrition.[7] It appears that adequate nutrition is an important factor in preventing major complications, particularly of viral infections.

REFERENCES

1. Ambrus JL Sr, Strandstöm HV: Susceptibility of old world monkeys to Yaba virus. Nature. 211:876, 1966.
2. Ambrus JL Sr, Strandstöm HV, Kawinski W: Spontaneous occurrence of Yaba Tumor in a monkey colony. Experientia. 25:64-65, 1969.
3. Stranstöm HV, Ambrus JL Sr, Owens G: Propagation of Yaba Virus in embryonated hen eggs. Virology. 28(3):479-481, 1996.
4. Strandstöm HV, Ambrus JL Sr, Pickren JW: Susceptibility of various strains of chicken to the oncogenicity of Yaba virus. Experientia. 25:769-771, 1969.
5. Ambrus JL Sr, Ambrus CM, Kulaylat M, Dembinski W, Akhter S, and Chadha KC: Effect of Nutritional Status and of a Carcinogenic Pox Virus Infectino on Interferon Producing Capacity and Mortality. J Med. 36(1-6):107-119.
6. Ambrus JL Sr, Ambrus CM: Burkitt's lymphoma. J Med. 12(6):385=413, 1981.
7. Ambrus JL Sr, Ambrus JL Jr: Nutrition and infectious diseases in developing countries and problems of acquired immunodeficiency syndrome. Exp Biol Med. 229:464-472, 2004.
8. Ambrus JL Sr, Ambrus CM: Yaba pox virus induced tumor in men – long term follow up and possible biowarfare role. J Med. 35:277-279, 2004.
9. Chadah K, Dembinski W, Dunn CB, Aradi J, Bardos TJ, Dunn JA, Ambrus JL Sr: Effect of increasing thiolation of polycytidyic acid strands of Poly I:Poly C on the α, β, γ interferon inducing properties, antiviral and antiproliferative activity. Antiviral Res. 64:171-177, 2004.
10. Ambrus CM, Ambrus JL Sr, Horvath C, Pedersen H, Sharma S, Kant C, Mirand E, Guthrie R, Paul T: Phenylalanine depletion for the management of phenylketonuria. Use of enzyme reactors with immobilized enzymes. Science. 201:837-839, 1978.
11. Ambrus CM, Horvath C, Kalghatgi K, Clowsley M, Huzella C, Warner R, Ambrus JL Sr, Cooley CM, Mirand EA: Depletion of phenylalanine in the blood of phenylketonuric patients using a

PAL-enzyme reactor. An in vivo study. Res Comm Chem Path & Pharmac. 37(1):105-111, 1982.

12. Ambrus CM, Sharma SD, Horvath C, Kalghatgi K, Anthone S, Ambrus JL Sr, Cooley CM, Mirand EA: In vivo safety of hollow fiber enzyme-reactors with immobilized phenylalanine ammonia-lyase in a large animal model for phenylketonuria. J Pharm and Exp Therapeutics. 224(3):598-602, 1983.
13. Ambrus CM, Karakousis CP, Stadler A, Stadler I, Ambrus JL Jr, Anthone S, Ambrus JL Sr: Reducing toxicity of cisplatin in cancer chemotherapy by extracorporeal removal of excess cisplatin. J Med. 33:119-127, 2002.
14. Ambrus JL, Jr, and Scamurra, DO: Method for removing HIV and other viruses from blood. US Patent 6,528,057.

Coffee Houses in Budapest

Between the two World Wars, there was a great deal of "coffee house life" in Budapest. There were over 600 coffee houses, which were open 24 hours per day, all year round, and were closed only on Christmas Day. One could order a cup of coffee and sit over it for many hours reading the many international newspapers, which were all available. Many writers used the coffee houses as their offices. Many of the famous writers and artists sat in the Café New York, which was around the corner from our house in Pest. They were easily approachable; anyone could ask them questions about their latest play or have their latest book autographed. Well-known authors who spent most of their days there included Ferenc Molnár, Endre Ady, Zoltán Ambrus, and Tamás Yabor. There is the well-known story about an author who usually slept until noon, went to Café New York in the afternoon, and stayed there working on his books most of the afternoon and evening. One day, he was involved in a traffic accident and was summoned as a witness to appear at the court at 8:00 a.m. His friends knew that by himself he would never get up that early, and therefore rang his bell at 7:00 a.m., got him dressed, and accompanied him to the court house. He looked around with amazement to see the tremendous amount of traffic and all the people running to their jobs to be in their workplaces by 8:00 a.m. He said, "My goodness, so many witnesses." Molnár eventually wound up in New York City and lived in the Plaza Hotel until his death. His best known plays include "Liliom," which was adapted into the Rodgers and Hammerstein musical "Carousel," "The Swan," "The Guardsmen," and the "President," which is currently playing at the Shaw Festival near Buffalo, NY. One of his books, *The Boys from Pal Street*, is a classic translated in many languages and is required reading in many high schools in Europe.

Farms in Hungary

At times, I think back on the family farms of my youth, where I spent a great deal of time often assigned to definite labors. Our family farm consisted of two parts: Steven's Farm (István Major) and Margaret's

Farm (Margit Major); each about 10,000 acres. In the southern part of Hungary, which later became part of Yugoslavia, there was our boar-hunting forest called Mohol, near the village of Ajk. It also had a marble mine in it. Close to the family farm was the farm of my uncle Páhi (Páhi Puszta), another 10,000 acres. I was to inherit all of that, since I was the only child in the combined families. I was hoping to build a research hospital after graduating from medical school, and to provide free medical care for all who would come, and to spend my time doing basic research. All of that remained a dream. Close to the family farm were farms of close friends: Hypolit Farm of the Steven Elek family was close by; also the farm of Francis Elek. There was the farm of the Hajdu family and the farm of Count Zichy. We often got together and had great hunting parties.

All of these farms were taken away by the communist regimes that came to power after World War II. A very small nominal compensation was paid, which was actually left to my relatives still in Hungary. The communists also took away the family houses in Budapest; the villa on the top of Szécsényi Hill, with the extensive gardens around it; the family house on Terez Ring, where four generations of the family lived in the winter; and the two large houses with apartments for rent owned by my two uncles. The communists also "nationalized" the asbestos and fine chemical factory of another uncle. A great deal of the advanced machinery was packed up by the Russians and taken out of the country.

School Talks

Every year I am asked to go to one of the public high schools and give some talks to the students. I often take with me a couple of falcons, fly them over the heads of the students, and talk to them about avian biology. I discuss the possible origin of birds from the dinosaurs and the problems of birds spreading human epidemics, including avian flu. On my first visit, I was asked to talk a little bit about the need of learning foreign languages, since there seems to be some resistance of that on the part of the students. I mentioned how important it is to enjoy the great antique literature in the original language, to try to properly interpret religious texts by reading them in the original language, and how important it is for international good-will to be able to talk the language of host countries. I mentioned that English contains many words which are of foreign origin. There are a large number of words from the Latin and a few from the Greek, but there are very many from the French. When William the Conqueror occupied England, the language of the court and of the higher nobility became French-Norman, while the population-at-large continued to speak English, which is partly of Saxon origin. For example, "cattle" for the farmers was "cow," "bull," or "ox;" but when it was served to the court or the high nobility for their table, it became "beef," from the French "boeuf," or "veal," from the French "veau," and not "calf" as it was called by the farmers. "Sheep," when it was served in court, became "mutton," from the French "mouton," and "pig" or "swine" (from the Germanic "schwein") became "pork" from the French "porc," even though to the farmers it was "sow" or "pig."

I remember once at the family table I asked my French governess, who only spoke French and a little English, how do you say "ewe," the female sheep, in French. She said, "Brebis." I asked, "And how about 'lamb'?" She said, "Ausai brebis." How about "sheep" in general? The answer, "Ausai brebis." "And what do you call a young ram lamb?" The answer, "Ausai brebis." Since that time, "Ausai brebis" remained a family saying. If something was the same and the same again, we said "Ausai brebis."

2008 Meeting of the Catholic Academy of Sciences

At this meeting in Washington, D.C., I was asked to present papers on the status of health and education in the United States in comparison to other countries throughout the world. I was also asked to discuss the present status of research in genetics and genomics. There was a major discussion on evolutionary problems. Some participants pointed out that the human genome consists of 46 chromosomes, but non-human primates have 48 chromosomes, and this brings into question a human derivation from the non-human primates. I pointed out that while this is true, human chromosome #2 actually has 4 telomers and 2 centromers, indicating that it really has an entire chromosome transposed onto it and therefore there is no real contradiction on human derivation from an ancestral non-human primate. It is unusual to have two telomers laying on each other in a chromosome; this only occurs when a chromosome is superimposed to another. I pointed out that probably with the big bang, the basic laws of physics, chemistry, and biology were also laid down and evolution became a basic law of biology. For this reason, there are no contradictions between science and theology. Evolution is a procedure of creation, as probably the big bang also is.

Honors

As we get older, we get more honors (they may consider us as "has-beens"). I was made President-elect by the Catholic Academy of Science, in Washington, D.C. Both Clara and I were given the award of Laureate – the highest honor by the American College of Physicians at their meeting in Rochester. In Albany, we both received the Sofer Award for heroism during World War II. For that same heroism, Clara received an award from the ADL in Florida and in New York City. She also received the "Righteous of the Nations" Award from the Israeli Embassy, the highest award to Christians who saved Jews during World War II.

Poems

One of the literary clubs I belong to asked me to read some recent poetry. I was in a hurry and did not do it in my usual highly formal style, but did free verse. Here it is:

My Zoo in free verse

I used to write poems in five languages and strict, traditional forms.
These verses are as free as their subjects.
Written fast and carelessly on the spur of the moment.

My dog

My dog lays at my feet and looks at me with trusting eyes
He knows I love him and care for him
Sometimes I am kind
And sometimes strict
And sometimes I play with him
He knows not why
But to understand – he does not understand me
He accepts this as the tune of life
I wish I could be as simply trusting
In him who sometimes plays with me
Is sometimes kind and sometimes strict
I do not know why
I turn to him often
But I do not understand him as my dog does not understand me.

My horse

My horse is much bigger and stronger than I
But he obeys me and seldom tries to dump me
Sometimes he just plays with me, shows his strength and swinging moods
But at most times he remains obedient – I don't know why
He flexes his neck as I ask him to do
To make his side laying eyes see forward

To be able to judge the jump into which I take him
Sometimes when I lose the way
He finds it in the woods and takes me home
We care for each other and go along in life.

My camel

The dromedary I rode in the desert
Looked back at me with his big eyes
But never spit at me as his cousins often do
He probably never understood what life is all about
As I don't much understand either
We just trudged along together in the desert.

My parrot

My parrot talks a few words and barks with my dogs
He does not know what the words mean
Sometimes I wonder whether I fully know.

My falcon

My falcon flies high in the sky but returns to my glove
For the tasty morsel on it
If she is not hungry she does not come back
She takes off and I never see her again
If I could fly I wonder whether I would come back.

My chimpanzees

My chimps in the lab are my cousins
Ninety-nine percent of our genes are the same
They can learn many things
They can sometimes trick me
I wonder what they think about life and death,
About the experiments of which they are part
And the people who experiment on them
Sometimes I wonder it would be nice
To know more about him who experiments with me.

Days in Paris

We were recently notified that Professor Luc Montagnier received the Nobel Prize in Medicine for his discovery of HIV-1, the causative agent of AIDS. We used to work in his laboratory many years ago, and welcomed him when he visited Buffalo some years ago and gave a lecture at the University. I remember in those days we used to work very late in the laboratory. After everyone left, the night watchman came around and said that he himself had to leave but that we should just lock up the laboratory and leave the key under his doormat. We did, and that key under the doormat opened the door to a laboratory which had enough viruses in it, including some unknown ones, to kill all of humanity. At that time, shortly after the war, transportation was still spotty and the metro stopped working after 10:00 p.m. We had to walk home, a long walk through largely abandoned streets in Paris. We lived in the house of my uncle, who was president of the French-Japanese bank. By the time we got home, the doors were locked. We rang the bell, and out came a very sleepy concierge who said he had to report to the police everyone who arrived after 10:00 p.m. and why. We told him that we were working late at the Pasteur Institute and had to take a long walk home. We did not have much time to spend with family, except for an occasional Sunday dinner. Usually the whole family was assembled, including their daughter, Jacqueline, who was married to the son of the mayor of that particular part of Paris, and her young son. Raymond, the other son of my aunt and uncle, was part of the French resistance and was shot by the Germans. Our Sunday dinners sometimes included Simon Hantai, a painter from our old country. He eventually became famous and we found many of his works exhibited at the Vatican Museum in Rome. His wife, Susan, was Clara's classmate, and we thought she was an even better painter but she gave up painting not to compete with her husband. Four of their children formed a string quartet, and one of their children became a well-known harpsichordist. Another child became a physician. We also periodically saw an old classmate, Francis Maroti, who became a professor of architecture in Paris. At the Institute we collaborated with the Robert brothers, who eventually became heads of the Institute for Rheumatologic Research at the University of Paris, and when they retired they moved to the Hotel Dieu research laboratories. At the Institute, we worked with Dr. Jacob and colleagues at the hospital of the Institute, as well as the Hotel Dieu Hospital. We corresponded with many of them for a long time, but by now most of them have died. We still remember with great fondness our days in Paris.

Family Travels

At Christine's wedding at the Castle on the Hudson, the family gathered and we were told that Christine was going to the Equatorial Amazon on her honeymoon. On that occasion we talked about different family travels. A long time ago, Clara and I were working on a government contract on health problems in the Brazilian Amazon and the Peruvian Amazon. Kathy and Charlie were with us. Christine has worked previously on a school assignment in Costa Rica and Columbia, and on a UN assignment in Ruwanda. Her paper on the psychological problems of single mothers and their relationship to children resulted in an invitation to present a paper at an international meeting in Australia, representing (and paid by) Reed College. She also traveled with us in Europe, including Hungary, and rode with us on horseback at our excursion in the Hungarian Pampas. Sarah was also with us on that trip. Karen traveled independently with other friends to Hungary, Italy, Greece, and Austria. Steven also rode with us in the Hungarian Pampas, and later worked in Taiwan, Hong Kong, Venezuela, Brazil, Guatemala, and Columbia. He has visited the Columbian part of the Amazon Rainforest as a reporter. Peter also traveled with us in Europe, including Hungary; he and Claudia rode with us in the Hungarian Pampas. Also, Peter worked as a student/intern in South Africa and in the native homelands of South Africa. Julian Jr. worked as a student/intern at St. Thomas' hospital and medical school in London, and traveled with us extensively in Europe, including the horseback trip in the Hungarian Pampas. Kathy came with us during our lecture trip in West Africa, Senegal, and Ivory Coast, and continued with us to East Africa, including the Ugandan border, Kenya, and Tanzania. I've done visiting professorships five times in Japan. On one trip, Clara, Madeline, and Linda came with us, and we traveled extensively around Japan. Clara and I also worked in Hong Kong, Thailand, Singapore, and Egypt. I have worked several times in Uganda, Saudi Arabia, Quatar, Bahrein, Sudan, and Mexico. At one time in Mexico, we had Kathy, Linda, and Charlie with us. In Mexico, we went riding with General Mariles and attended several bullfights. Kathy and Tom were with us in Alaska, and we had a wonderful fishing trip. We were supposed to go dogsledding and hunting with our old associate, Elmer Feltz, but our time did not allow it. We did reminisce, however, about our old kayak trips to Hudson Bay with Elmer and all of the children. I have lectured in virtually all the countries in Europe and all states of our own United States. Clara and I have worked in Turkey, Jamaica, and the Dominican Republic. Several times over the years, we were supposed to go and lecture in India; but each time something happened and we never got there. Another place I never got to is Russia; I was on my way as a prisoner of war camp inmate, but I escaped. I was twice in Australia but never in New Zealand. Neither of us ever got to Antarctica, nor did anybody participate in space travel. I don't think we really want to do that, particularly with whatever they are charging for it now. So, there are several spots in the world we still have to visit. As we look back, most of our travels were working trips with honoraria paying for the expenses. Nevertheless, we always had a few days to take off and enjoy the local sites. We learned a bit about local peoples' customs and problems, and tiny bits of local languages.

Clara and I traveled at one point to the Holy Land. We also went to Palestine and some of the surrounding areas. We were hosted by Archbishop Michael Saba, the patriarch of Jerusalem. We also visited some old colleagues and ex-students who worked in the Hadassa University Hospital. We had guided tours from the Catholic, Arab, and Jewish points of view.

Education

At a medical meeting, I was asked to discuss the issue of why our entering first-year medical students are relatively weak in science and mathematics, even though they passed the entrance examination adequately. I consulted the statistics of the Organization of Economic Cooperation Development (OECD) Program for International Student Assessment. The first two tables below show the ranking of countries, both in the OECD jurisdiction and of the non-OECD jurisdiction. We are 21st in the combined science literary scale, and 19th in identifying scientific issues best. The third table below shows the average scores of 15-year-old students on the mathematics literacy scale. Again we are about 25th.

Combined Science Literacy Scale

Jurisdiction	Score
OECD average	500
OECD jurisdictions	
1. Finland	563
2. Canada	534
3. Japan	531
4. New Zealand	530
5. Australia	527
6. Netherlands	525
7. Korea, Republic of	522
8. Germany	516
9. United Kingdom	515
10. Czech Republic	513
11. Switzerland	512
12. Austria	511
13. Belgium	510
14. Ireland	508
15. Hungary	504
16. Sweden	503
17. Poland	498
18. Denmark	496
19. France	495
20. Iceland	491
21. United States	489
22. Slovak Republic	488
23. Spain	488
24. Norway	487
25. Luxembourg	486
26. Italy	475
27. Portugal	474
28. Greece	473
29. Turkey	424
30. Mexico	410

Non-OECD jurisdictions

1. Hong Kong-China	542
2. Chinese Taipei	532
3. Estonia	531
4. Lichtenstein	522
5. Slovenia	519
6. Macao-China	511
7. Croatia	493

Identifying Scientific Issues

Jurisdiction	**Score**
OECD average	499
OECD jurisdictions	
1. Finland	555
2. New Zealand	536
3. Australia	535
4. Netherlands	533
5. Canada	532
6. Japan	522
7. Korea, Republic of	519
8. Ireland	516
9. Belgium	515
10. Switzerland	515
11. United Kingdom	514
12. Germany	510
13. Austria	505
14. Czech Republic	500
15. France	499
16. Sweden	499
17. Iceland	494
18. Denmark	493
19. United States	492
20. Norway	489

21. Spain	489
22. Portugal	486
23. Poland	483
24. Luxembourg	483
25. Hungary	483
26. Slovak Republic	475
27. Italy	474
28. Greece	489
29. Turkey	427
30. Mexico	421

Non-OECD jurisdictions

1. Hong Kong-China	528
2. Liechtenstein	522
3. Slovenia	517
4. Estonia	516
5. Chinese Taipei	509
6. Croatia	494
7. Macao-China	490

Average scores of 15-year-old students on MathematicsLiteracy Scale, by jurisdiction: 2006

Jurisdiction	**Score**
OECD average	498

OECD jurisdictions

1. Finland	548
2. Korea, Republic of	547
3. Netherlands	531
4. Switzerland	530
5. Canada	527
6. Japan	523
7. New Zealand	522
8. Belgium	520
9. Australia	520

10. Denmark	513
11. Czech Republic	510
12. Iceland	506
13. Austria	505
14. Germany	504
15. Sweden	502
16. Ireland	501
17. France	496
18. United Kingdom	495
19. Poland	495
20. Slovak Republic	492
21. Hungary	491
22. Luxembourg	490
23. Norway	490
24. Spain	480
25. United States	474
26. Portugal	466
27. Italy	462
28. Greece	459
29. Turkey	424
30. Mexico	406

Non-OECD Jurisdictions

1. Chinese-Taipei	549
2. Hong Kong-China	547
3. Macao-China	525
4. Liechtenstein	525
5. Estonia	515
6. Slovenia	504
7. Lithuania	486
8. Latvia	486
9. Azerbaijan	476
10. Russian Federation	476
11. Croatia	467
12. Israel	442
13. Republic of Serbia	435
14. Uraguay	427

15. Thailand 417
16. Romania 415
17. Bulgaria 413
18. Chile 411
19. Republic of Montenegi 399
20. Indonesia 391
21. Jordan 394
22. Argentina 381

The following table shows the ranking of gross domestic products (GDP) – we are number 1. The table after this shows the ranking of GDP per capita; here we are only 8th.

GDP (2005) by Country

Rank	Countries	Amount
1	United States	12,416,510,000,000
2	Japan	4,533,965,000,000
3	Germany	2,794,926,000,000
4	China	2,234,297,000,000
5	United Kingdom	2,198,789,000,000
6.	France	2,126,630,000,000
7.	Italy	1,762,519,000,000
8.	Spain	1,124,640,000,000
9.	Canada	1,113,810,000,000
10.	India	805,713,800,000
11.	Brazil	796,055,200,000
12.	Korea, South	787,624,500,000
13.	Mexico	768,437,500,000
14.	Russia	763,720,000,000
15.	Australia	732,499,200,000
16.	Netherlands	624,202,200,000
17.	Belgium	370,824,300,000
18.	Switzerland	367,029,400,000

19.	Turkey	362,501,700,000
20.	Sweden	357,682,600,000
21.	Saudi Arabia	309,778,500,000
22.	Austria	306,072,900,000
23.	Poland	303,228,600,000
24.	Norway	295,512,800,000
25.	Indonesia	287,216,800,000
26.	Denmark	258,714,400,000
27.	South Africa	239,543,200,000
28.	Greece	225,206,300,000
29.	Ireland	201,816,900,000
30.	Finland	193,160,100,000
31.	Iran	189,783,800,000
32.	Portugal	183,304,800,000
33.	Argentina	183,193,400,000
34.	Hong Kong	177,702,600,000
35.	Thailand	176,633,600,000
36.	Venezuela	140,191,900,000
37.	Malaysia	130,326,100,000
38.	United Arab Emirates	129,701,600,000
39.	Czech Republic	124,364,500,000
40.	Israel	123,433600,000
41.	Colombia	122,308,600,000
42.	Singapore	116,763,700,000
43.	Chile	115,247,800,000
44.	Pakistan	110,732,100,000
45.	New Zealand	109,291,400,000
46.	Hungary	109,239,000,000
47.	Algeria	102,255,900,000
48.	Philippines	99,029,360,000
49.	Nigeria	98,950,500,000
50.	Romania	98,565,380,000

51.	Egypt	89,369,290,000
52.	Ukraine	82,876,290,000
53.	Kuwait	80,780,820,000

GDP (per capita) by country (2005)

Rank	Countries	Amount
1.	Luxembourg	$ 79,851.00
2.	Norway	$ 63,918.15
3.	Iceland	$ 53,290.28
4.	Qatar	$ 52,239.72
5.	Switzerland	$ 49,351.14
6.	Ireland	$ 48,524.18
7.	Denmark	$ 47,768.73
8.	United States	$ 41,889.59
9.	Sweden	$ 39,636.64
10.	Netherlands	$38,248.04
11.	Austria	$ 37,175.00
12.	Finland	$ 36,819.75
13.	United Kingdom	$ 36,555.19
14.	Australia	$ 36,045.99
15.	Japan	$ 35,484.25
16.	Belgium	$ 35,388.56
17.	France	$ 34,935.52
18.	Canada	$ 34,484.35
19.	Germany	$ 33,890.46
20.	Kuwait	$ 31,860.60
21.	Italy	$ 30,073.50
22.	United Arab Emirates	$ 28,611.84
23.	Singapore	$ 26,876.73
24.	New Zealand	$ 26,663.59
25.	Spain	$ 25,914.47

26.	Hong Kong	$ 25,603.82
27.	Macau	$ 25,162.16
28.	Greece	$ 20,281.55
29.	Israel	$ 17,827.95
30.	Bahrain	$ 17,773.38
31.	Portugal	$ 17,375.77
32.	Slovenia	$ 17,172.56
33.	Brunei	$ 17,120.55
34.	Korea, South	$ 16,387.64
35.	Equatorial Guinea	$ 14,935.72
36.	Malta	$ 13,803.35
37.	Saudi Arabia	$ 13,399.31
38.	Trinidad and Tobago	$ 12,417.20
39.	Czech Republic	$ 12,114.50
40.	Barbados	$ 11,465.29
41.	Hungary	$ 10,941.18
42.	Antigua and Barbuda	$ 10,578.50
43.	Estonia	$ 10,213.36
44.	Saint Kitts and Nevis	$ 9,437.50
45.	Slovakia	$ 8,803.08
46.	Croatia	$ 8,753.72
47.	Seychelles	$ 8,551.40
48.	Poland	$ 7,943.34
49.	Lithuania	$ 7,513.19
50.	Mexico	$ 7,446.86
51.	Chile	$ 7,297.15
52.	Palau	$ 7,197.26
53.	Libya	$ 7,118.31

It appears that, just like in health care, we are the richest and spend most of the money, yet our educational achievements are mediocre. Our medical students seem to come out of mediocre high schools, enter college to make up what they missed in high school, and after four years of college may enter medical school. After four years of medical school, most enter a three-year residency and a two-year subspecialty fellowship program (depending on the field chosen). Most of my medical students are 32 when they start their medical career. I was thinking that Mozart was 35 when he completed all of his superb work. Our students seem to spend their most creative years in school, memorizing and regurgitating. In most continental European countries, students enter medical school after high school. There is no intermediary college education required. Most medical schools are 5 years, including an internship. And most students then enter family practice, with only a limited number doing residencies and subspecialty training.

Examinations

At one point in my career, I was asked to coordinate the entire internal medicine training at SUNY at Buffalo for one year. At the end of the year, the fourth-year medical students took a major examination. I also asked that the faculty members take this examination as well. The results were startling. Most faculty members did reasonably well, except in their own field. For example, a case was described, then the questions were whether the diagnosis was "a, b, c, d, or e," and the answer was clearly "a." However, faculty members in their field knew too much, and they knew that a recent paper indicated that "b" was also a possibility, and they have seen a case that was actually "e," so they checked all of these and this resulted in points being deducted. So the conclusion was that if you knew too much, it was bad for a standard, multiple-choice examination. I also introduced to the system the practice that if a student was dissatisfied with his grades, he/she could come in and take an oral re-examination. The results of these examinations then were final. The oral examination allowed us to judge students much more accurately. If the student gave a correct answer to a question, I could then ask why this is so, and why it is not something else. In other words, I could go into more detail and explore the actual knowledge and thinking of the student. I introduced this procedure in all of my courses. At one point, the students complained about the oral examinations, including that they were stressful and subjectively judged. I received an order from the Dean, who stopped oral examinations.

In our literary club I was asked to review the Decline and Fall of the Roman Empire. My main source was, of course, the book by Edward Gibbon by this title. It was most interesting to consider parallels between the factors discussed by several authors and the present status of our own country. Many wars conducted by the Romans were partly to bring home slaves. The slaves were used for heavy labor, the kind Romans did not want to do (including construction, agriculture, and work in mines). They were household servants, and some were auxiliaries in the army. On the other hand, they also introduced highly-educated Greek slaves, who became tutors to the children of the nobility, teachers, inventors, and constructors of war machinery. We are allowing the influx of illegal immigrants to work at undesirable and sometimes dangerous heavy labor and service jobs in our country. We also have invited – particularly around the war years, highly-trained scientists who worked on critical projects during the war (e.g., the Manhattan Project), and later became university professors. Still at meetings of major universities, many foreign accents can be heard. The Romans recruited barbarians into the army, and eventually they represented a major part of the lower ranks. Roman citizens demanded special privileges; "civus romanus sum" – I am a Roman citizen – could be often heard. "Panem and circenses" – bread and circus entertainment – was considered to be their due. We have to think about entitlements, golden parachutes, and television nowadays. The country of hard-working citizen soldiers, honest office-holders who returned to their farms when their term expired, of early Rome, became a corrupt society of undeserved-pleasure seekers. "Romam omnia venalia sunt" – in Rome everything is for sale – went the saying. Political life in Rome became a series of intrigues, and sometimes murders, and citizens tried to avoid responsibilities, honest hard work, and self-sacrifice. Rome could no longer withstand the onslaught of barbarians; it was sacked by the ots of Alarich and nearly sacked by the huns of Attilla. The "invincible" Roman Empire started to suffer one defeat after another. It is said "those who cannot learn from history are bound to repeat it." There is much of this to think about.

The Olah Family

I just heard news from the Olah family. These letters come periodically. John was my classmate; we had many fights. He and his wife, Aniko, wound up in Toronto. He died of stomach cancer. Aniko remarried and lives in London. Peter Olah died in the war in Russian captivity. George Olah (also a schoolmate) received the Nobel Prize in Chemistry and works in the United States.

Falcon chicks hatching

I remember an episode when a number of falcon eggs were hatching in the loft of our mews (the proper English name of a barn in which falcons are housed) and I thought it would be an interesting experience for the children to see that. When I returned from work late at night I took the children to the loft to watch the chicks hatching. Most of them were actually already hatched and were peeping around the nest, but the last egg was just about to hatch. As the little latecomer emerged, and as our children watched, the mother falcon simply took the little newcomer, tore it apart, and started feeding it to the already hatched youngsters. Apparently, with several young ones in the nest, she didn't recognize that the newly-hatched chick was also one of her brood. This was a horrifying experience for the children. They had a hard time going to sleep at night in our farmhouse.

Testing Worms

It is strange how ancient memories emerge sometimes for no apparent reasons. I was thinking about an episode of my early childhood the other day. One morning, I found in the toilet a long worm and asked my parents to look at it. They were alarmed and immediately called the family doctor, Dr. Szölösi (who was also the family doctor for the regent of the country). Before he came, I went to some medical books in the library and identified the worm. It was ascaris lumbricoides, and I also found the proper medicine to take to get rid of this infestation. When the family doctor arrived, I presented him with the picture from the textbook and asked him to write the right prescription. He did so and then turned to my parents and said, "Your son made the right diagnosis and suggestion for therapy, so therefore I cannot charge you for this visit."

Declaration of Independence

The Declaration of Independence states "We hold these truths to be self-evident, that all men are created equal, that they are endowed by their Creator with certain inalienable Rights, that among these are life, liberty, and the pursuit of happiness." A modern interpretation of this includes that men have rights to adequate health care, freedom from hunger, and adequate housing. There is still a great deal of controversy about how all of that should be enforced. From a long experience of dealing with people, including students, patients, employees, colleagues, and superiors, I have developed the feeling that there is another important component involved. All people desire the feeling that they are important, they have a function, they have contributions to make, and for this they are to be respected. When giving instructions to people, it is important to point out that they are not commanded to do something, but that they are asked to cooperate and use their own talents to bring to fruition the desired goal. Patients have to cooperate with their own treatment in keeping records and discussing observations at subsequent visits. Employees have to use their own initiative, imagination, and talents to carry out the mutually agreed tasks. Superiors, when presented with a plan, have to receive suggestions that this was really inspired by them. Students are told that they are here only to learn principles; eventually they will have to work out applications by themselves. There is nothing worse than to make a person feel that he is unimportant. This is most important when dealing, for example, with unemployed youth or elders in nursing homes. Feeling unimportant is what drives people to become suicide bombers and engage in other kinds of criminality. My father used to say, "If a poor man comes to your house, you offer him two chairs." This means that you are extra kind, extra polite, and that you make the man feel wanted, important, and respected. I believe this is an additional interpretation of what our forefathers had in mind when they penned the Declaration of Independence.

Another problem is that we Europeans and Americans tend to be arrogant when we deal with people from other parts of the world. Ostensibly, or covertly, we consider them inferior and treat them accordingly. This results in a great deal of resentment and is part of the anti-American, anti-European, and anti-Israeli attitudes of many people. We don't want to be looked upon as inferior, unimportant, and second-rate. Honor is most important for them, and they are willing even to become suicide bombers in its protection. We really have to change our attitudes. Several recent Nobel prize winners are of Chinese or Indian origin, although admittedly, for some of them, we gave working opportunities in our country. Historically, it also appears that our culture, which we consider superior, is relatively recent. When the pharaoh of Khufu was building the largest of the pyramids at Gisa, in the 26th century B.C., the region bounded by the North Sea, the Atlantic, the Mediterranean, and the Black Sea was populated by pastoral nomads. When Hammurabi was presenting his code, in the 18th century B.C.E., the tribes north of the Alps were just making the transition from stone to bronze tools. When Ashoka was developing Buddhist principles to governing India and the subcontinent, and the Emperor started to build the Great Wall of China, in the 3rd century B.C., sun worshippers in the English isles were working their way South to make contact with Celtic tribes and to learn advanced weapon production from them. Greek tribes, which eventually laid the foundation of European civilization, came from Asia. When Hungarian tribes came from Asia, and eventually established the Hungarian Kingdom and an advanced civilization, primitive tribes in the English islands were still fighting each other with primitive weapons. When western medieval Christianity eliminated the early works of Greek philosophers and physicians, because they were pagan, they were preserved partly by Muslim scientists and partly by Irish monks who continued to copy them. We have to respect the accomplishments of other groups and make no one feel second-rate.

Another important psychological feature is that we all look around us and see people who are better off, and whom we want to emulate and eventually want to become comparative to. The bad part of this psychology is, however, that we also want to see many people to be below us in many respects. This thinking we have to try to eliminate. Imagine looking at humanity from a higher point of view. Differences which may seem large to us are really minimal. All of humanity is quite comparable from a higher point of view and we should never forget that. Working with primitive tribes in Africa, I was impressed by how similar we are instead of the clear-cut differences, which are really small from a higher point of view. I try to impress this on my medical students and impress upon them the importance of this point of view when we approach patients.

At our Literary Club, I was assigned to write a free verse poem which is travel-related. Here it is:

Silversword

Haleakala silverswords bloom only once in fifty years.
They rise high above the rusty red and black volcanic cinder.
They bring forth many most delicate purple flowers and then die,
together with their spiky silver skin and hairs which reflect the sun
and protect them from evening frost and grazing predators.
Haleakala, "hour of the sun" is a dire mother.
Its stingy nourishment does not feed many plants.
The silversword learns to bloom out of deprivation,
Like the genius who grows up among hardships and sometimes persecution.
And then amazes all with new vistas and productivity.
But does not wait for rewards, soon dies and is pushed aside.
A story we so often see among the greats of mankind.
As we rode among the cinder cones,
And cinders slid and crunched beneath the horse's hoofs.
I thought about it all.
Fortunate indeed I am to have seen the silverswords,
and have known some of their parallels in mankind.

Aramaic

In the Hadassa Hospital, I had to see a patient who was a refugee from Kurdistan in northern Iraq. He spoke only neo-Aramaic. We found a translator who translated into Hebrew, and another one who then translated it into English. His language came from old-Aramaic which later became official—Aramaic—the lingua franca and much of the diplomatic language of the near eastern empires, including Assiria. It then developed into middle Aramaic—the language of Jesus and parts of the Old Testament. It further developed into late-Aramaic and then to neo-Aramaic. There remained only small groups which still spoke this language. It will probably be one of the several languages which become extinct in the next century.

Catholic Physicians Guild

At the Catholic Physicians Guild-USA, I presented a Presidential Inaugural Address on health care in the United States and other countries. Following is the text and the tables referenced:

We reviewed recent health statistics from the World Health Organization (WHO), the National Centers of Health Statistics files, and the Organization for Economic Cooperation and Development health data (OECD). Some of these data are summarized in Table I-IX. It appears that we are the country with the highest expenditure for health in the world (Table II), as well as the highest level of sanitary factors; nevertheless, from the point of view of infant mortality (which is used by epidemiologists as an indicator of health standards) and from the point of view of maternal mortality after childbirth, we are only in the middle of the nations surveyed. Countries such as Cuba are far ahead of us. Survival, life expectancy for both men and women, also puts us about in the middle of the nations surveyed. A detailed list of survival rates by countries is seen in Table III. Countries such as Sweden and Japan far outdistance us. Survival rates are greatly influenced by our bad showing in infant mortality. Table IV shows infant mortality rates per 1,000 live births.

The major cause of infant mortality is premature birth, largely related to inadequate care and nutrition during pregnancy. Prematurity causes a high incidence of respiratory distress syndrome – hyaline membrane disease. We were anxious to investigate the causes and surveyed cases in the Women and Children's Hospital of Buffalo, which belongs to our University and the Kaleida Health System. We found that members of the fibrinolysin system develop only fully in the last days of pregnancy, and infants which are born prematurely have inadequate levels of plasminogen, devoiding them of a system which can dissolve pulmonary fibrin deposition during birth trauma. Accordingly, we went ahead and produced pure human plasminogen from outdated bank blood and used this in 500 premature babies. In the vast majority, we managed to prevent respiratory distress syndrome. In those who developed the syndrome in spite of treatment, we used ready-made fibrolytic enzyme, also produced in our laboratory, both by aerosol and by intravenous injection. This resulted in survival in the vast majority of even the infants who developed respiratory distress. We hoped very much that one of the pharmaceutical companies would proceed, after these data were published, to produce both plasminogen and plasmin for general distribution. Unfortunately, they were afraid of using human blood products because of the possibility of contamination in the early days of the AIDS epidemic and no commercial preparations were made available. It also appeared that inhalation of surfactant may be helpful in these conditions. In our experience, the best results were obtained when plasminogen was combined with surfactant therapy or plasmin when needed. All of these data were published, and we are still hoping for one of the large pharmaceutical companies to eventually return to manufacture these products (CM Ambrus, et al, 1963, 1965, 1966, 1967, 1968, 1970, 1974, 1977). Even in mortality rates of 1- to 4-year-olds (Table V) and 15- to 24-year-olds (Table VI), we lead the world.

There are a few other comments to be made to these statistics. As far as doctors per capita are concerned, we are 44th in the world. At one time, there was a tendency to reduce admissions to medical and nursing schools because it was thought that this would save healthcare costs. The consequences of closing several nursing schools and admitting less Americans to nursing education, became by now a significant crisis. We are importing nurses from many countries, including under-developed countries that need them very badly. The lack of approving extending medical school admission rates is now projected to become a significant problem in the next decade. In the meantime, we depend heavily on attracting qualified doctors from under-developed countries, again depriving them from probably some of their best graduates.

We are 50th in the number of hospital beds, among the countries for whom adequate statistics are available. We continue to close hospital beds on the idea that this would also save healthcare costs. We neglect to consider, however, that in case of major emergencies, earthquakes, floods, bioterror attacks, war, and other major problems, we need available spare beds; and if we cut the number to the minimal required under normal conditions, we may eventually be in great difficulty.

We are number one in calories consumed, and obesity is a major problem for us (Table VII). Interestingly enough, during our first assignments to African hospitals, malnutrition and associated diseases were a major problem. On subsequent visits, however, we found at least in some of the large cities, such as Nairobi and Abidjan of the Ivory Coast, childhood obesity appeared to be a problem. We studied this issue and found that if women are malnourished during pregnancy, their infants develop mechanisms that make utilization of nutrients more efficient. After birth, in the presence of adequate but not necessarily excessive nutrition, this may lead to obesity. In patients coming in from the outlaying areas, we still found malnutrition; so that strangely enough, in these same hospitals we found diseases related to malnutrition and obesity at the same time. In our country, women worried about pregnancy-related weight gain and possibly gestational diabetes may reduce caloric intake to the point when similar phenomena became operative, and this may be a factor in the relatively high incidence of childhood obesity. Relative malnutrition may also be a factor in increased susceptibility to infectious disorders (Ambrus et al, 2004).

In an interesting footnote, it may be mentioned that as far as average doctor's incomes are concerned, we lead the world (Table VIII).

It is thought that poor health status is related to poverty. Some of the relevant data are shown in Table IX. It appears that about 75 million Americans are uninsured at least some of the time and about 40 million people live on incomes below the poverty level. This, together with a low level of education and consequent inadequate nutrition, can set the stage for health problems (Ambrus, et al, 2004).

References

1. Ambrus CM, Weintraub DH, Dunphy D, Dowd JE, Pickren JW, Niswander KR, Ambrus JL: Studies on hyaline membrane disease. The fibrinolysin system in pathogenesis and therapy. Pediatrics 32:10-24, 1963.
2. Ambrus CM, Weinstraub DH, Niswander KR, Ambrus JL: Studies on hyaline membrane disease II. The ontogeny of the fibrinolysin system. Pediatrics 35:91-96, 1965.
3. Ambrus CM, Weintraub DH, Ambrus JL: Studies on hyaline membrane disease III. Therapeutic trial of urokinase activated human plasmin. Pediatrics 38:231-243, 1966.
4. Ambrus CM, Ambrus JL, Niswander KR, Weintraub DH, Pickren JW: Changes in the fibrinolysin system during experimental pulmonary hyaline membrane formation in guinea pigs. Proc Soc Exper Biol Med 125:13-16, 1967.
5. Ambrus CM, Pickren JW, Weintraub DH, Niswander KR, Ambrus JL, Rodbard D, Levy IC: Studies on hyaline membrane disease V. Oxygen induced hyaline membrane disease in guinea pigs. Biol Neonat 12:246-260, 1968a.
6. Ambrus CM, Weintraub DH, Niswander KR, Ambrus JL: Studies on the ontogeny and significance in neonatal disease of the fibrinolysin system and of fibrin stabilizing factor. Thombosis et Diathesis Haemorrhagica 19(3):599-600, 1968b.
7. Ambrus CM, Ambrus JL, Niswander KR, Weintraub DH, Bross IDJ, Lassman HB: Changes in fibrin-stabilizing factor levels in

relation to maternal hemorrhage and neonatal disease. Pediatr Res 4:82-88, 1970a.

8. Ambrus CM, Weintraub DH, Niswander KR, Fischer L, Fleishman J, Bross IDJ, Ambrus JL: Evaluation of survivors of respiratory distress syndrome at 4 years of age. Am J Dis Child 120:296-302, 1970b.
9. Ambrus CM, Weintraub DH, Choi TS, Eisenberg B, Staub HP, Courey NG, Foote RJ, Goplerud D, Moesch RV, Ray M, Bross TDJ, Jung OS, Mink TB, Ambrus JL: Plasminogen in the prevention of hyaline membrane disease. Am J Dis Child 127:189-194, 1974.
10. Ambrus CM, Choi TS, Weintraub DH, Eisenberg B, Staub HP, Courey NG, Foote RJ, Goplerud D, Moesch RV, Ray M, Bross IDJ, Jung OS, Mink TB, Ambrus JL: Studies on the prevention of respiratory distress syndrome of infants due to hyaline membrane disease with plasminogen. Seminars in Thromb Hemostasis 2(1):42-51, 1975.
11. Ambrus CM, Choi TS, Cunnanan E, Eisenberg B, Staub HP, Weintraub DH, Courey NG, Patterson RJ, Jockin J, Pickren JW, Bross IDJ, Jung OS, Ambrus JL: Prevention of hyaline membrane disease with plasminogen. A cooperative study. JAMA 237:1837-1841, 1977.
12. Ambrus JL, Sr., and Ambrus, JL, Jr.: Nutrition and Infectious Diseases in Developing Countries and Problems of Acquired Immunodeficiency Syndrome. Exp Biol Med 229:464-472, 2004.
13. National Centers for Health Statistics: Health USA Annual Report, 30th edition, 2006.
14. Organization for Economic Cooperation and Development. Paris, France. OECD Health Data, 1993: OECD Health Systems: Facts and Trends, 1993.
15. Weintraub DH, Ambrus CM, Ambrus JL: Studies on hyaline membrane disease IV. Diagnostic and prognostic problems. Pediatrics 38:244-253, 1966.
16. Srivastava, MD, Ambrus, JL: Effect of 1, 25 (OH)2 Vitamin D3 Analogs on Differentiation Induction and Cytokine Modulation in Blasts from Acute Myeloid Leukemia Patients. Leukemia and Lymphoma 45:2119-2126, 2004.

Table I
Rank of the USA Among Nations in Healthcare and Related Areas - 2005

	Rank
Money spent on healthcare per citizen	1 ($5,700)
Gross domestic produce % for healthcare	1 (15%)
National debt	1 (8.6 trillion)
Federal foreign debt	1 (2.1 trillion)
Trade deficit	1
Access to clean water and sanitation	1
Doctors per capita	44
Hospital beds	50
Infant survival rate	34
Maternal survival rate	29
Life expectancy for women	30
Women who already reached age 65	20
Life expectancy for men	28
Calories consumed	1
Murder rates	15
Rape rates	51
Gold reserves	1
Unemployment	38
Consumption of oil	1
Nuclear energy production	1
Solar and wind energy production	3
Incarcerations	1
Executions	4
Women in managerial or high government positions	5
Voting age citizens who vote	139

Table II
Health Care Expenditures (percent of GDP) – 1991

United States	**13.4%**
Canada	10.0
Finland	9.1
Sweden	8.6
Germany	8.4
Netherlands	8.4
Norway	7.6
Japan	6.8
United Kingdom	6.6
Denmark	6.5

Table III
Life expectancy at birth, years
(1991)

RANK	COUNTRY	YEARS
1	Japan	82
2	San Marino	81
3	Switzerland	81
4	Sweden	81
5	Andorra	81
6	Australia	81
7	Monaco	81
8	Bali	81
9	Canada	80
10	Singapore	80
11	Iceland	80
12	France	80
13	Israel	80
14	Spain	80

15	Netherlands	79
16	Belgium	79
17	United Kingdom	79
18	Germany	79
19	New Zealand	79
20	Austria	79
21	Finland	79
22	Norway	79
23	Luxembourg	79
24	Malta	79
25	Greece	79
26	Ireland	78
27	Cypress	78
28	Cuba	77
29	Portugal	77
30	Kuwait	77
31	United States	77
32	Slovenia	77
33	Costa Rica	77
34	Chile	77
35	Denmark	77
36	North Korea	76

Table IV
Infant Mortality Rate (per 1,000 live births) – 1991

United States	**10.4**
United Kingdom	9.4
Germany	8.5
Denmark	8.1
Canada	7.9
Norway	7.9
Netherlands	7.8

Switzerland	6.8
Finland	5.9
Sweden	5.9
Japan	5.0

Table V
Death rate of 1 to 4 year olds
(per 200,000 per year) - 1991

United States	**101.5**
Japan	92.5
Norway	90.2
Denmark	85.1
France	84.9
United Kingdom	82.2
Canada	82.1
Netherlands	80.3
Germany	77.6
Switzerland	72.5
Sweden	64.7
Finland	53.3

Table VI
Death Rate of 15 to 24 year olds
(per 200,000 per year) - 1991

United States	**203**
Switzerland	175
Canada	161
France	156
Finland	154
Norway	128
Germany	122
Denmark	120
United Kingdom	114

Sweden	109
Japan	96
Netherlands	90

*Note: The murder rate for the above age group is 48.8 per 200,000 in the USA

Table VII
Percent of people with normal body mass – 1991

	Men	Women
Germany	53%	37%
Finland	51	37
United Kingdom	46	38
Canada	52	29
Switzerland	49	30
France	44	30
Denmark	44	25
United States	**47**	**22**
Sweden	44	25

Table VIII
Doctors' Incomes – 1991*

United States	**$132,300**
Germany	91,244
Denmark	50,585
Finland	42,943
Norway	35,356
Sweden	25,768

*Means including residents, fellows and equivalent

Table IX
USA Status
Approximate Number (in Millions)

Uninsured, part of the time	75
Uninsured, all times	40
Lives on/under the poverty line (<$20,000)	40
Lives on less than twice the poverty line	90
Illegal immigrants	12

AIDS Research

Since our publication on AIDS (Ambrus, et al, 2004) we have received many phone calls, e-mails, and faxes requesting information on the present status of our AIDS-related studies. Here is a brief outline:

1. AIDS patients were shown to develop resistance of interferons induced by HIV – this may be a "virus against host defense mechanism." Modified double-stranded RNAs have been found effective in inducing α, β, and γ interferons and inhibiting reverse transcriptase of HIV. One of these compounds, termed MPC at 7.4% thiolation, was effective against multi-drug resistant HIV and VSV in vitro (Ambrus, et al 2007, 2006, 2004a, 2004b, 2004c, 2004d, 2003).
2. Another compound of this series (Suligovir, 4-thio-deoxyuridylate (S^4dV)35) (Horvath, et al 2006) inhibited the penetration of HIV through its receptors.
3. Interleukin 14 (IL14) increased immunity and was found in preliminary animal experiments to activate otherwise inactive AIDS vaccines (Ambrus, Jr., et al, 1985, 1990, 1993; Shen, et al, 2006).
4. HIV antibodies insolubilized in dialysis cartridges removed HIV from blood (but not from intracellular sources) (Ambrus, Jr, et al, 1985).
5. New non-calcemic vitamin D derivatives increased resistance to infections. Seventy percent (70%) of our population was deficient in vitamin D (Ambrus, et al, 2005; Srivastava, et al, 2004).

References:

1. Ambrus J Jr, Jurgensen C, Brown E, and Fauci A: Purification to Homogeneity of a High Molecular Weight Human B Cell Growth Factor: Demonstration of Specific Binding to Activated B Cells and Development of a Monoclonal Antibody to the Factor. J Exp Med 162:1319-1335, 1985.
2. Ambrus J Jr, Chesky L, Stephany D, McFarland P, Mostowski H, Fauci A: Functional studies examining the subpopulation of human B lymphocytes responding to high molecular weight B

cell growth factor (HMW-BCGF). J Immunol 145:3949-3955, 1990.

3. Ambrus J Jr, Pippin J, Joseph A, Xu C, Blumenthal D, Tamayo A, Claypool K, Srikiatchatochorn A, McCourt D and Ford R: Identification of cDNA for a Human High Molecular Weight B Cell Growth Factor (Interleukin 14). Proc Natl Acad Sci (USA) 90:6330-6334, 1993.
4. Ambrus J Jr, Pippin J, Joseph A, Xu C, Blumenthal D, Tamayo A, Claypool K, Srikiatchatochorn A, McCourt D and Ford R: Identification of cDNA for a Human High Molecular Weight B Cell Growth Factor (Interleukin 14). Proc Natl Acad Sci (USA) 90:6330-6334, 1993.
5. Ambrus JL, Sr., Dembinski W, Ambrus JL, Jr., Sykes DE, Akhter S, Kulaylat MN, Islam A, Chadha KC: Free interferon-α/β receptors in the circulation of patients with adenocarcinoma. Cancer 98:2730-2733, 2003.
6. Ambrus JL, Sr., Ambrus JL, Jr., Bardos TJ, Dembinski W, Chadha KC: New approaches to the treatment of AIDS with special reference to overcoming interferon resistance. J Med. 35:201-209, 2004.
7. Ambrus JL, Sr., Dembinski W, Chadha KC, Ambrus JL, Jr.: Resistance to interferons. Discovery Medicine. 4:310-314, 2004a.
8. Ambrus JL, Sr., Ambrus JL, Jr.: Nutrition and acquired immunodeficiency syndrome. Exp Biol & Med. 229:865, 2004b.
9. Ambrus JL, Sr., Ambrus JL, Jr.: Nutrition and infectious disease in developingcountriesandproblemsofacquiredimmunodeficiency syndrome. Exp Biol Med. 229:464-472, 2004c.
10. Ambrus JL, Ambrus CM, Akhter S, Srivastava M: Attempts to induce differentiation of neoplastic cells to normal. Discovery Medicine 5:405-406, 2005.
11. Ambrus JL, Sr., Chadha KC, Akhter S, Islam A, Ambrus JL, Jr.: Treatment of viral and neoplastic diseases with double-stranded RNA derivatives and other new agents. Exper Biol Med. 231:1283-1286, 2006.
12. Ambrus JL, Sr., Ambrus JL, Jr., Islam A, Kulaylat MN, Bardos T, Ambrus CM, Aszalos A, and Chadha KC: Disease Related

Resistance to Interferons. IN: Interferons: Current Status. KC Chadha (ed), Research Signpost, India, 2007.
13. Chadha KC, Dembinski W, Dunn C, Aradi J, Bardos TJ, Dunn JA, Ambrus JL: Effect of increasing thiolation of polycytidyic acid strands of Poly 1:Poly C on the α, β and γ interferon inducing properties, antiviral and antiproliferative activity. Antiviral Research 64:171-177, 2004.
14. Horvath A, Beck Z, Bardos TJ, Dunn JA, Aradi J: Effect of the extent of thiolation and introduction of phosphorothiolate internucleotide linkages on the anti-HIV activity of Suligovir [(s^{4}dU)]. Bioorg Med Chem Lett. 16:5321-23, 2006.
15. Shen L, Zhang C, Wang T, Brooks S, Ford RJ, Lin-Lee YC, Kasianowicz A, Kumar V, Martin L, Liang P, Cowell J and Ambrus J Jr: Development of Autoimmunity in Interleukin-14 alpha Transgenic Mice. J Immunol 177:5676-5686, 2006.
16. Ambrus CM, Islam A, Akhter S and Kulaylat M: Interferon Resistance in AIDS Patients—Studies on Therapeutic Approaches. A Review. Journal of Medicine (in press).

Arab Horses

I remember we had some Arab horses on our farm in Hungary. Several were named after the horses of historic figures. One was called Al-Borak (named after the horse of Mohamed); another was named Bukephalus (after the horse of Alexander the Great). My first horse (at age 3) was a half Arab named Sari. My second horse was an Arab stallion named Harun (after Harun al-Rashid).

Uganda

I recently received a call from a colleague from the Meharry Medical School in Uganda consulting me about some difficult medical problems. He also told me a few things about the present status of Uganda. They are in continuous fear of civil war, particularly because of the land claims of the Kabaka against the government and the government settling of poor, non-baganda pasturalists in Bugandan territory. There is also continued war by the Lords Resistance Army in the Congo and also in Acholi territory, where there are close to two million displaced people living in Uganda refuge camps. It appears that the Lords Resistance Army slaughters entire villages just to get enough food for a short time. Then they go on and slaughter everyone in the next village. They spare only young boys whom they train as their advance lines of fighting, with the older ones behind them slaughtering them if they turn back and run. They also keep some of the young girls and boys for sex slaves and kill them off when they don't want them anymore. The United States sent a few instructors to train Ugandan, Congolese, and Ruwandan soldiers to fight the Lords Resistance Army, but so far with not much success. They have a way of melting away in the jungle and then assembling again where they are not expected. Uganda used to be the bread basket for East Africa; however now there is hunger in certain parts. Fishing success has also decreased in Lake Victoria; this is partly due to over-fishing and pollution. Tourism, a major income for Uganda, has decreased recently partly because of fear of various epidemics, including a recent outbreak with Ebola virus. There is a great deal of AIDS and related multi-drug-resistant tuberculosis. We discussed various aspects of treatment and prevention.

Family Reunion

At a recent family reunion, we talked about various schools which our family has attended. The first two years of elementary school, I was taught at home. My teacher was called Ms. Flora, but I had a separate teacher for mathematics which my father thought to be particularly important. I was raised by a Scottish nurse who left after a while but continued to come back once a week to keep up my English. Her name was Elizabeth Bremner. She was eventually followed by a French madam, who also came around once a week long after she left to keep up my French. My third nurse was Miss Helen, who spoke with me in German. By the time I entered regular elementary school at grade three, the Sajo school, I spoke four languages. From the elementary school I remember Miss Anna and Miss Jolan as teachers. Elementary school was followed by eight years in the Evangelic gymnasium, a church school which was thought to be one of the best in central Europe, particularly in science. I passed the Matura examination and received the B.A. diploma. I entered the University of Budapest and studied there from 1942 to 1945, with two semesters spent at the University of Szeged Medical School. In 1945, I received a fellowship to the University of Zurich in Switzerland and completed medical school and an internship there, and graduated in 1949. I passed the Swiss Medical State Board. In Switzerland, the diploma indicated you were a physician but didn't give you the M.D. title. For that you had to spend an extra couple of years doing research and presenting a thesis. I did work, however, during medical school in the evening, weekends, holidays, and summers in the Department of Pharmacology at the University of Budapest and University of Zurich, under Professors Ubekatz and Fischer, respectively. I published several papers and had the thesis ready by the time I completed my exams, so I received the M.D. title. My thesis was supervised by Professor Fisdher and Professor Moser, of the Rickettsia Moseri fame. Professor Loeffler, of Loeffler's syndrome fame, Chairman of Internal Medicine, wanted me to join his department. I was also asked by Professor Frommel in Geneva to join him as Chef de Travaux in the Department of Pharmacology of the University of Geneva. I did, however, choose to accept a Fellowship to the Sorbonne-University of Paris, with assignment to the Pasteur Institute, the Pasteur Hospital, and the Hotel Dieu Hospital. I worked there with Professor Jacob in Medicinal Chemistry and Professor Montagnier (who discovered HIV, the cause of AIDS) in Virology. We published several papers, but I then accepted a fellowship to Jefferson Medical College in Philadelphia, PA. In those days fellows did not receive a stipend, and for that reason arrangements were made to teach Pharmacology in the associated Philadelphia College of Pharmacy and Science and to supervise graduate students. I did a fellowship and thesis research under Professor Gruber, Chairman of Pharmacology; Professor Leonard; and Professor Erslev, of the Department of Medicine Hematology/Oncology. In Buffalo, I had three assignments. I was Principal Cancer Research Scientist, and later Director of Cancer Research at the Roswell Park Cancer Institute; Professor of Internal Medicine at SUNY at Buffalo School of Medicine; and Professor and Chairman of Experimental Pathology at SUNY at Buffalo Graduate School. In the latter position, I was also asked to allow graduate students from Niagara University and D'Youville College to attend some of our courses and work with us on thesis research. Accordingly, I was given the title of Professor at both of these schools, and received an honorary Doctor of Science Degree from Niagara University.

Clara M. Ambrus attended a German Sister's Elementary School in Rome, Italy, and returned to Hungary at age 10. She graduated from the Zriny gymnasium for girls, one of the best girls' schools in Hungary, and entered the University of Budapest. She studied there from 1942 to 1945 with the exception of two semesters which she spent at the University of Szeged Medical School. In 1945, she studied in the University of Zurich, did an internship, and received a medical degree in 1949. She was asked by Professor Amsler in Ophthalmology and Professor Fanconi (of the Fanconi Syndrome fame), Chairman of Pediatrics, to join their department. She was also asked to join the department of Professor Frommel in Geneva. However, she came to the Sorbonne-University of Paris and worked at the Pasteur Institute, the Pasteur Hospital, and the Hotel Dieu Hospital. At the end of 1949, she was given a fellowship at the Jefferson Medical College, where she worked under Professors Gruber, Leonard, and Erslev, and obtained a PhD in medical sciences in 1955. She also taught Pharmacology at the Philadelphia College of Pharmacy and Science, and advised graduate students. In 1955, she came to Buffalo and worked at the Roswell Park Memorial Cancer Institute and became a Professor of Pediatrics, Obstetrics/Gynecology (Neonatology), and Pharmacology at SUNY at Buffalo Medical and Graduate Schools.

Madeline Susan Ambrus Lillie started at the Chesterfield Nursery School and Kindergarten in Philadelphia. She started elementary school in the Smallwood School in Philadelphia and continued in the Elmwood Franklin School in Buffalo. In 1964 she entered the Buffalo Seminary and graduated in 1968. She entered the Wellesley MIT program and was in residence on the Wellesley campus, with the exception of one year which she spent in residence at the MIT campus. She graduated in 1970. Madeline then entered the SUNY at Buffalo Graduate School, Roswell Park Division, and continued on at the Wayne State Medical School in Detroit. She obtained her medical degree in 1976; and in 1975, a PhD from SUNY at Buffalo. She did a pediatric residency at St. Christopher's Children's Hospital and a fellowship at the Children's Hospital of Philadelphia – University of Pennsylvania, completing her work in 1981, qualifying for the Pediatric and Allergy-Immunology boards.

David Day Lillie completed public schools in Hamburg, New York, and entered Princeton University in 1967, graduating with a BA degree in 1971. He entered SUNY at Buffalo Medical School, but transferred to the Wayne State Medical School in 1973, graduating with a medical degree in 1975. He completed a residency in urology at Temple University Medical School in Philadelphia, completing his work in 1980. He is on the urology faculty of SUNY at Buffalo.

Peter S. Ambrus started out at the Chesterfield Kindergarten in Philadelphia and the Smallwood School in Buffalo, New York. He transferred to Elmwood Franklin School and entered Nichols in 1961, graduating in 1969. He entered Yale University, and graduated in 1973 with a BA degree majoring in molecular biology. He entered SUNY at Buffalo Medical School, and graduated with a medical degree in 1977. He did a surgical residency at the Beth Israel Hospital in Boston, and a fellowship in head and neck surgery and otolaryngology at the Massachusetts Eye & Ear Infirmary.

Claudia Ambrus met Peter when she worked with him as a nurse anesthetist, and they were married in Boston. They have two children: Melissa Ambrus, who graduated from the Southfield School in Boston and is currently a student at the Milton Academy in Milton, MA; and Peter Ambrus, Jr., who graduated from the Dexter School in Boston and was just admitted to the Milton Academy in Milton, MA.

Julian L. Ambrus, Jr., attended the Smallwood Drive School in Buffalo, and continued at the Elmwood Franklin Elementary school in Buffalo, NY. He graduated from Nichols School and attended Yale University, earning a BA majoring in molecular biology. He entered Jefferson Medical College and obtained a medical degree in 1979. He did his residency in internal medicine at SUNY at Buffalo, and obtained the title of "Best Medical Resident." He did a fellowship at NIH and qualified both for the Boards of Internal Medicine and Allergy/Immunology. Sarah Ambrus graduated from the Buffalo Seminary, and obtained a BA degree from the University of Rochester in 1985. She received her MBA from the Simon School of Management of the University of Rochester in 1986.

Linda C. Ambrus-Broenniman went to the Westminster Nursery School and Kindergarten, the Elmwood Franklin Elementary School, and the Buffalo Seminary, and graduated from the Swarthmore College with a BA degree and from the Carnegie-Mellon University in Pittsburgh, PA., with an MBA. Linda's husband, Ed Broenniman, graduated from Yale University and obtained an MBA degree from Stanford.

Steven Ambrus graduated from the Westminster Nursery School and Kindergarten, the Elmwood Franklin Elementary School, and attended Nichols School and Hotchkiss Boarding School. He obtained a BA degree from Cornell University and an MS Degree from the Columbia School of Journalism.

Katherine Ann Ambrus-Cheney graduated from the Westminster Nursery School and Kindergarten, the Elmwood Franklin Elementary School, and attended Nichols School and The Schipley Boarding School in Bryn-Mawr, PA. She graduated from Cornell University with a BA degree, from the University of Gödellö in Hungary with a PhD in Agriculture, and a JD degree from the Lewis and Clark Law School in Portland, Oregon. Her husband, Tom Cheney, graduated with a BA, an RN, and an NP degree in Portland, Oregon. He is about to receive a Master's Degree as well.

Charlie Ambrus graduated from the Westminster Nursery School and Kindergarten, the Elmwood Franklin Elementary School, attended Nichols School, graduated from the Park School, and then received a BA degree from American University and an MBA degree from Canisius College in Buffalo, New York.

Christine Lillie graduated from the Elmwood Franklin Elementary School, from Nichols School in Buffalo, from Reed College with a BA, from the University of Massachusetts with an MBA degree, and is about to graduate from Case Western Law School with a JD degree.

Sara Lillie graduated from the Elmwood Franklin Elementary School, Nichols School in Buffalo, and Vassar College with a BA degree. She then received an MA degree in Public Health from the University of North Carolina in Chapel Hill, and is currently working at the University of Michigan in Ann Arbor for a PhD in public health.

Karen Lillie graduated from the Elmwood Franklin Elementary School, the Buffalo Seminary, and graduated with a BA degree from Princeton in 2009. She is currently a medical student at SUNY at Buffalo.

Alexander and Christopher Cheney are currently attending public high school in Portland, Oregon.

Cortney Lloyd Ambrus graduated from the Elmwood Franklin Elementary School and is currently a first year student at the City of Honors School in Buffalo, NY.

Invitation to Deanship

Unexpectedly, a group of people appeared in my office and said that one of the large universities north of New Delhi, India, has all type of schools except for a medical school. They decided to start a new medical school which would teach in English and concentrate on international studentship, admitting students not only from India but also from elsewhere in the world, including the United States. They asked whether I would be willing to be the founding Dean and help them organize and initiate the school. I told them that at this point I don't think that I want to move to India but I would be happy to help them with advice or whatever I can do from my present location.

Old Horses

We were talking with the children and reminiscing about old times and our best past horses. Some of them have interesting stories. At one time Julian Jr. needed an additional polo pony, as we all played on the East Aurora team. Louie Smith was the manager of the team and we asked him to look for a not-too-expensive pony. He was on an international team; at the time he was considered to be the best player in the country. He talked to the manager of the opposing team who said that he had two ponies that were quite unmanageable. One of them was very difficult to handle and the other one couldn't be taught about changing his leads when needed. Louie bought them for $500 each. He picked them up and spent about three months re-educating them. Conquistador turned out to be a magnificent polo pony, mostly played by Julian Jr. Color-Me-Lightly finally learned to change his leads when needed and I played him most of the time. Some time later, our team played out of town and Julian performed magnificently on Conquistador. The manager of the opposing team came along and said that he was in need of an additional pony and he would like to buy this excellent mount. He offered $22,000 for it. He asked where the pony came from. Julian replied that he had bought it from him for $500 about a year prior. Julian would not sell him because Conquistador had become a part of the family.

Another pony which I played often was Pancho Villa. This was a magnificent pony, particularly good at leaning in and pushing the opposing pony away. Another horse we talked about was Red Fox. This was a magnificent jumper, an ideal three-day event horse, and a wonderful hunter. Peter won a large number of prizes with him. The other horse we talked about was Impending Storm. This was a 17-hand-tall thoroughbred and turned out to be a magnificent jumper. Julian won many championships with him. He sailed over five foot jumps with an extra foot to spare all of the time. We eventually sold him to the Olympic team. He was a great hope for a gold medal but was injured before the game and could not compete. Another horse we talked about was Angel Dark. She was a granddaughter of Man of War, which was considered to be the best race horse ever in our country. Her daughter, Angel Dark, also turned out well. She was born with a somewhat difficult assisted delivery at our farm.

Another favorite polo pony was On Time; his nickname was JR because this was his tattoo. He was mostly played by Peter. He went with him to Yale and played in the college tournaments.

Medicine in the Field

I've told the story of saving my friend who had been stung by wasps on a fox hunt, and I wanted to write about another episode on a different hunt. There is a tradition in our family for a boy's eleventh birthday: he has to shoot a boar. At the Kentucky-Tennessee line there is an open season on Russian boars. We hired a guide whose hounds located and surrounded a boar. We rode behind in the woods; my son Peter shot his boar and the guide said, "One of the hounds was eviscerated by the boar before you arrived. Please give him a coup de grace shot and put him out of his misery." I said, "No, I have equipment in my saddlebag and we will try to save him." I gave the hound an intravenous anesthetic. My son held the retractors and I sutured the hound together. The guide gave us a hunt breakfast; and when we left his hut, there was the hound wagging his tail. My son said, "I am going to be a surgeon." He is now on the surgical staff of Harvard.

Medical Reimbursements and Libraries

In a small group of physicians, we talked about medical reimbursements. Internists complain that with restrictions by insurance companies, after paying office rent, nurses, secretaries, and other expenses, little is left. Academicians complained of increasing pressure to see more patients in less time, without changes in fixed salaries, and prohibition of private practice. I was thinking of an historic event: Sancho I of Leon (956-960), "the fat" Christian King of Navarra (Northern Spain), was brought to the Muslim medical school in Cordoba, and the physician of Abdel Rahman III, Amir of Andalus (Southern Spain), took care of him. He suffered from a number of obesity-related diseases, but all were cured. He returned home, and as an honorarium gave the physician 10 villages and the surrounding fields. At that time, the Muslim medical school was considered the best; it had a library with 400,000 texts penned on paper (making it was a secret formula). At the same time, for example, the medical and general library of the Benedictine Abbey of St. Gallen (Switzerland) was the most famous of the West and had 600 volumes all on calfskin. Interestingly, our library at the Buffalo General Hospital, part of the State University of New York at Buffalo Medical School, is getting rid of many of its books and journals, and most texts are available only on the computer. When I was in boarding school in St. Gallen we wrote term papers using some of the ancient texts which were still preserved. Today, I have to ask for printing out texts from the computer and have them photocopied to be distributed to students and fellows.

Major Catastrophes - What Have We Learned From Them

The following is a summary of my presentation at the Presidential Symposium of the Catholic Academy of Sciences (based on inaugural presentation after being elected president of the Catholic Academy of the Sciences - USA at Washington, DC):

There were a large number of manmade and non-manmade major catastrophes during the last few decades. What have we learned from them and how can we prevent recurrences?

One of the not-well-known natural episodes was the Tunguska incident in the early 1900's in Siberia. Several thousand square kilometers of forest were devastated. Fortunately, the area was very sparely populated, and there were not many deaths. It was thought that if this was due to an asteroid, which if it had flown a few more minutes before disintegrating, it would have destroyed St. Petersburg and killed several million people. The possible cause is still being investigated. Some of the theories are summarized (in Table 1).

Table 1
Some Theories on the Tunguska Incident

Large areas of Siberia forest destroyed. If it would have hiT minutes later and further it would have destroyed St. Petersburg. No significant crater found.

1. Asteroid disintegrated in the air.
2. Comet.
3. Meteoroids (small craters found).
4. Antimatter shower (magnetic cones).
5. Volcanic eruption.
6. Extraterrestrials destroying asteroid to save us.
7. Extreterrestials bombing and bioterror (Russian's find of table with script).

It might have been an asteroid which disintegrated in the air, and for this reason there are no large craters left behind – but just a few small meteoroid-type craters were found. It might have been a comet or an antimatter shower. Even less likely it might have been related to a volcanic eruption. Some of the more outlandish theories include the possibility that it might have been a large asteroid which could have destroyed humanity, but it was actually destroyed by extraterrestrials who wanted to save us and only its disintegration in the air resulted in some consequences. Another outlandish hypothesis is that it might have been a bioterror attempt on the part of extraterrestrials. Some Russian investigators claim that they found some fragments of a table with strange script on it.

Certainly we have to worry about many potential cosmic episodes in the future. These include cosmic gamma ray showers, giant asteroids, earthquakes, tsunamis, newly emerging mutant infectious diseases, and attempts at bioterror, chemical and nuclear warfare

(Table 2). We certainly have to consider establishing international organizations which would monitor such features. We also have to establish organizations which would study potential defensive mechanisms, including procedures to alter the flight path of threatening asteroids.

Table 2
Some Major Potential Dangers For The Future

Cosmic Gamma Rays
Giant Asteroids
Earthquakes
Tsunami's
New Emerging Infectious Disease
Chemical Warfare
Nuclear Warfare

In the past decades, there were several epidemics in our country, mostly part of world-wide episodes. These are summarized (in Table 3). For example, the epidemic Typhus and its late consequence, Rickettsiae Prowazekii, spread by lice, was the cause of deaths of a large number of people after World War II in Europe (Table 4). Assisting the chief camp doctor in a Russian prisoner of war camp, I saw the deaths of hundreds of people. There were, however, some medical accomplishments of which we can be proud of. For example, in 2003-2004 there was a major epidemic in China, severe acute respiratory syndrome (SARS). It was rapidly discovered that this was caused by a newly described coronavirus and that the reservoir was probably that of horseshoe bats, which transmitted it to the palm civets, in which angiotensin converting enzyme acts as a virus receptor; it becomes amplified, and when civet meat is sold in local markets it is transmitted to people. People develop interferon resistance and a multiple-antibiotic-resistant infection with very high mortality. However, after discovering the epidemiology of the disease, it was quickly eliminated by simply prohibiting the sale of palm civets and related wild animals in local markets. The potential major epidemic was prevented by a single public health measure (Table 5).

Table 3
SOME AMERICAN EPIDEMICS

DISEASE	YEAR & AREA	WORLDWIDE DEATHS
Cholera	1892 Worldwide	2 Million
Bubonic plague (Yersinia Pestis)	1900 San Francisco	113
Typhus (Rickettsiae Prowazeki)	1917 El Paso, Texas	3
"Spanish" Influenza	1918 Worldwide	100 Million (600,000 in US)
Swine Flu	1976 Fort Dix, N.J.	Guillian-Bare' Syndrome following vaccination
Aids (HIV)	1982 Worldwide	32 Million
Sars (Sars Coronavirus)	2003 Worldwide	916 (74 in U.S.)

Table 4
Epidemic Typhus and Brill-Zinsser Disease

- Rikettsia Prowarzeki
- Spread by lice (resistant to DDT susceptible to melathion
- and lindane)
- Incubation 7-14 days
- Susceptible to chloramphenicol and tetracyclines
- Vaccination (not readily available

Table 5
SARS Coronavirus

- 2003-2004 epidemics in China
- SARS-CoV discovered in 2005
- Reservoir: horseshoe bats
- Transmitted and amplified by: civets
- IFN type 1 resistance
- Multiple antibiotic resistance
- Subunit vaccine: being developed
- Virus Receptor: Angiotensin converting enzyme

(Table 6): Shows the number of soldiers killed and wounded in action during recent wars and the percentage of victims who died of war wounds. Over the years these situations have improved very significantly, and while in the Revolutionary War of 1775, 42% of the wounded died, in the current wars in Iraq and Afghanistan the death rate was 10%. This certainly indicates improvement in medical care on the battlefield.

Table 6
Lethality of War Wounds among U.S. Soldiers

War	No. Wounded or Killed in Action	No. Killed in Action	Lethality of War Wounds (%)
Revolutionary War 1775-1783	10,623	4,435	42
War of 1812 1812-1815	6,765	2,260	33
Mexican War 1846-1848	5,885	1,733	29

Civil War (Union Force) 1861-1865	422,295	140,414	33
Spanish-American War 1898	2,047	385	19
World War I 1917-1918	257,404	53,402	21
World War II 1941-1945	963,403	291,557	30
Korean War 1950-1953	137,025	33,741	25
Vietnam War 1961-1973	200,727	47,424	24
Persian Gulf War 1990-1991	614	147	24
War in Iraq and Afghanistan 2001-present	10,369	5,004	10

(Table 7): Indicates that during World War I, approximately ten million soldiers died but the " Spanish" Flu after the war killed 50 million documented, and probably an additional 50 million undocumented patients worldwide. In our country, 600,000 died. In certain Inuit villages, the death rate was 85% of the population. Recently, the virus (H1N1) was recovered from frozen cadavers and is being studied. Live virus was reconstructed and genetics and molecular biologic studies are underway.

Table 7
Estimates of Number of Casualties in Some Recent Historic Events

World War I	1914-1918	10 million
"Spanish" Flu Epidemic	1918-1919	50 million (500,000 in USA including 85% in certain Inuit villages. Virus – recovered from frozen cadavers – under study.)
World War II	1939-1945	50 million

(Table 8): Shows influenza pandemics since that time.

Table 8
Influenza Pandemics

Time	Name	Type	Notes
1918	"Spanish"	H1N1	About 100 million fatalities
1957	"Asian"	H2N2	
1968	"Hong Kong"	H3N2	
1977	"Russian"	H1N1	Genetically altered
1977-2004	"Avian"		32/44 deaths
2004	"Canadian-Avian"	H7N3	
2004	"Netherland-Avian"	H7N7	
2004	"Mild"	H3N2	
2004	"Classical influenza strains"	Various	USA: 36,000 deaths World: 500,000 deaths

(Table 9): Shows some potential pandemics in the last few years. This does not include the current (H1N1) which has spread to over 100 countries and involves a very large number of people. The disease is relatively mild, with relatively low mortality; however, the past experience is that most flu epidemics start as a relatively mild disease, but after a latent period with further mutations it becomes much more aggressive with a second wave involving high mortality. It appears that people who fall under the early form of the epidemic are lucky because they probably become immunized before the second more lethal phase of the epidemic develops. It was pointed out that the majority of patients who died of the "Spanish" influenza after World War I probably died of super infections at the time when no antibiotics were available and certainly there were no antiviral drugs.

Table 9

Influenza Pandemics			
Year	**Designation**	**Type**	**Remarks**
1918-1920	"Spanish"	**H1N1**	About 100 million deaths
1957	"Asian"	**H2N2**	
1968	"Hong Kong"	**H3N2**	Being attenuated
1977	"Russian"	**H1N1**	Being attenuated
Potential Pandemics			
1997-2004	"Avian" South East Asia	**H5N1**	About 50 deaths About 120 million birds ill, dead, or slaughtered
2004	"Avian" Canada	**H7N3**	
2004	"Avian"	**H7N7**	

Some of the problems of war-related medical problems are shown as an example (in Table 10). This is a story of a 56-year-old Vietnam

War veteran who was exposed to Agent Orange and gunshot wounds; however, when he returned home, he developed a large number of medical problems. When he came to our clinic, we diagnosed pulmonary nocaradiosis with an ileal abscess, thrombophlebitis, trichophyton rubrum, onycomycosis, carpal tunnel syndrome, arthritis, diabetes mellitus Type II with neuropathy, 1st degree AV block, bilateral hearing defect, hemochromatosis (and he was heterozygote for Hi 563 Asp mutation), and adenocarcinoma of the lung that was metastatic to adrenals and the liver. He also had activated protein C resistance. Some of these many problems might have been independent from his wartime experience, but some might have included mutations induced by exposure to Agent Orange. This is still under study.

Table 10

56-year-old White male Vietnam War veteran exposed to Agent orange and gunshot wounds

- Pulmonary nocardiosis and ileal abscess
- Thrombophlebitis
- Trichophyton rubrum onycomycosis
- Carpal tunnel syndrome
- Arthritis
- Diabetes mellitus Type 2
- Neuropathy
- 1st degree AV block
- Bilateral hearing defect
- Hemochromatosis, heterozygote for Hi 563 Asp mutation
- Adenocarcinoma of the lung, metastatic to adrenals and liver, APC resistance

Selected laboratory data:

- Ferritin: 456.9 μg/ml
- Glyco Hemoglobin A_1C: 8.4%
- Resistance to activated protein C
- High α /β circulating IFN receptors

There are several ongoing studies in our laboratories to prevent future catastrophes.

For example, one of the problems in the battlefield is that severely wounded patients are bled out. Their veins are collapsed and medics, particularly under fire, were unable to cannulate veins and infuse electrolyte solutions or blood. We have developed a needle which was to be easily inserted into bone marrow and, with the aid of hyaluronidase, infusions, can be given directly into the marrow. When the patients are transported to first aid stations, the needle is securely anchored into bone and is unlikely to be moved out or pulled out by semi-unconscious patients. This simple device saved the lives of many patients (Table 11).

Table 11
For patient with collapsed, hard to find veins on the battlefield:

Disposable bone marrow injection needles, blood or physiologic salt solution with hyaluronidase suitable for patients with difficult to find veins or to undergo transportation.

A major problem is the appearance of new mutant viruses about which little is known. There are no known antidotes and it takes a very long time to develop appropriate vaccinations. We developed a compound which is a thiolated double stranded RNA (Tables 11a and 12) which increases α, β,γ interferon production, which is a most powerful natural antidote against viral infection in patients. It also has many other characteristics as summarized (in Table 12). It inhibits reverse transcriptase, and thus it is a powerful inhibitor of HIV (AIDS); it activates natural killer cells and macrophages, which are also important defense factors. Besides many other biochemical effects, we have found that in our studies it inhibits vesicular stomatitis virus and human colon adenocarcinoma transplanted into nu/nu mice. In preliminary experiments, it inhibited multidrug resistant HIV from AIDS patients in vitro, and in small clinical studies decreased circulating malignant blasts in acute myeloid and lymphoid leukemia. This is still an early study, but it is hoped that it will be developed into a general antiviral agent which may be effective against newly emerging mutant infections.

Table 11a

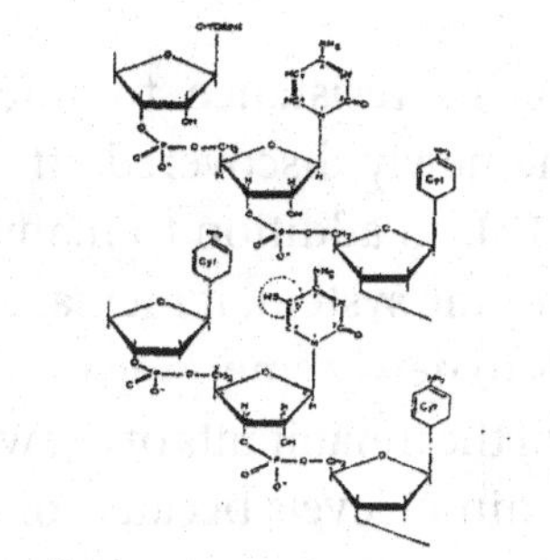

Figure 1. A schematic representation of the partially thiolated polynucleotide.

Table 12
Thiolated double stranded RNA – Poly (i)–7.4% thiolated Poly (c) (MPC)

- Increases α, β, γ interferon (IFN) production
- Inhibits reverse transcriptase (of HIV)
- Activates IFN induced ds RNA dependent protein kinase which decreases protein synthesis
- Activates $2^1 5^1$ oligoadenylate synthetase which activates latent endoribonuclease (RnaseL)
- Activates adenylate cyclase
- Activates natural killer cells
- Activates macrophages
- Stimulates TNFγ production
- Is less attacked by ribonucleases than native poly(i)—poly(c)
- In vitro inhibits human lung cancer (A549) and colon cancer cell lines
- Inhibits vesicular stomatitis virus (VSV)
- In vivo in nu/nu mice, inhibits transplanted human colon adenocarcinoma cells

- In patients with ALL and AML decreases circulating malignant blasts and causes 5/18 CR or PR
- In preliminary experiments, it inhibited multi-drug resistant HIV
- In man, dogs, rabbits, guinea pigs and mice MPC is of very low toxicity as opposed to native poly(i)—poly(c)

Another general factor in resistance to infections is related to Vitamin D. Many of the newly discovered effects of Vitamin D are summarized (in Table 13). In addition to many effects it appears to be a regulator of the immune system, it increases immune resistance, which of course extends to newly emerging mutant infections. In our experience, about 70% of the inhabitants of the western New York area have relatively low vitamin D levels because of inadequate exposure to sunshine. This certainly increases susceptibility to infections, and possibly neoplastic and autoimmune diseases. We have developed and studied a number of Vitamin D derivatives which are summarized (in Table 14). These are less likely to produce hypercalcemia than in native Vitamin D and are more powerful in acting on the immune system and have the characteristics of promoting differentiation of neoplastic cells. These are studies still in progress.

Table 13
Functions of Vitamin D

- Calcium absorption and utilization (prevention of osteoporosis)
- Suppression of PTH
- Contributes to the regulation of the immune system and immune surveillance
- Decreases TH1 activity; increases TH2 activity
- Increases regulatory T cell activity
- Induction of a differentiation of cancer cells (non calcemic derivatives more active)
- Regulation of pancreatic β cell function and insulin sensitivity
- Contributes to the regulation of the renin-angiotensin system; it may decrease hypertension

- Possible prevention of breast, prostate, colon, pancreas and ovarian cancers
- Possible reduction of autoimmune diseases (e.g., Crohn's disease, rheumatoid arthritis, type 1 diabetes mellitus, MS) possible prevention of muscle and joint pain

Table 14

Compounds Tested for Induction of Differentiation

A) 1,25 $(OH)_2$-Vitamin D_3
B) 1,25 $(OH)_2$-22(Σ) dehydro-24-monohomo-Vitamin D_3
C) 1,25 $(OH)_2$-22(Σ) dehydro-24 dihomo-Vitamin D_3
D) 1,25 $(OH)_2$-23-yne-Vitamin D_3
E) 1,25 $(OH)_2$-16-ene-23-yne-Vitamin D_3
F) 1,25 $(OH)_2$-16-ene-Vitamin D_3

1,25 $(OH)_2$-Vitamin D_3

1,25$(OH)_2$ Vitamin D_3 and five of its analogs tested for induction of differentiation of blasts from AML patients.

Discovery Medicine, Volume 5, Number 28, August 2005

Turning from medical emergencies to manmade disasters, I will quickly summarize a few factors about recent wars.

(Table 15): Shows that the three major dictators of the past decade killed a large number of civilians, in addition to soldiers and civilians who died in their wars. Hitler and his Nazi regime killed about 10,000,000 civilians, and another approximately10 million died in World War II. Stalin caused the deaths of 20 million civilians, mostly before the war, and approximately 20 million died during the war. Mao in China caused the deaths of about 40 million civilians and about 10 million in various wars. After World War II, we said, "No more wars." However, since that time, a large number of wars developed.

Table 15
Approximate Number of People Who Died (in Millions)
Due to Actions of:

Hitler/Nazis		Stalin/Communists		Mao/Communists	
Civilians	War	Civilians	War	Civilians	War
10	10	20	20	40	10

(Table16): Lists those in which over one million deaths occurred. This does not include such wars as the Gulf War, the Spanish Civil War, the Israeli Wars, the Armenian genocide in Turkey after World War I, and many other episodes in which the total number of victims was less than one million. There were virtually very few years since World War I when wars were not raging somewhere and a large number of people were not killed.

Table 16
WARS SINCE WORLD WAR I WITH MORE THAN 1 MILLION TOTAL DEATHS (MILITARY AND CIVILIAN)

- Mexican Revolutionary War (1910-20)
- Russian Civil War (1917-21)
- Chinese Civil War (1926-37)
- World War II (1939-45)
- Korean War (1950-53)
- Rwanda and Burundi Wars (1961-95)
- Indo Chinese Wars (1960-75) including Viet Nam
- Ethiopian Civil War (1962-92)
- Nigerian Civil War (1966-70)
- Bangladesh Independence War (1971)
- Mozambique Civil War (1975-93)
- Afghanistan War (1979-2001-present)
- Iran-Iraq War (1980-88)
- Sudan Wars (1981-present)

- Congo Wars including Lord's Resistance Army War (1998-present)
- Iraqi War (1974-present)

Not included e.g. Gulf War, Pirate Wars, Zimbabwe Rebellions, Somali Wars, Serbian Wars, Armenian Genocide Turkey, Israeli Wars, Spanish Civil War (1936-39)

(Table 17): Shows the civilian and military deaths in World War II. They estimated a total of 59 million people died. In Russia 35 million people (10%) of the population died, of which 20 million were soldiers and about 7 million were civilians who were deported and died in the Gulag. In Germany (including Austria), about 5 to 10 million people died in wars, and about 10 million were deported into death camps. The highest number of war deaths occurred in Poland, where 19% of the population was killed. In Hungary 8% of the population was killed. In large countries, the death rate was less. In the United Kingdom 0.7% and in the United State 0.2% of the population died on the fronts.

Table 17
Civilian and Military Death in World War II
(% of population) best estimates
59 million (2.6% of the world's population)

- Soviet Union 35 million (10%), deported and died in Gulag 7.5 million
- Germany (including Austria) 5.3 million (10% died in the war); in death camps Germans and non Germans 10 million (including Jews, mentally impaired, homosexuals, gypsies, church leaders, resistance members, certain SA groups)
- Japan 2.9%
- China 5%
- Poland 19%
- Hungary 8%
- Rumania 6%

- Czechoslovakia 3%
- Finland 2%
- Bulgaria 0.3%
- France 1%
- Italy 1%
- United Kingdom 0.7%
- United States 0.2%

I will now switch briefly from a medical aspect to a more general historic aspect. After World War I, heavy fines were imposed on the devicted nations and a large number of territories were taken away from them.

(Figure 18): Shows an example of the original borders of Hungary which extended to the Adriatic Ocean in the South, and to Poland and Ukraine in the North. About two-thirds of the territory was given to its neighbors, including about 3 million of Hungarians who found themselves in foreign countries. All this resulted in severe economic depression and unemployment throughout central Europe. In desperation, the population turned to Hitler and to Nazis in Germany, to Mussolini and the Fascists in Italy, and ultimately resulted in World War II.

Figure 18

(Figure 19): Shows a geographic map of Hungary surrounded by the Carpathian Mountains. It was a well-defended geographic unit. The Hungarians originally came from Asia and occupied this area in the 900s. There is an old legend that they were guided to this area by a hunting falcon. It was probably a Steppe eagle. It is interesting to note that for many years we bred Steppe eagles on our farm.

Figure 19

(Figure 20): Shows my son Peter and daughter Madeline mounted with a hunting eagle at our farm.

Figure 20

(Figure 21): Shows one of the border castles which guarded Europe for over a hundred years from invading Osman Turks. Finally, the central part of Hungary was occupied by the Turks and held for over 150 years before they were expelled jointly by the Austrian-Hungarian Army.

Figure 21

During World War II large parts of Budapest were destroyed including all the bridges of the Danube.

(Figure 22): Shows one of the destroyed bridges and part of the destroyed city. The country was then occupied by the Russians, and then in 1956 there was a major revolution which cleared the country of Russians (Figure 23) but they soon returned with vengeance and killed and imprisoned large numbers of the citizens. During all these terrible times, there were many people killed or imprisoned and forced into hard labor. There were, however, small groups of resistance, of which my family and my wife's parents were part. They managed a large textile factory which stopped working in World War II because of lack of materials, and all the workers were let go. The large factories and warehouses stood empty. My wife and her parents used this facility to hide many of the persecuted, including Jews, priests, and members of the resistance. She also went to concentration camps and bribed the guards to let out prisoners for one golden guilder about ($5.00) a piece. Some of them were hidden in their factories, some were taken to other areas, including a large house of one of my uncles who worked for the Italian Embassy, and nunneries of the Gray Nuns of Social Services. One of these nunneries was invaded by German soldiers. Everybody was killed, including the head nun, Sr. Sara Salkahazi, who was recently beatified and is on her way to sainthood.

Figure 22

Figure 23

(Figure 24): Shows my wife Clara in front of a statue erected in gratefulness for the passing of plague in the middle ages. She should probably also be selected for sainthood; if not for her war time services, but for putting up with me.

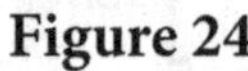

Figure 24

Finally, as a matter of interest, I want to show (on Table 25) some of the factors that were thought to have contributed to the demise of the Roman Empire, and some interesting parallels in our country at the present time. We have to think about some of these factors and consider remedies.

Table 25

ROME	USA
Gibbon E:	N Ferguson:
"The history of the decline & fall of the roman empire" 3 Vol 1781	The war of the world, 20th century conflict and descent of the West 2006
Citizens no longer serve in the military or in office and then return to their farms. Barbarians serve mostly in the ranks of the military.	No obligatory military service. Politician's major efforts are directed toward being reelected.
Most of the low level and service work is done by slaves.	Much "undesirable" work is done by illegal immigrants.
Much of the advanced teaching and medical jobs are done by Greek slaves or immigrants.	Many high level university and research positions filled by immigrants. Many medical residents and nurses are from abroad.
"Civus romanus suim" "panem et circenses" Romans demand special privileges and entertainment. Roman citizens received regular grain allotments. The Circus maximus seated 200,000 and the Coliseum 50,000 people.	Much time is spent watching television and team sports. Entertainment and sports stars find excessive renumerations.
Most functions of elected consuls are replaced by unelected emperors many of whom want to be considered Gods.	Executives and politicians award themselves excessive privileges, perks and compensations.
Much of the food needed comes from abroad (e.g. Egypt).	The economy depends on imports. Many jobs are exported.

Continuous warfare is aimed partly at importing slaves.	Much global expansion
Barbarians invade Rome or its environment repeatedly (e.g. Visigoth under Alaric, Huns under Attila).	Multiple wars (e.g., Korea, Vietnam) and terrorist attack (9/11/01)
Multiple internal fighting	Some internal problems
Climate change decreased food production.	Climate changes initiated
Over taxation of farmers.	Some tax problems.
Class Tensions	Racial tensions
Increasing difference between the wealthy and on the top (senators, equestrians) and on the bottom, "capite censi" of society.	Increasing difference in income between the executives and the workers (60 xs in an example).

Finally, I want to show (on Figure 26) a couple of rhinoceros looking in a human camp and saying to each other, "As I understand it they are also in danger of becoming extinct."

Figure 26

"As I understand it, they're in dang
of becoming extinct, too."

Total honoraria of chief executives of some managed care companies for 2007 and 2008

CEO	Company	Total Compensation (millions) 2007	Total Compensation (millions) 2008
Ronald Williams	Aetna	$23.05	$24.3
H. Edward Hanway	Cigna	$25.84	$12.24
Dale Wolf	Coventry	$14.87	$9.05
Jay Gellert	Health Net	$3.69	$4.43
Michael McCallister	Humana	$10.31	$4.77
Stephen J. Hemsley	United Health Corp.	$13.16	$3.24
Angela Braly	Wellpoint	$9.09	$9.84

Feeling of Importance In Comparison to Neighbors

I discussed with medical students how important it is to get all of our patients well and to make clear to them that they are important to us – they are not handled like numbers in a clinic, but they are appreciated as individuals. It is important to impress upon them that they are important in life, that they have contributions to make, and they certainly should not think of terminating their life due to a serious illness. Part of our psychology includes the factor that wants us to feel important but also to feel like we want to be better than our neighbors. I told them a joke on this last point. The story is about a Russian farmer plowing his field with a donkey-drawn plow when he throws up a bottle. He opens it up and out comes a genie. The genie says, "I can grant you three wishes; however, anything I grant you I will grant your neighbor twice as much." The farmer said, "I'm getting tired of plowing my field with this one little donkey. Can you possibly give me a new tractor?" Within a minute a brand new tractor appears in his field. But across the fence, two tractors appear in the yard of the neighbor. "My second request is a brand new barn.

Mine is getting old and I have a hard time continuously repairing it." Within a minute, a beautiful new barn appears in his yard, but as he looks across the fence he sees two brand new barns appear for his neighbor. The farmer then thinks what his next wish should be and finally he says, "Oh Genie, can you make me blind in one eye?"

I'm telling my medical students that we should learn not to try to be better than our fellow man. We may feel that as physicians we are above our patients. But if you look at it from a higher perspective, the possible differences are so small that they are almost insignificant. We should learn to become humble and to be brothers to our patients rather than their superiors.

Indian Health

When I was teaching an introduction to medicine class, I took my students to an Indian reservation and showed them something about Indian medicine. The vast majority of the patients suffered from obesity. This was due to junk food and an inactive lifestyle; it's possible that genetic factors were also involved. Originally, they were programmed over thousands of years to exist on low calorie diets and to use food efficiently. When calories became high, this genetic background contributed to obesity. Consequently, there was also a very high incidence of diabetes, mostly of Type 2. There was also a great deal of unemployment, a few suicides, and a great deal of alcoholism. Many of the patients had hepatomegaly and liver function deficiencies. Frustration, feelings of inadequacy, and the lack of educational opportunities also contributed to this phenomenon. Even though tribal leaders did well financially with casinos, untaxed cigarette sales, and other enterprises, little of that trickled down to the average tribe members. There was a significant amount of tuberculosis, including a few cases of the multi-drug-resistant type. We did not see too much of a problem with intestinal parasites or multi-drug-resistant AIDS. We also didn't see any influenza; but the tribe elders remembered that after World War I, the Spanish Flu claimed a large number of tribal members. I understand that farther North, some Inuit villages were decimated by the Spanish Flu – up to

85% of the population died in some villages. Some frozen cadavers were unearthed recently and the original H1N1 Spanish Flu strain was isolated and is presently being studied.

Our Chiefs at the Pasteur Institute

Today is the 20th anniversary of the death of Pierre Lépine. At the Pasteur Institute we also worked in the Virology Department, headed by Pierre Lépine MD. Those were great days. It was a time when Dr. Lépine developed the first polio vaccine, close to the development of the killed and live vaccines in the United States by Drs. Sabin and Salk. It was suggested that the Lépine vaccine had less side effects and was safer than the American vaccines. Extensive clinical trials in 1955 seemed to prove this point as well as efficacy. The Lépine vaccine was double-inactivated, both with formaldehyde and propiolactone. Dr. Lépine was born in 1901 and started to study medicine in Lyons at the age of 17. By the age of 24, he was appointed to the faculty of the medical school. He participated in a research project in Central America. He studied the relationship between hygiene and disease. At age 27, he became laboratory chief at the Institute Pasteur. Afterwards, he was appointed Director of the Pasteur Institute in Athens, Greece; a position he held from 1930-1935. In Greece, he studied typhoid, leprosy, and polio. He returned to the Institute Pasteur and became head of the rabies research section, and soon thereafter of the entire viral research department. He also became a teacher at the medical school. He did a one-year fellowship in Canada, where he studied the epidemiology of polio. He also was virology consultant and infectious disease chief of the hospital of the Pasteur Institute, which after the war was treating primarily soldiers returning from captivity in Asia and suffering from various tropical diseases. He was a great teacher, mentor, and friend in research and tropical medicine.

At the same time, Luc Montagnier also working at the Institute, started studies which led to the isolation and identification of the HIV-1, the causative agent of AIDS. Later, he was involved in a controversy ending in a compromise with American investigators about priority of isolating this virus. Montagnier visited us later in Buffalo, and he received the Nobel Prize in Medicine.

Dr. Lépine was also in contact with Dr. Hillary Kaprovsky, a pioneer of polio research, with whom we were also in frequent contact during our work in Philadelphia and later in Buffalo.

Brief Autobiography of Clara M. Ambrus, MD, PhD, FACP, LCsHS

I was given a medal in Albany for war-time services and was asked to present a brief description of my life's story. "Je me suvier du jour ancient:"

I was born in Rome and baptized in the Basilica of St. Peter in the Vatican. We lived close to the Vatican, and later by the Villa Sara on top of the hill Giannicolo, one of the seven hills on which Rome was built. I remember beautiful peacocks in the garden and a magnificent view from the terrace of all of Rome. I was cared for by a housemaid called Dennice, whom we imported from Venice. She spoke Italian with us but a Venetian dialect with her friends, which we could not understand. I went to a private elementary school run by German nuns. By the time I was 10, I spoke Hungarian, Italian, and German. When I was 10, the family moved back to Budapest. My parents were Hungarian but on assignment in Italy. I was sent back before the rest of the family moved, and I stayed with my grandmother. She was the widow of a famous architect and worked at the Wander Pharmaceutical Company. My mother's sister, Vilma, and her daughter, Nora, also stayed with us. I attended the Zrinuyi Ilona Gymnasium, which was considered one of the top schools in Budapest. My cousin, Nora, had some problems in mathematics, and although she was a year older than I was, I spent some time tutoring her. Later, I tutored several of my schoolmates and made a little pocket money that way. On weekends, we always went hiking in the Buda hills, guided by my scout cousin, Laszlo (whom we visited much later during a visiting professorship in Australia). Interestingly enough, we always passed the great villa which belonged to the family of my future husband. My family soon returned to Budapest, including my parents and my brother, Ivan. At age 16, I was diagnosed to have tuberculosis and was sent to the school sanitorium in the Buda hills. I was reading Zauberberg, by Thomas Mann, which described a similar experience. After a year, I was considered cured and returned to my regular school. After completing high school, I enrolled in the medical school of Budapest. There was a small group of close friends who were all interested in research and volunteered to work in various departments after the school day was over, on weekends, and on holidays. This group included the following: my future husband, Julian; Andrew Szent-Gyorgyi, whose uncle won the Nobel Prize for studies on cellular metabolisms and the discovery of Vitamin C – he later became Professor at Brandeis University and we spent several summers at his summer home in Woods Hole; Ivan Beck, who became Professor of Gastroenterology at Queens University in Canada; Maria Fabinyi and Szebehelyi, who later became Professors of Pharmacology in Stockholm and later married; Eva Fischer and George Klein, who later became Professors at the Department of Oncology of the University of Stockholm, and married; Nicholas Talley, who later became Professor of Gastroenterology in Sidney, Australia; four friends who became general practitioners in Hungary: Polarecky, Sommer, Somay, and Eros; and one dear friend who became infected with tuberculosis during our assignment to a tuberculosis hospital. Julian's uncle, who was Chief of the University Tuberculosis Hospital, took care of him, but he died while hospitalized.

In my first year of medical school, a great deal of time was spent in anatomical dissection. However, Julian, who was assigned to the same group, worked in part with the second professor of anatomy, Dr. Szentagotai, using the Hoarsley-Clark apparatus on cats to map the various areas of the brain. This was in collaboration with Dr. Jack Eccles, who later received the Nobel Prize for this work. Since Julian was often in the research lab, I did most of the dissection that Julian was supposed to do. We all took the demonstration and bi-weekly examination together, and Dr. Szentagotai always gave us top grades.

In 1944 the Germans invaded Hungary. My family and Julian's family were part of the resistance. My family managed a large textile factory which stood empty because of the lack of material. It was decided that this would be a good place to hide persecuted people, such as Jews scheduled to be taken to extermination camps, members of the resistance, priests, and many others. Some stayed there throughout the German occupation; some wandered in and out to various hiding places not feeling safe in one place. I was also assigned to go to concentration camps and bribe the guards to let people out, whom we then hid in my family's home or textile factory or with others who were cooperating with the resistance, including the nunneries of the Gray Nuns of Social Service, and the palace of Julian's uncle, who was an officer of the Italian embassy. Julian and his resistance group wound up in a German prisoner of war camp, from which they escaped but then wound up in a Russian prisoner of war camp. They escaped from there as well and managed to go to the southern town of Szeged where the University was already functioning. When we found out about this, my friend Eva Fischer and I partly hitchhiked and partly walked and arrived in Szeged. We also enrolled in the medical school. It turned out that the Russians were forcing unmarried female medical students to join their mobile hospitals, which at that time stood under Vienna. Julian and I decided we would quickly get married. We were under the legal age of 21; but the mayor of the city, who was a friend, assigned the Dean of the medical school to become guardians for both of us and he gave the necessary permissions for both sides. We continued our studies there; but when the Russians started to recruit all medical students, we returned to Budapest and stayed with our parents. We continued medical school and worked on research in the Department of Pharmacology under Professor Issekutz, who developed the first diuretics. In 1947, we received fellowships to continue our studies in the University of Zurich in Switzerland. In Zurich, medical school was seven years, including a year of internship. When students graduated and became physicians, they could not use the title "doctor." For that, they had to spend a couple of additional years in research and write a thesis. Julian and I worked in the Department of Pharmacology under Professor Fischer, spending evenings, weekends, and vacation time in the laboratory. We wrote several papers; and when we completed medical school, we already had a thesis ready to present and thus got the MD title simultaneously. We then went to Paris to do postgraduate work at the Sorbonne University of Paris and to do research at the Pasteur Institute and the Pasteur Hospital. We worked in the Department of medicinal chemistry under Professor Jacob and Madame Trefuel, the wife of the institute director. We also worked in the virus department under Dr. Lépine, who was developing a polio vaccine, and under Dr. Luc Montagnier, who isolated HIV, the causative agent of AIDS, for which he later received the Nobel Prize. These were very exciting times in the laboratory. In the Pasteur Hospital there were mainly French GIs who returned from Japanese prisoner of war camps and suffered from multiple tropical diseases. It was a great time to learn tropical medicine. We wrote several papers and published them together with our mentors. This probably resulted in an invitation to Jefferson Medical College in Philadelphia, PA, to do postgraduate studies, and also to work in both at the Department of Pharmacology under Professor Gruber and the Department of Hematology-Oncology under Professors Ewell and Tocantins. At the time, there was a program at Jefferson Medical College where MDs could receive postgraduate training and at the same time do research, write a thesis, and receive a PhD degree. We both received a PhD degree in medical science, and completed our work in 1955. At that time we were invited to the newly-reorganized Roswell Park Memorial Cancer Institute in Buffalo, New York. We rose in the ranks, and Julian became Director of Cancer Research, and I became a Senior Cancer Scientist. The Institute was also associated with the University at Buffalo, which later became a part of the State University of New York. Julian became Professor of Internal Medicine in the medical school, and Chairman of the Department of Experimental Pathology in the graduate school. I became Professor of Pediatrics and Obstetrics/ Gynecology (Neonatology) in the medical school and Professor of Pharmacology in the graduate school. We retired form Roswell Park in 1992 and moved our headquarters across the street to the Buffalo General Hospital, the main teaching hospital of the university. One of our sons, Julian Jr., joined us there; he is in charge of the Clinical

Immunology/Rheumatology Clinic and the Systemic Autoimmune Disease Research Center. Our oldest daughter, Madeline, also works here periodically in Pediatric Allergy-Immunology, as well as her husband, David Lillie, in Urology.

Although I have seen many things in life, I feel that my major contribution is seven outstanding children and eight wonderful grandchildren. Our children were raised partly on the family farm in Boston, New York. They learned how to handle cattle, sheep, horses, and falcons, which we bred. They participated in training horses. We sold trained horses to the Olympic equestrian team, and developed a line of great polo ponies. Depending on their age, all the children had significant work assignments at the farm. This taught them a great deal of responsibility. They participated in delivering calves and foals, in immunizing animals, and in developing diets. This was a little bit of introduction to medicine. They also worked under the National Science Foundation program for high school and college students in our research laboratories at the Roswell Park Cancer Institute.

Ecumenical Meetings

During a visiting professorship in the Netherlands, I was invited to participate in an evening ecumenical meeting. At the meeting, I was asked that since I was from far away, would I say a few words. I was, of course, unprepared, but I tried. Looking around, I said "I see many groups of people, of many denominations; but of course, there are so many branches of Protestantism that all cannot be represented. The French say about my country that America is home to 300 religions but only one sauce (catsup); by contrast, France has 300 sauces but only one religion (this was, of course, at that time). I will start my theme with what I had to say before each class session in the medical school of Riyadh: "Bism Illah el raman el rahim' (in the name of God, the merciful, the compassionate). My second theme verse is from the Hebrew prayer I heard often while working in the Hadassa hospital in Jerusalem: "Semaj Isroel Adonaj elauchenu Adonaj echod' (Hear ye oh Israel the Lord your God is one). At the time this was first said, it was important because most neighboring people believed in many gods. Today, the problem is not so much this, but the fact that many people don't believe in any God at all. As in so many biblical passages, this was important when it was written; but it is still important, although in a different way. It can be interpreted as saying, "God is one" whether we call him Lord, Yaveh, Adonai, Alah, or by any other name. We are all children of the same God – we should all follow his teachings and should not have differences and fights among ourselves. We often think that there are only three groups of religions which believe in one God (monotheism) but for example, the Hindus point out that Vishnu (the Creator), Brahma (Teacher and Preserver) and Shiva (the Destroyer) are a trinity, three manifestations of the same God, and all the others are comparable to the Saints in Catholicism. When Vishnu comes to earth to inspect his people, he is Krishna or Rama. We should not exclude Hindus from our ecumenical communities. Many of our important persons and prophets are common. For example, Holy Mary is mentioned more often in the Koran than in the Bible. The Bible and the Koran are big books and one can find sections for almost any interpretation one chooses. The important thing is not to use isolated sections taken out of context, but to look at the spirit of the whole. In this way, we may find fewer differences between ourselves.

When I was in the Netherlands for a second visiting professorship, they again invited me for an ecumenical evening meeting. They might have liked my earlier presentation and asked me to speak again. This time I had advance notice and had some time to look up a few things in the library in my spare time. I said that one of our basic tenements, the "golden rule," was set down by Matthew (7:1-2) and Luke (6:27-36): "And as you would that men should do to you, do you also do to them likewise." Interestingly enough, the same theme is found in many other religious opuses. For example, it occurs several times in the Old Testament: Kings 6:8-23; Psalms 109:5; Proverbs 21:13, 24-29; Obadiah 15; Leviticus 19:18; and the following:

Hinduism (c. 13th century B.C.): "Do not do to others what ye do not wish done to yourself…this is the whole Dharma. Heed it well," the Mahabharata. Judaism (c. 13th century B.C.): "What is hateful to you, do not do to your neighbor; that is the entire Torah; the rest is commentary; go learn it," the Babylonian Talmud. Zoroastrianism (c. 12th century B.C.): "Human nature is good only when it does not do unto another whatever is not good for its own self," the Dadistan-i-Dinik. Buddhism (c. 6 century B.C.): "Hurt not others in ways that you yourself would find hurtful," the Tibetan Dhammapada. Confucianism (c. 6th century B.C.): "Do not do to others what you do not want done to yourself," Confucius, Analects.

But, G.B. Shaw rewrote the golden rule: "Do not do unto others as you would have others do unto you – they may have different taste."

In a new book on Neuroscience, Donald W. Pfeff discussed the "golden rule," and suggested that this is universally embedded in the human brain and that we have an instinct for "fair play" by learning our own identity with the identity of another person. For example, if we attack another person we instinctively envision the fear that the other person would experience. Scanning studies show the anterior cinanate cortex in the insular area (a site of emotional quality and activity) lights up in these areas in response to perceiving someone else's pain.

Well-known Hungarians

In addition to those famous Hungarians discussed in an earlier part of Babel, there are several more we should mention.

At the last meeting of the Hungarian-American Medical Association, we talked about Hungarians who significantly contributed to our country and our allies, but yet were not properly recognized.

Peter Lux was a mathematician who significantly contributed to the Manhattan Project. He received the Abel Prize, the highest award mathematicians can receive.

Nicholas Kléber and Thomas Balogh were economists who contributed significantly to reorganization procedures. They were both appointed to Lordship by Queen Elizabeth.

Robert Capa and his brother Cornel Capa were photographers. Robert contributed significantly to demonstrate the horrors of war during the Spanish Civil War. His picture of the falling soldier was widely distributed. Pictures of the horrors of war and inhumanity of the axis powers were said to contribute significantly to the will of the American people to enter World War II. He was involved in storming the beaches of Normandy and the documentation of D-Day. He was killed in 1954 after stepping on a land mine during the war in Indochina.

Cornel Capa, founder of the International Center of Photography in New York, worked in Paris. He started to study medicine but abandoned it and became a full-time photographer. He emigrated to the United States and became a photographer for the US Air Force Intelligence Unit. He later became a staff photographer for Life magazine and documented the six-day war in the Near East. He documented life in the Soviet Union.

Few people know that Fred Astaire, who was considered a very anglo-saxon artist, originally came from the Austro-Hungarian Empire and his original name was Frederic Austerlitz.

Tony Curtis was born to Hungarian immigrant parents. His original name was Bernard Schwartz.

Another actor, Leslie Howard, considered to be one of the most classically British, was also born in Hungary (Laszlo Steiner).

Arthur Koestler was a writer, journalist and revolutionary activist. He was born in Budapest. His book, "Darkness at Noon," a condemnation of the Soviet communist system, was most famous. In a semi-humorous essay, he compared prisons in various countries in which he spent time, including Franco's Spain (during the civil war there) and France (during the Nazi occupation). He was also detained in England (for drunk driving). His brother-in-law was jailed in Russia (the doctors plot accusations). He wrote more than 30 books. He described modern astronomy and predicted many scientific advances.

Nobel Prize Winners at the Roswell Park Cancer Institute

While we worked at Roswell Park Cancer Institute, Metcalf from Australia was a visiting fellow. We had many interesting discussions. He is now a candidate for the Nobel Prize for his work in immunology. The two Cori's, Gerty and Carl (originally from Austria), did basic biochemical work (including the Cori cycle) while at Roswell Park, for which they later received the Nobel Prize (while in St. Louis). They warned us not to go to Roswell Park; they felt that it was a terrible place and that they discriminated against the foreign-born.

Madame Curie worked at Roswell Park briefly to engage in clinical studies on radium therapy (she was not allowed to do this in France since she did not have a medical degree).

There was collaboration with Herbert Hauptmann at the nearby Crystallography Institute. Some joint studies with his staff still go on.

There were many studies going on which may eventually be considered for a Nobel Prize. For example, interferon β was first produced, and its therapeutic activity in MS demonstrated, with collaborators at the State University of New York at Buffalo hospitals. Our group identified the four factors through which cancer cells, viruses, and autoimmune processes (including MS) produce interferon resistance, and remedies have been developed (MPC). This group also developed therapies for respiratory distress syndrome – hyaline membrane disease and fibrinolytic therapy with locally-developed new agents for thromboembolic diseases.

Syndromes By Former Teachers

A few of our former teachers in medical school were busy naming new syndromes after themselves. Fanconi, our Professor of Pediatrics, was of course famous for Fanconi Syndrome 1 to 4, the Fanconi-DeToni Syndrome (reno-tubular disease), the Fanconi-Hegglin Syndrome (pneumonia causing positive syphilis laboratory reactions); Fanconi-Bickel Syndrome (hepatic glycogenosis with Vitamin D unresponsiveness); the Fanconi-Tuerler Syndrome (ataxia, diplegia); and Fanconi adult renotubular disease. Löffler, our Professor of Internal Medicine, was less busy – only two syndromes were named after him: Löffler I (idiopathic eosinophilic lung disease) and Löffler II (eosinophilic endomyocarditis). Another rare syndrome is Binswager Syndrome (subcortical arteriosclerotic encephalopathy), named after Dr. Binswager. We had to know all about these for our examinations; but we thought that they were very rare and it would be unlikely that we would see many of them during our active careers. It just so happens that I wrote a paper about Fanconi's anemia and new approaches to its treatment and new approaches on the treatment of Löffler's I Syndrome. If you live and work long enough, you are likely to see all kinds of rare diseases. But, even more often, we have a chance to discuss these as part of differential diagnosis considerations with our medical students.

Origin of the Names of Hungarians

Hungarians call themselves "Magyars." I often wondered where that name came from. I discussed it with a friend who is a Sumerian scholar. He thought the name came from the Sumerians with whom the Hungarian tribes were associated. There were seven Hungarian tribes, of which the "Magyar" was the leading tribe. The Sumerians called them "Dientu muhger." "Di" means law; "en" means his; "tu" means makes; "muh" means exalted, and "ger" means son. In other words, they are "the sons who make the laws and are exalted." Later, this was abbreviated to "Muhger" or "Mager." This is where "Magyar" comes from.

There were several Sumerian cities whose names became Hungarian words. For example, the Sumerian capital city's name "Ur," means "Lord" in Hungarian. The second city, "Kis," means "small" in Hungarian. "A'rpadu" became the name of the Hungarian leaders, A'rpád (Gyula and Harka), when they occupied the land of Hungary.

American History

I was helping our children in elementary school with homework. One of the questions was, "Who was the first President of the United States of America and what do you know about him?" Of course, the children knew that it was George Washington, but they wanted to know more about him. In Hungary, when I learned American history, we were told that the first President was John Hanson, who in 1781 was elected "President of the United States in Congress Assembled." While Washington, Commander of the Continental Army, was still fighting the British, Hanson was followed by six more Presidents before Washington was elected President under the new American Constitution in 1789 (which replaced the Articles of Confederation). These former Presidents were more like "speakers of the house;" nevertheless, their title was "President." What do I tell my children? What everybody expected? – Or the complex situation which the elementary school teacher was probably unaware of?
The second question was, "Who discovered America and what do you know about him?" Of course everybody knew it was Christopher Columbus in 1492. He actually landed in San Salvador and, in spite of several voyages, never set foot on the main American land. Of course, before him there were the Siberian tribes (including the Pima Indians related to the Hungarians), Eskimos, Aleuts, Viking explorers (including Leif Erikson), the Chinese Admiral Zheng He (who was claimed also to have discovered Africa and Australia),and Richard Amerike (a British man who sponsored the Italian Captain John Cabot). He might have named our country. On the other hand, Amerigo Vespuci (named after the Hungarian Prince Saint Emeric) made the first map using his own name for our country. So what is the right answer?

DNA

When the children were in high school they were supposed to write about the discovery and the discoverer of DNA. Again, they asked for my help. The expected answer was "Watson and Crick." DNA was actually identified by the Swiss scientist, Johann Friedrich Miescher in 1869 (a great, great, great grandson was one of my professors). Rosalind Franklin (1920-58) did the first crystallographic identification. Her assistant, Maurice Wilkins, took her picture (photo 51) to Watson and Crick in King's College, London. The three of them got the Nobel Prize in 1962. They never mentioned Rosalind Franklin, who by that time had died from ovarian cancer, which she probably acquired from experimental x-ray exposure.

Some Major Cosmic Catastrophes

At the Gross Medical Club meeting, we discussed limits on human and other activities. I presented evidence that there are many factors which limit human life span. Shortening of the telomers after each cell division may be a major factor. Considering many of these factors, it is possible that even with most advances active, we could not live longer than a definite time, e.g., if life span could be extended to 150 years, 100% of the males would develop prostate cancer. There are also limits to the life span of our universes.

- **"Big Bang"** 14 billion years ago, accelerating expansions since then, in 100 trillion years the Universe will be a largely empty space.
- **Black hole areas** in 10^{40} years.
- **Protons decay** in 10^{45} years.
- **Changes in the sun**. Now 4.6 billion years old, will be largely unchanged for 6 billion more years. It will continue to brighten as helium in the core is compressed. It will become extreme in 8 billion years. In 10 billion years, it will become a sub-giant and in 12 billion years a red giant and it will engulf its planets. In 12.4 billion years its helium will be exhausted and it will become a white dwarf.

- **Supernovae form** in neighboring galaxies and send gamma ray bursts to Earth.
- **Collision with other galaxies**, e.g., with andromeda, in 5 billion years.
- **Rebirth.** Universes in other of the 11 dimensions on the branes may collide with ours in 10^{100} years and may start a new big bang. This process may continue cyclically forever. This theory is supposed to substitute for the one-time creation idea.

Plant Hormones

As a high school student, I was asked by my Biology Professor, Dr. Sarkany, who was also at the same time Assistant Professor of Botony at the university, to work on our weekends and vacations in his university laboratory. He had isolated auxins and studied other plant hormones. I was interested in whether any of these hormones have an effect on human cells as well. In first year medical school, I took a course in pathology. I received permission from the department head to do a study on rats, producing burn wounds and exploring the effect of plant hormones on healing. This appeared to be of interest, since during the war many soldiers came back with injuries from flame throwers. Unfortunately no significant effect was detected. We did some additional studies while working at the University of Zurich, and later at the State University of New York at Buffalo. We tested the effect of plant hormones on several established and newly developed normal and pathologic cells in tissue culture. At the same time, Japanese investigators reported that certain plant hormones had a differentiation inducing effect in certain human cell lines. I'm just about to correct the galley proof of a paper we have submitted to a medical journal on our studies. Interestingly enough, this was one study started in high school and continued for several decades.

Linguistics

An old friend, who is an academic linguist, visited me because of some medical problems. We chatted about many things, including an interest that certain words mean one thing in one language, and the same word has an entirely different meaning in another language. For example, one of my daughter's names is Linda, which in Spanish means beautiful. Interestingly enough, in Swahili it means "to guard" or "the guards." My other daughter is named Kathleen, which in Hungarian is Kati, or its diminutive is Katika. Interestingly enough, in Swahili this is both "come in" and "come out of the cold." For example, in the morning when my barefoot houseboy brought the morning tea to my tent while on medical safari, he knocked on the tent post and I said, "Karibu," which means "near" or "come in," or if I wanted to be more precise, I said "Karibu Katika," which means "come in out of the cold." We also talked about the relationship of the Hungarian language to the Sumerian. According to one set of old stories, due to the pressure of attacking surrounding groups, some of the tribes related to the Sumerians, the Szubars, escaped to the East and settled near the Kaukazus. Presumably they were the ancestors of both the Huns and the Hungarians.

Interestingly enough, there are many words similar in Sumerian and Hungarian. For example, one interesting group of words is related to falconry. Falconry was introduced into Europe when the Crusaders came back from the Holy Land and brought with them falcons and Arab falconers. On the other hand, Hungarians traditionally came to Europe before that with their falcons and traditionally many families continued to breed them. I grew up with falcons and professional falconers on our farm. For example, one of the falcons that we used, the Saker falcon, is called "Kerecseny." The word comes from the Sumerian "kerhecnen." The Sumerian "ker" means turning around; "he" means place; the "c" means in; and "nen" means going. In other words, this refers to the waiting on of the falcon when he circles around and waits on for the quarry to flush. The name was preserved in the family name of some of our friends, and one of my professors of literature, named Kerecsényi. The word falcon in Hungarian is "Solyom," which comes from the Sumerian "suilhuum," where the "su" means hand; "il" means to lift up; "hu" is bird; and "um" is his. In other words, it refers to the bird which flies up from the gloved hand. In later Sumerian, this would be "Soljom," which is very close to the Hungarian "Solyom." There is a district in Hungarian called

Zolyom, which probably comes directly from the name of this bird. According to the legend, the Hungarians were guided from Asia to Hungary by a hunting eagle (Stepe eagle) or a falcon. We later bred Stepe eagles on our farm in Boston, New York.

Zoo Studies

For many years I served on the Scientific Advisory Board of our zoo. We developed a scientific collaboration where we obtained samples of various zoo animals for research purposes. Among others, we found that raptorial birds have a deficiency of Hageman's factor, whose lack in humans results in hemophilia D, yet the birds had no bleeding problems. We are still studying their defense mechanisms, which may eventually be useful for our patients.

There were a number of interesting episodes. I was consulted about a gorilla, which was found to have a cancer for which we decided radiation therapy would be most effective. We took the anesthetized gorilla to the Roswell Park Cancer Institute, covered him with a sheet, and pushed him along the corridor in a cart toward the Radiation Therapy Suite. An old female patient came by and said, "You have this poor patient completely covered; he shouldn't have the sheet over his face." She pulled off the sheet and much to her surprise there was the gorilla. She was really frightened.

Another interesting episode was when I was called to consult for a lion, which seemed to have a tumor in the oral cavity. I examined the anesthetized animal, and it turned out that it was not a tumor but an abscessed tooth. We did a quick tooth extraction and everything looked all right. When we were working on the anesthetized lion, some of my grandchildren sneaked into the cage and sat on the lion. Madeline, their mother, was outside of the cage and took pictures of all of that. The lion did well and the children treasured the pictures.

Falconry

I was asked to talk to various groups of students about falconry. I pointed out that this is a noble sport, a character-builder, and it followed a great tradition. Falconry was brought to Europe by knights returning from the Crusades, who brought with them Arab falconers and falcons. Also, Eastern tribes which invaded Europe and settled there (e.g. Hungarians) brought with them falcons and eagles and continued to breed them. In those days, falconry had several useful functions. Before the days of shotguns, it was almost impossible to bag flying birds with bows and arrows. The only way to hunt pheasants, quail, and other tasty snacks for the people was by catching them with falcons. Falconry also played an important military function. Most armies had "Falconry Corps." When forts were besieged, members of this corps continuously circled the fort on horseback with falcons on their fists. If they saw messenger pigeons fly out of the fort, the released their trained falcons and captured the messenger pigeons and deciphered the message and certainly prevented it from arriving to its goal. Falcons and eagles were also used to hunt large mammals, including foxes and wolves (and they are still being used for this purpose by the Kyrges). It was the origin of a lucrative trade in furs.

Falconry was a type of hunting which was readily available to ladies. In the middle ages up to the early modern times, they participated usually on horseback.

Classic falconry in central Europe required three animals: falcons, hunting dogs, and horses. When the dogs found and pointed game (e.g. a pheasant), the hood was removed from the falcon and it was made to fly up and start circling. At that point, the pointing dog was told to lay down and stay still while the falconer on horseback rode closer to the quarry and cracked his whip to make it fly. The falcon came down, dropping like a stone, tumbling down with the quarry sometimes a mile away. At that point, the hunter canters "hell bent for leather" in order to get there before the hungry falcon eats his catch, in which case he takes off and may never return. The hunter then dismounts, picks up the quarry, and gives a small wedge of liver to the falcon so that he gets a reward but does not get sated and is ready to continue to hunt. The rest of the bird goes into the hunting bag, the falconer remounts, and the hunt resumes. This classical type of hunt is only seldom practiced today. I was lucky to have participated in this type of falconry early in my life.

European Falconry Association Meetings

I participated in European Falconry Association meetings in Hungary in 1986, 1989, and 1994. There was a great deal of difference between them. In 1986, the meeting was at Szarvas near the Tisza River. There was still communism, and hunting and gun licenses were greatly restricted. They were mostly for the government elite and their cronies; consequently, there was relatively little regular hunting and a great abundance of game. The government wanted to impress foreign visitors and unlimited permits were made available. At the end of the first day, for example, we wound up with about 300 pheasants and a few deer caught by the eagles. In tradition, at the end of the hunt, Taps was blown on horns at the piles of birds and deer, and the quarries were honored. I participated with a tiercel peregrine falcon and a golden eagle. I also entered the mounted division. The stallion station nearby lent me a mount, a great grandson of Kincsem, which was supposed to be the best thoroughbred racehorse in central Europe. My horse turned out to be a magnificent jumper; it sailed through small rivers and local fences. The only problem I had with him was that it was hard to make him stand still when needed. At the end of the hunt, we paraded through the local village. We stopped at the local hospital and showed our birds to the patients, telling them stories about them. We also stopped at the local high school. I let some of the children hold a falcon with a glove and let the local teacher take pictures. We talked about the need for conservation and care of wildlife.

I did not bring my birds back to the United States because of the lengthy (and expensive) quarantine procedures and the fact that they often fly against the cage walls and break their feathers. I donated my birds to the local breeding program, and I understand that they sired many young over a long period of time.

The second and third meetings I attended were very different. Communism was gone, and one consequence was that game and gun licenses became readily available. There were many hunters out in the field, much before our meeting started, in contrast to when the first meeting started, Thus, in contrast to the first meeting, there was relatively little game available. We also had a great deal of difficulty with birds landing on electric wires and windmills and being electrocuted.

We made many friends as falconers from all over Europe. One of the German falconers, a retired colonel whom I later visited at his facility, developed an excellent breeding program for falcons and eagles. He put on a magnificent show for tour groups whose cruise ship regularly stopped at this facility. A falconer from Scotland had probably the best-trained raptors and gave a great talk on training methods. I talked about diseases in raptors, treatment, and breeding methods. With a colleague, we gave demonstrations on artificial insemination. One of the breeders presented a talk on captive breeding methods. I met him later when I was a visiting professor in Saudi Arabia and he brought some falcons for sale. A colleague from Northern Ireland visited me later at my farm in Buffalo and we had a great time hawking.

With travel becoming easier for central Europeans (under communism it was nearly impossible), I hope to host several colleagues in the near future and show them something about American falconry.

The Olive Trees of Gethsemane

During a medical meeting in Jerusalem, one of our hosts took us to the Mount of Gethsemane and showed us the olive trees, which were presumably over 2000 years old and most likely had seen Jesus. We took some photographs and got a special permission to cut a few branches and take them home. At one of our host's research laboratory, we put together a special nutrient medium and put them in it. We had no difficulty bringing them back home and continued putting them in nutrient media. We consulted with some of our plant physiology colleagues and continued them in liquid nutrient medium for a while. Then, we planted them out on our farm and continued applying specially-designed nutrient media. They grew for a while, but then in spite of all kind of care and consultation with experts, they did not survive. We do have, however, photographs of the original trees hanging on our wall.

The Oldest and Largest Organisms

There are many arguments on what is the oldest being at present on Earth. Some oceanographers think that there are deep sea tube worms which hold the record; they may be many thousand years old. There are also arguments which are the largest presently living organisms. Again, oceanographers pointed out to us while diving on the Great Barrier Reef of Australia, that the Great Barrier Reef can be considered as a continuous organism ranging from islands around Northern Australia to Indonesia, several thousand kilometers in length. On the other hand, it was also pointed out that there are deep sea micro-organisms which hang together forming large curtains close to the size of Greece, which also can be considered as one being. If that is true, it is certainly the largest.